Germany in Europe in the Nineties

Edited by

Bertel Heurlin

Research Director, Danish Institute of International Affairs
Jean Monnet Professor of European Integration and Security
Institute of Political Science
University of Copenhagen
Denmark

First published in Great Britain 1996 by
MACMILLAN PRESS LTD
Houndmills, Basingstoke, Hampshire RG21 6XS
and London
Companies and representatives
throughout the world

A catalogue record for this book is available
from the British Library.

ISBN 0–333–66074–9

First published in the United States of America 1996 by
ST. MARTIN'S PRESS, INC.,
Scholarly and Reference Division,
175 Fifth Avenue,
New York, N.Y. 10010

ISBN 0–312–16148–4

Library of Congress Cataloging-in-Publication Data
Germany in Europe in the nineties / edited by Bertel Heurlin.
p.   cm.
Includes bibliographical references and index.
ISBN 0–312–16148–4
1. Germany—History—Unification, 1990.   2. Germany—Foreign
relations—1990–   3. Germany—Foreign relations—Europe.   4. Europe-
–Foreign relations—Germany.   I. Heurlin, Bertel.
DD290.29.G493   1996
943.087'9—dc20
                                                                    96–9308
                                                                    CIP

Selection and editorial matter © Bertel Heurlin 1996
Chapters 1–11 © Macmillan Press Ltd 1996

10   9   8   7   6   5   4   3   2   1
05   04   03   02   01   00   99   98   97   96

Printed in Great Britain by
The Ipswich Book Company Ltd
Ipswich, Suffolk

Contents

Notes on the Contributors

Yves Boyer is currently Deputy Director of CREST, a French think-tank dealing with international affairs and security issues. He is teaching international relations at the Ecole Politechnique and the French army academy in Saint Cyr. He has been Research Associate at the International Institute for Strategic Studies in 1982/83 and Senior Researcher at IFRI. He has also been Wilson Research Associate. He has published regularly in French and foreign magazines such as *Politique Etragère, Defense National, Europa Archiv* and *The Washington Quarterly.*

Lily Gardner Feldman is Senior Scholar in Residence at the Center for German and European Studies, Georgetown University. She has been the Research Director of the American Institute for Contemporary German Studies, Johns Hopkins University (1991–95), and a Professor of Political Science at Tufts University (1978–91). Her work on German foreign policy and on the European Community includes *The Special Relationship between West Germany and Israel* (1984), *The EC in the International Arena: A New Activism?* (1992), *Germany and the EC: Realism and Responsibility* (1994), and *Transatlantic Relations* (1995).

Helga Haftendorn is Professor of International Relations at the Free University of Berlin, and Director of its Center for Transatlantic Foreign and Security Policy Studies. From 1989 to 1991 she was President of the International Studies Association. She earned her Ph.D. at the University of Frankfurt, and her Habilitation (post-doctorate degree) at the University of Hamburg. Her best-known publication is her book *Sicherheit und Entspannung. Zur Aussenpolitik der Bundesrepublik Deutschland 1955–82* (2nd ed., Baden-Baden: Nomos 1986). Her most recent publication is *Kernwaffen und die Glaubwürdigkeit der Allianz. Die NATO-Krise von 1966/67* (Baden-Baden: Nomos 1994).

Bertel Heurlin was born in 1935. He is Research Director, Danish Institute of International Affairs and Jean Monnet Professor of European Integration and Security at the Institute of Political Science, University of Copenhagen. From 1992 to 1996 he was Director of CORE, the Copenhagen Research Project on European Integration. Until 1995 he has been co-Chairman of SNU, the Danish Committee on Security and Disarmament. He was a member of the Danish Defense Committee of 1988. He is author, editor and co-author of 35 books and numerous articles dealing with international politics and foreign policy, security and strategy. His latest book is *Security Problems in the New Europe*, 1995.

Christopher Hill is a Montague Burton Professor of International Relations at the London School of Economics and Political Science. Among his best-known publications are *National Foreign Policies and European Political Cooperation* (ed., 1983), *Cabinet Decisions on Foreign Policy; the British Experience 1938–1941* (ed. with Pamela Beshoff, Cambridge University Press, 1991), and *Two Worlds of International Relations: Academics, Practitioners and the Trade in Ideas* (Routledge, 1994). He has held visiting positions at the Royal Institute of International Affairs (London), the Woodrow Wilson International Center for Scholars (Washington, D.C.), Dartmouth College, New Hampshire and the European University Institute (Florence). He is currently Convenor of the Department of International Relations, LSE.

Josef Joffe is columnist and editorial page editor of the *Süddeutsche Zeitung* in Munich, Germany's largest quality paper. Previously, he served as a senior editor of *Die Zeit*. He has taught international relations at Harvard, the School of Advanced International Studies (Johns Hopkins) and the University of Munich. His journalistic work has been published in major newspapers on either side of the Atlantic. His scholarly work appears in *International Security, The National Interest, Foreign Affairs* and *Survival*. He is the author of *Limited Partnership: Europe, America and the Burden of Alliance.*

Michael Kreile is Professor of International Politics at the Humboldt Universität in Berlin. He was educated at Tübingen,

Paris, Heidelberg and Harvard. Dr Kreile was Professor of International Politics at the University of Constance (1982–92), the Visiting Konrad Adenauer Professor at Georgetown University, Washington, D.C. (1980–81), and Assistant Professor at the Institute of Political Science, University of Heidelberg (1974–82). His publications include *Gewerkschaften und Arbeitsbeziehungen in Italien 1968–1972* (1985), *Europa 1992 – Konzeption, Strategien, Aussenwirkungen* (ed., 1991), *Die Integration Europas* (ed., 1992).

Ekkehart Krippendorff was born in 1934. He is a Professor of Political Science at the Free University of Berlin. He is also an author of various books in this field, ranging from *International Politics, Critique of the Military* and works in peace research to books on *Goethe* (1988), *Politics in Shakespeare* (1992) and other political interpretations of literature.

Roger Morgan is a Professor of Political Science in the European University Institute in Florence. He previously held senior research appointments at the Royal Institute of International Affairs and the Policy Studies Institute, London. He has also held teaching or research appointments at a number of British and American universities, and has published numerous books on European and international affairs. These include *The United States and West Germany, 1945–73: A Study in Alliance Politics, West Germany's Foreign Policy Agenda: The Political/Economic Balance* (1978), and *New Diplomacy in the Post Cold War World* (co-author and co-editor, 1993).

Richard Münch was born in 1945. He is Professor of Sociology at the University of Bamberg. From 1976 to 1995 he was a Professor at the University of Düsseldorf, and from 1974 to 1976 at the University of Cologne. Some of his major publications are *Theorie des Handelns* (1982), *Die Kultur der Moderne* (1986), *Dialektik der Kommunikationsgesellschaft* (1991), *Das Projekt Europa* (1993), *Sociological Theory* (1994), and *Dynamik der Kommunikationsgesellschaft* (1995).

Vitaly Zhurkin was born in 1928 in Moscow. He became a Doctor of History in 1975, and has been a Professor since

1977 and a member of the Russian Academy of Science (RAS) since 1984. He has been a Director of the Institute of Europe, RAS, since 1987 and Head of the Division of World Economy and International Relations, RAS, (7 institutes) since 1991. He became a member of the European Academy of Science, Art and Humanities in 1990, and of the World Academy of Art and Science in 1994. His publications include *International Conflicts* (1972), *Strategic Stability* (1985), *Reasonable Sufficiency and New Political Thinking* (1989), *Building the Greater Europe* (1991), and *The European Integration and its Impact on Experience of Russia and CIS* (1993).

An Introduction

Bertel Heurlin

THE GERMAN QUESTION THEN AND NOW

The 'German Question' (die Deutsche Frage) haunted decision-makers in the East and the West during the cold war. The main players in the big game were, of course, the United States and the Soviet Union. But the two Germanys were in a crucial way the manifestation of bi-polarity, and divided Germany constituted the real content of the German Question. East Germany, the GDR, was an extremely artificial creation of bi-polarity, acting as the Soviet Union's obedient puppet, playing no independent international role. West Germany, the FRG, was also, on vital issues, deeply dependent on the United States. It did, however, influence the German Question by continually reminding its Western allies – primarily the USA – on what had been agreed policy. Not least, the vision of reunification as embodied for a very long time in the 'Alleinvertretungsrecht' (the Hallstein doctrine) was emphasized by the FRG. Reluctantly giving up this policy after being convinced about the virtues of *détente,* the FRG attempted to stick with *détente* even after the USA had renounced it.

The FRG's vital interest was certainly not to bring about reunification immediately. Rather it was to remind Western partners and Eastern opponents that reunification still remained the long term goal. The policy was no longer isolation as in the Hallstein doctrine days. Rather it was to embrace the East Germans through increased human contacts and economic relations to avoid ultimate alienation.

Without any decisive German impact or influence, the international system was transformed. The Soviet Union gave up in the cold war, gave up its empire in Eastern Europe. Suddenly Germany emerged as the real winner of the war. Through an extremely expedient process, the German Question was solved. What nobody had expected became a reality: a united Germany.

1

This solution, however, brought about a new German Question. What will happen to Europe and to the world when Germany re-enters European and world politics with its full powers, its new regained capabilities? Those who counted the most, feared reunification the least. The two most positive powers were the two former main competitors: the Soviet Union and the United States. The Soviet Union saw in united Germany a partner and a tool with which to break Soviet regional and international isolation. The United States saw the new Germany as a partner in leadership. The immediate reaction of France, and to some extent Britain, was concern. However, both came to realize that, under the new conditions, the solution to the new German Question lay in maintaining and broadening European and Atlantic integration – a policy of 'embeddedment'.

But how long will Germany accept a self-restraint considerably greater than that of comparable countries – a self-restraint which could be considered a 'singularization' of Germany? The fact is that, for the time being, this policy seems to serve German interests very well. But will the new 'Berlin Republic', which is certainly different from the 'Bonn Republic' – not just in terms of external but also in terms of domestic developments – follow European trends of 'renationalization' entailing a new role for Germany in the centre of Europe?

The new German Question is: How will Germany behave in its new position and how will the world react to the new position of Germany? Basically it is a question of the impact of the new international structure, new international processes and the reaction of the units.

GERMANY AS WINNER, LOSER, WINNER: THE DICHOTOMIES

Given the double focus on what unit is Germany and what are the reactions to this unit one has to consider the last century of German history. The years 1870–71 and again 1989–90 are the extremes: the moments of big gains for Germany, the winner position. In the 19th century Germany became a victor through her own efforts. In 1989–90 – which the Germans call 'die Wende' – victory came as an unexpected gift from on high.

From 1870 to 1871, Germany presented itself as a potential world power. But the first attempt to gain that status failed. In 1918 Germany was the loser, regionally and globally. The second attempt to gain world power status also failed and Germany was heavily punished. In 1945, as a double or triple loser, the German State ceased to exist. This certainly was 'Stunde Null'.

This event led to the total surrender of German integrity: both Germanys became victims of 'penetration'. The winners of the Second World War – manifested in the United Nations and, in practice, in occupation status – forced their norms and values upon Germany. In this way a new Germany, different in scope and content from the Third Reich, emerged. This is the reason that most Germans do not refer to the transformation in 1990 as 're-unification' – but rather as 'unification'.

Reflecting on the general position of the new Germany it is impossible to avoid conceptual dichotomies: winner and loser; world power and no power. For as long as Germany has existed as a nation state, it has been interpreted in contradictary terms. Its structure and organization, too, are based on a certain polarization. For example, on the one hand there is a German perception of the civilian state à la Friedrich der Grosse's Prussia; on the other hand we have the nation (Blut-und-Boden) – a Herder-like state of the German Romantic, regarding the state as an organism, not as an organization. On the one hand, there is the cultural Germany of classicism and humanism (das Land der Dichter und Denker) and, on the other hand, Germany exposed as the racist, inhuman Nazi regime (das Land der Richter und Henker).

The current dichotomy is between normal great power status, assuming full global and regional responsibility including the hard security issues on the one hand, and, on the other hand, a civilian, economic power trying to exert influence by financial, economic, societal and non-military means.

In regional European terms – with federalism and hegemonism as the poles – the dichotomy is expressed in a simple way by distiguishing between the European Germany and the German Europe.

Another perspective from which a dichotomy is emerging is, on the one hand, that of normalization, the status and the behaviour of a normal state in an anarchical system, exerting full freedom of action. Yet, on the other hand, there is the special status, the voluntary 'embeddedment' and restraint, the uniqueness and singularization in international politics. And linked to this dichotomy are two kinds of options: on the one hand, stability, the status quo, adaptation, soft security; on the other hand, change, transformation, new opportunities, hard security.

Finally one can point to the dichotomies in policy orientation – between Europeanism and Atlanticism, materialized in the choice between France and the United States, and also between the widening of the German/European sphere of influence towards Central and Eastern Europe on the one hand, and on the other the traditional anchoring to the Franco-German entente.

All these dichotomies are to be found in this book, directly or indirectly. And these considerations have been part of the basic idea behind the book. The focus of the book is twofold: it relates to and analyses the impact of the transformed international system – and thus also the impact of the similarly transformed European sub-system – upon the German position and role, and upon German policy.

CONTENTS

This book attempts to present contrasting analyses of the general political dimension and position of united Germany in Europe, at different levels. In Part I, the position and role of the new Germany is identified and analysed, emphasizing identity, national interests and Germany's new position in European and world politics.

Part II deals with German foreign and security policy, policy *vis-à-vis* the European Union and, finally, domestic policy as a determinant of foreign and European policy.

Part III looks at the policies of the great powers towards Germany, encompassing chapters on American, Russian,

British and French policy.

Part IV deals briefly with the future of Germany, particularly Germany's future status in international politics.

Part I: Germany's Position and Role

Part I consists of three chapters. Richard Münch tries to establish a conception of German identity. How do the Germans conceive of themselves? How do they see their role in the European Union and how are they perceived by other people? How has this identity been affected by unification and how far can the new Germany be characterized as a 'normal' state? Taking its point of departure in historical developments from the formation of the idea of the German nation to the defeat of the Nazi regime and the separation into two states, Münch uses public opinion surveys to analyse identity problems in recent, crucial years. He emphasizes the remarkable gap between the political élite and public opinion, particularly on European integration.

The main purpose of Bertel Heurlin's chapter is to identify the national interests of the new Germany. This is conducted on the basis of an analysis showing in how many ways Germany and the position of Germany have changed and are fundamentally new after 1989–90. Using a modified version of neo-realism, six national interests are identified and analysed. The author concludes that, despite unification, Germany still has a road to travel before it can be considered a 'normal' state. The chapter ends with a discussion about whether Germany will remain a 'post-sovereign' state or strive for 'normality'.

The third chapter consists of Ekkehart Krippendorff's analysis of Germany as a world power and as a European power. Whereas the previous chapter was an attempt to give an overview of Germany's interests, Krippendorff concentrates more on the current situation. Can Germany after unification be defined as a world power or is the term 'European power' more appropriate? After an attempt to clarify the criteria for the concept of a world power, the author concludes that Germany does not meet the criteria. To a certain extent Germany has, however, achieved a hegemonic position in Europe. The chapter ends with a discussion of the emerging disjunction between the German political élite, which favours a more active foreign policy, and public opinion, which prefers a continuation of current foreign policy.

Part II: Germany's Policy

Part II also consists of three chapters. While Part I focusses on the position and interests of Germany, Part II is about policy. In Chapter 4, Helga Haftendorn examines the content of German policy. What has Germany actually done after unification in terms of foreign and security policy? After an overview of the transformation in the structural framework, she analyses German options and initiatives in the European Union, NATO and the OSCE. She also investigates and assesses Germany's policy towards France, Central and Eastern Europe, the United States and Japan. She concludes that a policy of multilateralism has, despite unification, been continued and that German power has been weakened by the absence of clear priorities. 'It is not the dwarves that tie Gulliver down, but he himself does not yet know which bindings he has to cast away, and which institutional or multilateral bonds he has to accept ... for his own good.'

In Chapter 5, Michael Kreile assesses whether Germany will assume a leadership role in the European Union. On the basis of the theory of hegemonic stability, Kreile looks at the leadership role of Germany in a European context. Is Germany, post unification, in a position to reach and develop the hegemonic position previously unattainable due to the unresolved national question? His main argument is that there is no convincing evidence for the thesis that the Federal Republic is about to assume a leadership role. This is also due to European unwillingness to follow the German lead.

In Chapter 6, Roger Morgan analyses the interplay between German foreign policy and domestic politics. The point of departure is the claim that German foreign and European policy normally arouses minimal political controversy and that there is little reason to expect the national consensus to disappear. But Morgan asks whether the internal balance is likely to be permanent. He analyses the coalition-effect and the phenomenon of 'capture' of policy by an interest group, as in the case of German policy *vis-à-vis* Croatia. The role of the Länder and the role of the 'extreme' parties are also examined. He concludes that foreign policy itself is evolving in ways which make it likely that the involvement of domestic political forces will continue to grow.

Part III: Policy towards Germany

The third part deals with the policies of the great powers towards Germany. Lily Gardner Feldman investigates US policy towards Germany, posing the question: What is the impact of German unification on German–American relations? Is it to be understood in terms of alliance, estrangement or partnership? The point of departure is a description and typology of recent, mostly American, literature on the topic. She compares and contrasts the two more traditional conceptions of dyadic relations – alliance and estrangement – and then argues for widening the scope of enquiry to view the relationship as what has officially been labelled 'partnership'. Included in the analysis is a review of policy implications. She concludes that Germany has been able to balance its multiple identities and partnerships. It is now up to the United States to elaborate a more fully 'layered partnership' with Germany and Europe.

Chapter 8 is Vitaly Zhurkin's essay on Germany and Russia. He analyses how two practically new states – Russia and united Germany – have reacted to each other in the post-cold war era. A major part of the chapter deals with the interplay of the new relationship between the two states and the historical experiences of their predecessors. The author concludes that the relationship has better prospects than usually forecast, due in particular to their economic links, the moral–psychological *rapprochement* of the civil societies of both countries and the multiplicity of common interests in Europe.

In Chapter 9, Christopher Hill outlines the Anglo-German relationship. The main objective of this chapter is to relate the powerful historical experience of Britain and Germany to the apparent discontinuity represented by the end of the cold war and German unification. How has unification affected Anglo-German relations? Hill deals particularly with British attempts to build a special relationship with Germany. He concludes that these attempts have failed, mostly due to misunderstandings which are rooted in very different outlooks and historical experience.

Chapter 10 deals with French policy towards Germany and the relationship between the two countries. The main question in this analysis is: What is the resilience of the link which continues to bind the two countries? Yves Boyer argues that, for a variety of deep-rooted reasons, the marriage of interests between France and Germany is so solidly rooted that the current phase of turbulence will again lead the two countries to realize that neither Berlin nor Paris have any credible political alternative to deepening their relationship. The chapter examines the many institutionalized ties and their political role and impact.

Part IV: Prospects

Part IV contains only one chapter. In this final chapter, Joseph Joffe tries to take a look ahead. He claims that 30 June 1995 is a watershed in post-war German history. After this date, the Bundestag could authorize the deployment of German troops out-of-area for the first time since the Second World War. Now Germany is exposed to the pulls and pushes of world politics. Now Germany has also to consider a grand strategy. Current strategy is to 'keep all options open'. Joffe concludes that German autonomy is growing and old parameters are re-emerging due to the disappearance of bipolarity.

BACKGROUND

In preparation for this publication, an international conference entitled 'Germany in Europe in the '90s' was held at the Institute of Political Science, University of Copenhagen, in November 1994. The conference was arranged by the Copenhagen Project on European Integration (CORE). Some of the chapters in this publication are revised versions of papers presented at this conference.

I want to thank the participants in the conference for

their contributions, and to thank the authors for their revisions, their prompt delivery of manuscripts and their patient cooperation. Further thanks go to Research Fellow Lykke Friis who has functioned as a highly competent and professional co-editor and to the CORE secretariat, especially Tina Schou, for valuable help in the administrative and editorial process.

This book is a publication in the CORE research series.

Part I: Germany's Position and Role

1 German Nation and German Identity: Continuity and Change from the 1770s to the 1990s

Richard Münch

How do the Germans conceive of themselves? How do they relate to other people? How do they see their role in the European Union and how are they perceived by other people? These are the questions which come up when we want to know what constitutes the specific German identity. I will deal with these questions in six steps.

First I will look back to the formation of the idea of the German nation and of German identity in the historical process from the German Enlightenment, beginning in the 1770s, to the founding of the nation state in 1871, and to the further shaping of this idea by the Kaiserreich, the Weimar Republic and the regime of Nazism. In the second step I will ask how the Germans related to their nation and their identity after the defeat of the Nazi regime and after their separation into two states. In the third step I will deal with the question of how the Germans' view of Nazism developed in the post-war decades from the fifties to the nineties. The question of the fourth step will be the Germans' relation to immigrants to their country. The fifth step will be concerned with how the Germans' values and their commitment to democracy have changed in the post-war decades. Finally, the sixth step will turn to the Germans' attitude towards the European Union.

1. THE IDEA OF THE GERMAN NATION: HISTORICAL ROOTS

Patriotism

At the time when the Western European nation states of Spain, Britain, France and the Netherlands emerged in the 17th and 18th centuries, Germany remained divided into a plurality of individual states. There was no centralization of power and no corresponding establishment of an embracing political unit on a larger territory. The people were subjects of monarchs who exerted absolute power over their territories, and they conceived of themselves as members of local, regional and state units but not as members of a larger unit of 'Germans' or 'Germany'. The Holy Roman Empire of the German Nation, created in the Middle Ages and formally existing until 1806, after its confirmation in 1648, did not penetrate the populations of individual states. It was a nation only for the élites who were able to communicate across the borders of individual states.[1]

It was Martin Luther, with his translation of the Bible into the German language, who created a common language for the German people beyond their regional and local dialects and against the ruling Latin language which was the clergy's means of communication. However, Luther divided the Germans in religious terms. The religious split remained an obstacle for German unity up to the building of the first German nation state in 1871.[2]

In the 17th and 18th centuries France established a political and cultural hegemony on the European continent. This situation changed in the second half of the 18th century. There emerged an élite of writers who began to speak for the value of German language and culture against the French language and culture then dominant at the courts of the German kings and principalities. The language and culture of the aristocracy was French but, adopting the French idea of the Enlightenment, German writers longed for liberation of their own language and culture and claimed equal rights for every culture. In their view, every language and culture has its own character and beauty which deserves to be preserved and cultivated in its own right. Johann Gottfried

Herder[3] was in the forefront of this movement and celebrated these views in his collection of Volkslieder (folk songs) and in his articles on 'German character and art'.

The movement for the German language makes patriotism a central virtue. Patriotism establishes a link between people across the borders of the individual states. It creates a feeling of commonality between the people who still belong to different states and it marks a difference between these people, who have a language and culture in common, and those who are united by other languages and cultures. This patriotism of the German writers was not conceived in narrow particularistic terms. It drew a distinction between the dull celebration of Germanhood at the one extreme and the loss of the bonds of a common culture in an empty cosmopolitanism at the other. Patriotism, as these writers conceived it, sought to be an educated and enlightened link between primordial Germanhood and an all-embracing cosmopolitanism. It was not understood as a rejection of cosmopolitanism but as a substantial addition to it. For Herder, every language and every culture was valuable in its own right. The cultivation of one's own language and culture would have to fit into a plurality of others. True cosmopolitanism would not subject the world to the domination of one language and culture but would acknowledge the right of every other language and culture and thus argue for a world of pluralism in languages and cultures.

Because of this linking of patriotism and cosmopolitanism, drawing a boundary between the German and the then dominating French language and culture did not imply a sense of superiority. In the first instance, it was a defensive position to permit the development of the German language and culture. In the second instance, it was a comparative position. Comparing French and German language, literature and arts enabled a better understanding of the unique character and beauty of each. Wilhelm von Humboldt and Goethe felt that the growing dialogue between the writers of different languages would contribute to a growing knowledge of the unique character of different national literatures. On the one hand, nations would be able to discover their specific identity. On the other hand, they would be led to learn from one another. An all-embracing European civilization would emerge out of mutual comparison and learning. However, as Humboldt recognizes, this process would also contribute to a reflected individuation and mutual distinction between the different nations. Within the emerging European civilization the different national cultures would try to survive as distinct cultures and would emphasize those qualities which make them unique and distinct. Goethe developed his notion of world literature in this context. In the process of mutual comparison, correction and learning the different national literatures discover the key to their unique character and strength and they learn to acknowledge the worth of other national literatures. Thus a sense of one's national identity grows along with the realization of a wider civilization of world literature. National identity does not exist in and for itself, but only in its linkage to cosmopolitanism, to a sense of world citizenship.[4]

Romanticism

The first construction of the German idea of the nation was by the writers of the German Enlightenment and neo-classicism from Herder to Humboldt and Goethe. Under different historical circumstances, the Romantic movement towards the end of the 18th and right into the beginning of the 19th centuries[5] was a further influence. Friedrich von Schlegel[6] and Novalis (Friedrich von Hardenberg)[7] were spokesmen of the Romantic movement who gave the idea of the German nation an aesthetic turn. They not only compared German and French culture but began to see in German culture the carrier of truth, morality and beauty, whereas, in their view, French culture stood for the superficial, the untrue, for immorality, pretension, business and narcissism.

The German identity became the key to what was called the Erhabene (sublime): a key that can only be grasped by being enlightened and achieving a higher position of perception, understanding and feeling. One turns into oneself and recognizes in oneself the whole world as one unites with that whole world. In this process German culture shows the way to an all-embracing European, or even world, culture.

Pre-March Liberalism

The period between the French liberal Revolution in July 1830 and the outbreak of the Revolution in March 1848 is called 'pre-March' and is linked with the growth of a movement towards establishing a German democratic nation state.

The disunity of the major forces of the revolution; the lack of a charismatic leader; its scattered occurrence throughout the country with no concentration in a centre of revolution; the separation of the Frankfurt parliament from the action on the streets all led finally to its failure. The principalities were able to restore absolutist rule.

The Prussian Historical School and the Nation State

In the Frankfurt parliament there was also a division between the supporters of the so-called Greater German Nation State, which included Austria, and the smaller German nation state without Austria. After the revolution had failed, the smaller German nation state was propagated by a new group of intellectuals, the Borussian historians, including Christoph Dahlmann (1785–1860), Maximilian Wolfgang Duncker (1811–66) and Johann Gustav Droysen (1808–84), who had all been members of the Frankfurt parliament, and, later on, Heinrich von Sybel (1817–95), Ludwig Häusser (1818–67) and Heinrich von Treitschke (1834–96).

What the Borussian historians argued for was a political nation state, one that was powerful enough to survive in the competitive European state system. This was not the cultural nation of the Enlightenment and Romantic intellectuals; it was not the democratic republic of the pre-March radical democrats, and it was not the republican nation in the sense of the French Revolution of 1789. Their work and their lectures legitimized what was realized by Bismarck after the war against France in 1871.[8]

Identity-Shapers: Literary Men, Civil Servants, Landowners, Officers and Industrialists

In practice, the modern German nation state was created by warfare within the competitive European state system.

The educated bourgeoisie had to share its leading role with those forces that were able to guarantee the nation state's position in that system: the Prussian landowners of the Eastern Provinces (the Junkers), the Prussian officers' corps, and the large-scale industrialists. It was the power of these four major strata that the new nation state was grounded on, and that shaped the nation's identity well into the 20th century. Because of the predominance of these strata, the petite bourgeoisie of artisans and small businessmen did not develop a self-assured role in society. The same is true of the small-holding peasants. The workers had to struggle up to the First World War to be accepted as citizens with equal rights. The Social Democrats voted for the war budget of the government in August 1914 in order to achieve full acknowledgement of their existence. German identity was shaped in the Kaiserreich (empire) by these four major status groups.

The influence of the educated bourgeoisie can be traced back to the Enlightenment in the second half of the 18th century. It's contribution to German identity is the conception of the nation as a cultural unit with a common language and cultural heritage. The vehicle for creating the corresponding sense of German nationhood is education in its language and culture. Education is the central virtue of the good citizens of that nation. Through the struggle against French and British competitors, the German idea of culture and education was transformed into the claim of a higher validity and deeper truth of German culture in comparison to French and British civilization. French culture was denigrated as the formal etiquette of courtiers without substance, and British as the profit-seeking commercialism of tradesmen. In this way, the nation of culture was used as an instrument for rejecting foreign elements as endangering the higher German culture, including the people who could introduce such foreign elements. The nation of culture was used as an instrument for legitimizing the German crusade against French and British supremacy. Distinguishing German culture from French and British civilization became very common right into the 20th century.[9] Thus it was not by accident that a writer of the repute of Thomas Mann cultivated this distinction in his *Betrachtungen eines Unpolitischen.*[10]

A secondary trait of German identity rooted in the educated bourgeoisie but spreading out well into every strata
of the bourgeoisie (though in a trivialized version) is the
love of Geselligkeit (conviviality) as it was first celebrated in
the Lesegesellschaften (reading societies) of the educated
bourgeoisie but extended to the broader bourgeoisie by the
Gesangsvereine (choral societies) and Turnvereine (gymnastic
clubs).

Along with the Geselligkeit of the Vereine (associations)
came the Gemütlichkeit (cosiness) loved by the people when
they were sitting together drinking beer or wine and sing-
ing their Volkslieder.

The Romantic movement celebrated the devotion to nature which became trivialized into the love of the German
land and its beauty. Another virtue cultivated by the Romantic movement was the devotion to true and deep love
and friendship as distinct from purely legal marriage or the
French superficial and short-lived passion.[11]

The landowners' (Junker) conception of the nation was
territorial in character. In their view, the conception of the
nation was intimately linked to a territory and space was
needed in order to secure its livelihood. For the Junkers,
competition between nation states was competition about
space claimed by the nation in order to maintain its position in the state system. They saw the nation's identity rooted
in a commonly cultivated territory and the virtues of the
good Germans in their rootedness in the soil of their homeland (Heimatland), in their commitment to the traditions
of their homeland, in the cultivation of their land and in
guarding that land against invaders. Their perspective on
the linkage between nation and soil was expansive with regard to land needed for bettering the competitive position
of the nation in the inter-state struggle, and it was protec-
tive with regard to cultivating and defending the land against
competitors. In its orientation towards the soil, the landowners' idea of the nation merged with the earlier Romantic devotion to nature as the Erhabene into which one has
to sink oneself (hineinversenken) for the sake of complete
fulfilment (Erfüllung). Romantic admiration of nature was
transformed into the love of the German soil the more it
became trivialized in the process of diffusion throughout

society. In this way, commitment to one's homeland and love of the German land (including the protection of its beauty) became a durable feature of German identity. Its linkage with the Prussian landowners' commitment to soil fuelled Germany's struggle with its competitors in the late 19th and early 20th centuries.[12]

The contribution of the officers' corps is the conception of the nation as a unit prepared to fight against competitors who could endanger its position in the nation state system. The officers' corps is the bearer of belligerent nationalism. In its view, the nation stands together and comes to itself in warfare: that is, the people become conscious of being a nation and of what it stands for. The virtues here demanded from the good member of the nation are the soldier's virtues of courage, fearlessness (Unerschrockenheit), discipline and obedience to orders. In these last two features, the officers' conception of virtue merged with the discipline and obedience of the legally trained civil servant.[13]

The large-scale industrialists had direct access to the power centre and took part in preparing Germany for its struggle with its competitors in the European state system. They led their companies in a similar way to officers leading their corps in warfare. Strategic planning, directing people in the interest of a higher goal, absolute devotion to that goal and perseverance in its realization were the virtues they required. Their idea of the nation was one of busy workers submitting themselves to the leadership of statesmen and large-scale industrialists, who directed the ship of the nation through the storms of fierce competition in an expanding world economy, with nation states as the main economic and political units. Their ethical catalogue included the complementary virtues of leadership and obedience, strategic planning and hard work. Steel and iron became the symbols of the large-scale industrialists' wealth, of the strength of the army's weapons and of the virtues of the German army's officers and ordinary soldiers.[14]

From Nationalism to National Socialism

Three forces influenced the further development of the German idea of the nation and of German identity after the foundation of the German nation state in 1871: intensified international competition, Social Darwinism and mass culture.

There was, firstly, the intensification of economic and political competition in the European state system towards the end of the century, to which the growing German industry and the German politics of armament and late-coming colonization contributed its part.

There was, secondly, the success of Darwin's theory of evolution. In a climate of increasing economic and political competition, the vulgarization of Darwin's theory led to its translation from biology to social and political theory. Competition between nation states was interpreted as a process of natural selection, one in which the fittest survive and the weak die out. In its most extreme version, Social Darwinism argued that the strength of the nation state in that struggle for survival was rooted in the biological structure of the nation.

Thus the nation became interpreted in biological terms as a species, as a community of common descent tied together by blood and linked in its existence to the soil that nurtured the species. The Kulturnation (culture nation) and the Staatsnation (state nation) now were primordially rooted in a Volksnation (folk nation). The Volk (folk) was not simply conceived of as people but as a community of common blood, the roots of which had to be traced back to its biological ancestors.

The third factor was the growth of mass culture. An increasing number of writings were no longer addressed only to an educated élite, but to a growing mass of people. Therefore the intellectuals – scholars, writers and artists – were replaced to a considerable degree by popular writers like Lagarde, Langbehn and Chamberlain in influencing public opinion. This change in the formation of public opinion implied that the reflection of the educated élites played a less important role and simplification, as well as dramatization, a more important one. There was no civic and republican sense of the nation as a community of citizens, the

idea of the Kulturnation became Germanized and bound
to the Volksnation in the primordial sense of blood ties,
and this Volksnation served as the sub-structure of a forceful Staatsnation.

Nazism made the Germans a Volksnation in the most
extreme form of blood ties and racist purity. That Volksnation
received some legitimizing support as a Kulturnation by right-
wing Hegelians like Karl Larenz (1935) and Julius Binder
(1934).[15] The Volksnation also took on the form of a thoroughly militarized Staatsnation that used capitalist industrial
growth, modern science and technology to realize its goal
of German predominance.[16]

2. GERMAN NATION AND GERMAN IDENTITY AFTER
NATIONAL SOCIALISM

After the end of the Hitler regime in 1945, the questions
'Who are the Germans?' and 'What is the German nation?'
were determined by two facts of history: the Holocaust and
the division of the nation into two states – one part of the
democratic West, the other part of the communist East.[17]
Both the German linkage of Volksnation, Kulturnation and
Staatsnation and the virtues that constituted German identity were discredited by the Holocaust. The German idea of
the nation had been manipulated by racist ideology and
Hitler's politics of world domination, and the German virtues had been used to justify the Holocaust. Too many well-
educated, courageous, disciplined, hard-working, obedient,
true-love-and-friendship-cultivating and homeland-loving
Germans had carried out the Holocaust.

What was left of the German nation and the German identity that was not discredited? What could have been an inspira-
tion for a new beginning, the republican idea of the nation
and the civic virtues, had failed in German history in 1848–49
and in 1919–33. They were now imposed by the Western
allies in West Germany, and in East Germany the Socialist
state was imposed by the Soviet Union. In the West, the
majority of people solved the identity crisis by way of public
disengagement, by a retreat into private life and by concentration on the economic reconstruction of their personal

situation and of the country. As a discredited people, they had become insecure about showing overt commitment to their nation and to German virtues. This insecurity is still alive. According to a survey conducted in December 1988/ January 1989 in West Germany, a majority of 52 per cent saw in the Nazi regime the specific difference of German history compared to the history of other nations. It is, however, remarkable that only 4 per cent of East Germans shared this view of German history, according to a survey conducted in December 1990. For the East Germans, the division of Germany after 1945 was of the greatest importance. In January 1989 and December 1990 respectively, 74 per cent of West Germans and 79 per cent of East Germans assigned to the separation of Germany the greatest importance for their history out of a list of 21 historical events.[18] In public opinion polls carried out at different times in the post-war period and right up to 1990, we find that the lowest percentage of people saying that they are proud of their nation are German, the major reason being awareness of Nazi crimes. The degree of pride expressed was at its lowest immediately after the war and has increased until 1990, but it was still below the rate of any other country in the polls. According to surveys, 73 per cent of West Germans were proud to be Germans in 1959, 57.2 per cent in 1982, 63.9 per cent in 1988 and 66 per cent in 1990. The East German comparable figure in 1990 was 68 per cent. The EC average for national pride was 80.7 per cent in 1988.[19]

3. THE GERMANS AND NATIONAL SOCIALISM

The division of the country with regard to the question of drawing a line under the Nazi past is remarkable: 53 per cent vote for such a line, 41 per cent against. There is a great difference here between East and West. In the East, only 39 per cent argue for drawing a line, and 58 per cent against, in the West 56 per cent for and 37 per cent against. Level of education is an important factor in this context, the vote against drawing a line increasing from the lowest (23 per cent), to the middle (45 per cent) and to the highest level of education at 61 per cent.

This division of the population reflects the intellectual debate of German historians on that topic in the mid-eighties and the continued conflict between efforts of right-wing conservative intellectuals and left-wing intellectuals after unification. The crux of this debate is about regaining a national historical consciousness that gives the Nazi regime not the one and only place but only a place side by side with other periods in the totality of German history.[20] The one side of this debate argues that the nation has the right to establish a positive self-conception after it has paid off its guilt. Those who take this position demand justice in the judgment on Germans' involvement in the Nazi crimes. They call for 'comparable justice' by seeking to classify Nazi crimes in the context of other major crimes of the 20th century, such as the Osmanian Turks' massacre of the Armenians or the murder of thousands of people who were regarded as a danger to the Stalinist regime. And they want to do so by embedding the Nazi regime in the context of German history as a whole, emphasizing Germany's positive contributions to world history as well as it's negative contributions. The intention here is to regain a positive identity for the Germans and their nation. The consequence of such a redefinition should be more positive self-consciousness of the German people and of their political representatives in playing their part and pursuing their interests in European and global politics. According to this view, German foreign policy should no longer be paralyzed by the abnegation of the Holocaust identity.

The other side of the debate argues that the claim for 'comparable justice' and the attempt at 'historicizing' the Nazi regime would entail an external and internal relativization of the Holocaust as just another collective crime and one to be weighed against the other features of German history. Such a relativization could easily be misused in attempts to play down Germany's responsibility for the Nazi crimes. The Holocaust would lose its incomparable character and Germany its incomparable moral obligation to do everything feasible to atone for its guilt and to be particularly bound by ethical standards in its politics. In this view, the German people have to keep in mind the incomparable character of the Nazi crimes in order to feel their special moral obligation, as part of working on the construction of a positive national identity for a better future. This should, however, not preclude the Germans from trying to relate to and renew their positive contributions to world history.

The sharp division of the whole nation on the question of drawing a line under the Nazi past indicates that this debate will be part of the construction and reconstruction of German identity for a long time to come.

4. THE GERMANS AND THEIR IMMIGRANTS

In the light of the Holocaust, it has always been an important issue as to how the Germans deal with immigrants to their country. After the relatively unproblematical absorption of about eight million German refugees from former German territory and from special areas of German settlement in Eastern Europe between 1945 and 1950 (another four million settled in East Germany), three types of immigrants have attracted special attention in post-war West Germany: guest workers, resettlers of German origin and those seeking political asylum. Since 1955, guest workers have come into the country because of special agreements with southern European countries in order to meet the demand for unskilled labour by an enormously growing economy. The number of guest workers rose from 100 000 in 1955 to 2.6 million in 1973. Further recruitment was stopped by a ban in 1973 in reaction to the economic crisis in the early seventies. Since the end of the seventies, immigration of resettlers and asylum seekers has grown, with about 50 000 resettlers and 30 000 to 100 000 asylum seekers arriving per year until 1987. From that year on there was a dramatic increase in immigration of first resettlers and then asylum seekers, up to more than 600 000 in 1992. The number of resettlers rose to almost 400 000 in 1990 and levelled off well above 200 000 in 1991 and 1992. The number of asylum seekers increased to 438 191 in 1992.[21] A much debated change of the law in 1993 that permits the deportation of any asylum seeker intending to enter Germany from a so-called safe country, and a quota of 225 000 per year for resettlers has diminished the wave of immigration. By the end of 1992, the foreign population of Germany was 6.5 million (that is, about 8 per cent of the total population); 97 per cent of foreigners lived in West Germany.

The influx of immigrants in those years was accompanied by a dramatic increase in the number of attacks, riots and crimes against foreigners, reaching its peak between mid-1992 and mid-1993, and decreasing since then. From 1991 to 1992, a growth in the number of right-wing violent acts of 54 per cent to 2285 was registered.[22] Public debate was preoccupied by the dramatic growth of both immigration and right-wing extremism. Had the Germans again demonstrated their inability to accept aliens in their country? Is their idea of the nation (as rooted in common origins and culture) an obstacle to the integration of a society that has become ethnically and culturally pluralistic due to the Europeanization and globalization of modern life, a process fuelled by economic growth and the expansion of communication? Do they fail in the integration of their society because they have summoned guest workers for economic reasons, resettlers for political reasons and asylum seekers because of the formal humanism of their constitution, but are unprepared and unwilling to conceive of their community of citizens in the same pluralistic terms that correspond to the reality of the people living in Germany? Are they unable to transform the factual pluralism of their society into the normative pluralism of a civil society integrated by a notion of citizenship that is independent of ethnic and cultural origin? Are they unable to conceive of the nation as just that citizens' community because they have always interpreted the nation as a community of people tied together by common origin? Are they less prepared for such a pluralistic notion of citizenship as a multicultural society than other Western nations like France, Britain and the United States which have much more experience in defining the nation as a community of citizens willing to live together, independent of their origin?

German law reserves citizenship predominantly for people of common origin. This law has been responsible for an insufficient integration of guest workers into German society thus far. Guest workers were expected to return to their home country so no special arrangements were made for their naturalization until 1991. However, most of them did not go back but stayed in the country without citizenship. Though foreigners share many rights with the native population, they lack political rights and therefore cannot participate in political decision-making. This is particularly a problem in the big cities where up to 26 per cent of the inhabitants are foreign.[23]

If we look at the data on attitudes towards foreigners, however, we discover a striking development. Contrary to the impression given by the wave of right-wing violence against foreigners, the acceptance of foreigners by the native population generally grew in the decade between 1980 and 1990 and remained at the level of 1990 in the early nineties or increased or decreased only slightly, depending on the foreign groups in question and the questions asked. According to Allbus surveys conducted in 1980, 1984, 1988 and 1990, restrictive attitudes towards guest workers decreased from about 55 to about 35 per cent of the respondents. Four statements were combined to indicate a restrictive attitude: guest workers should (1) better adjust to the German style of living, (2) be sent back if their jobs are needed, (3) not be allowed any political activity, (4) marry among their own.[24]

The data show that the reaction of the Germans to foreigners is no different from that of their European neighbours. A Eurobarometer survey conducted in December 1994 shows, for example, 43 per cent of respondents in the EU average who say that there are too many foreigners in their country. With 40 per cent, Germany (West and East) is below that average.[25]

A multivariate model of the above mentioned Allbus data explains negative attitudes towards foreigners in Germany by four main variables: the lower the educational level achieved, the more the political orientation leans towards the right, the higher the level of relative deprivation and – with the smallest effect – the higher the age, the more negative the attitudes towards foreigners expressed. This result is also corroborated for all member states of the European Union with a multivariate analysis of the Eurobarometer data.[26]

Thus the recent wave of xenophobia and violence against

foreigners has to be explained by socio-structural variables that are effective in all countries, independently of cultural differences. Contemporary German identity does not produce any more xenophobia, right-wing extremism or violence against foreigners than the identity of the other nations compared here, though there are still differences in the concept of the nation.

5. THE CHANGE OF VALUES

Has there been a change in the Germans' character, in their values and attitudes and typical behaviour of which the sharp rejection of National Socialism and a greater tolerance towards aliens is a reflection?

If we look at the stereotypes used by others and by Germans to characterize the Germans, little change seems to have occurred. According to a survey conducted in seven Western European countries in 1963, the Germans are particularly hard-working and busy, disciplined and self-controlled, scientific and exact, forceful, active and dynamic. According to the Italians and French, however, Germans are also frigid and stiff. And in the view of all, not very reliable, not life-loving and sensuous, not humorous and cheerful, not romantic and emotional, not easily excitable and hot-headed, not chasing girls, not superficial and prone to flattery, not lazy and indolent. The Germans described themselves in much the same way, except that they regard themselves as pretty reliable and not as frigid and stiff as the Italians and the French do.[27]

Nearly 30 years later, Germans still describe themselves by the same character traits: in 1991, more than 80 per cent said that they are hard-working and busy, love order, and are clean and efficient. According to 62 per cent, they are also disciplined. Less than 40 per cent characterize themselves by traits such as life-loving and romantic.[28] They see themselves as particularly qualified for building cars, industrial plants and homes; a bit less so for composing music, doing scientific research, constructing safe nuclear reactors, writing books and making inventions; and much less so for staging theatre plays, cooking, painting, producing films and creating fashion.[29]

However, a change *has* occurred in the values, attitudes and dispositions of the German people in the post-war decades. This is confirmed by a number of surveys which report a decline in hard work, discipline and obedience as well as law and order as dominating value-orientations, in favour of an increased emphasis on freedom and autonomy, self-realization, participation in decision-making, permissiveness and tolerance. According to surveys, the idea of life as a task was expressed by 59 per cent of the respondents in 1959, by 60 per cent in 1964, 58 per cent in 1968, and only 43 per cent in 1982. A 1952 survey shows that 59 per cent of respondents wanted schools to train pupils to obedience, order and discipline; but only 28 per cent said so in 1973, 30 per cent in 1979 and 32 per cent in 1986. The percentage of people who reported that they go rarely or never to church services increased from 13 to 44 per cent between 1953 and 1988. When asked to select two out of four policies – namely (1) law and order, (2) participation in decision-making, (3) fighting inflation and (4) protection of free speech – the percentage of 'materialists', according to Inglehart's terminology, choosing law and order and fighting inflation decreased from 42.2 to 20.7 per cent between 1970 and 1990, the smallest percentage in the European Community after Denmark, Luxemburg and the Netherlands.[30]

The decline of the law and order mentality has been accompanied by the rise of the mentality of autonomy and self-realization. The percentage of people who are in favour of educating children for autonomy grew from 28 to 66 between 1951 and 1989.[31]

At the same time, participation in public affairs and the appreciation of democratic rights have become more and more important. A major visible change came with the student movement in the late sixties and the extension of participation in informal political groups, citizens' groups and new social movements in the seventies. Like other Western societies, Germany went through a 'participatory' revolution at that time.[32]

As the surveys indicate, Germany has become a 'normal' member of Western democracies with citizens who are committed to the rules of democracy and who make use of their rights to participate: at least like the average of the populations of other EU member states, and in some aspects more than the average for other European societies.

6. THE GERMANS AND EUROPE

The Germans are considered as promoters of European integration, and the Germans see themselves in the same way. According to a survey, conducted in 1986, the highest percentage of Europeans and Germans, namely 41 and 77 per cent, placed Germany in the first rank with regard to the country's efforts in integrating Europe.[33] This might be a reflection of the real efforts of the German political leadership from Adenauer to Kohl. The reasons for this have always been among the premises of German foreign politics, accepted by all major political parties: the acceptance of Germany after the Second World War and the Nazi crimes; support for Germany in its exposed position *vis à vis* the Soviet bloc; the need for its long-term goal of reunification to be guaranteed by its absolute loyalty to its Western Allies and by playing a constructive role in building and maintaining supranational Western institutions, particularly the European Community and NATO. Until the Soviet bloc broke down, West German politics had been primarily directed at keeping the European and the North Atlantic loyalties in balance. Since 1989, however, there has been a clear priority for the further development of the European Union. The relationship to the USA will unavoidably turn more towards economic competition in the triangle of Japan, the USA and the European Union.

Compared to the priority of European integration for the political leadership, the attitude of the German population to European integration is no different from that of the average citizen of the member states. The difference between the political leadership and the population is accompanied by a similar difference between the business élite and the population. Asked whether German unification or the EC single market is more important for them, 53 per cent of the West German population chose unification, 20 per cent the internal market; 19 per cent of business managers chose unification, and 63 per cent the single market, in 1989/90.[34]

Together with Denmark and the United Kingdom, the Germans give the lowest level of support to a common European currency. The net vote for a single currency started at about +22 per cent, about 10 per cent below EU average, in 1990 to go down to -20 per cent, nearly 40 per cent below EU-average, in 1994.[35] The Germans were the only ones who mentioned that they would have to pay for the others – with more money transfers from Germany to Brussels than vice versa – as one of the three most important fears regarding the single market in a 1992 Eurobarometer survey. After too much immigration (44 per cent) and criminality because of insufficient border control (43 per cent), it was the third major problem (42 per cent) that troubled the Germans. For the West Germans, it was the second most important troubling problem (44 per cent), right after too much immigration (45 per cent). The EC average was only 20 per cent.[36] Thus it is no surprise that we find the second highest percentage of people perceiving the single market as disadvantageous in Germany at 34 per cent, right after France at 39 per cent, and also the second lowest percentage perceiving the single market as advantageous at 38 per cent, also right after France at 33 per cent. These are Eurobarometer results in the autumn of 1993. Half a year later, the Germans had the second smallest percentage expressing hopes and the second highest percentage expressing fears with regard to the single market with 51 per cent hopes and 41 per cent fears, close behind the French. The EU average is 54 per cent hopes and 35 per cent fears.[37]

The Fragile German–EU Relationship

The survey data show a remarkable gap between the conventional view that Germany promotes European integration and the population's attitude to that integration: the latter is no more than average in the general question of integration and quite below the average of EU member states in more specific questions like the single market and a single European currency. The fears regarding closer integration are, particularly, fears of too much immigration, increasing criminality and, very distinctly, of the presumed obligation to pay for the other members.

This characterization of the fragile German relationship to the European Union is supported by the fact that the Germans are part of the group of nations that are least interested in European politics and least informed about that politics.[38] The lower level of knowledge is accompanied by a lower level of identification with Europe, compared to most other countries. According to a spring 1992 survey, the Germans saw themselves as often or sometimes Europeans (37 per cent) or never Europeans (59 per cent), which was quite below the average of 46 to 51 per cent and came right after the British and the Irish people. Asked about their future identity, 41 per cent of Germans regarded themselves as Germans only, 43 per cent as Germans and Europeans, 9 per cent as Europeans and Germans and 3 per cent as Europeans only. The average of the EU countries were 38 per cent, 48 per cent, 7 per cent and 4 per cent respectively.[39]

The lower percentages of people interested in and informed about European politics, people identifying with Europe and people wanting local and European rights across borders in Germany indicate that the German citizens lack affiliation to the integrationist policy of their political leaders. This has been the case with regard to Western European integration in the past, and it seems to be the case with regard to the integration of the Eastern European nations in the European Union in the future. The German political leadership takes a leading role in opening the doors of the European Union for Eastern Europe. It aims at deepening and extending the integration of Europe at the same time, which requires an integration process at 'different speeds'. Such a policy has its complications and insecurities and is feared by those member states that are more reluctant with regard to the integration of Eastern European countries. In taking this lead, the German political leadership is once more well ahead of the population. There is, however, a striking difference between East and West Germans in this regard. According to an autumn 1992 survey, the East Germans are more in favour of the integration of Belarus, Bulgaria, Estonia, Hungary, Latvia, Lithuania, the Czech Republic, Russia, Slovakia and the Ukraine, and Poland than the EU average. However, the West Germans are only in favour of EU extension with regard to Estonia, Latvia, Lithuania and the Czech Republic. Only in regard to Hungary are they nearly as favourable as the EU average. In all other cases they are well below average.[40]

The gap between political leaders and citizens in identifying with Europe and advancing its integration calls for more inclusion of the citizens in European matters. The media have the task of dealing more with European politics. Politics has to bring European affairs back from the meetings of élite politicians and élite administrators to the national arena by including the national parliament much more in the process of decision-making. Public debate and political decision-making have to turn the citizens' attention to the level of European politics in order to allow them to keep pace with the factual transmission of politics to the European level.

CONCLUDING REMARKS

The German idea of the nation and the identity of Germany experienced a remarkable transformation without, however, doing completely away with their historical roots, from the 1770s to the 1990s: the transformation of the Kulturnation (culture nation) to the Staatsnation (state nation) from the 1770s to the 1870s, and of the Staatsnation to the Volksnation (folk nation) from the 1870s to 1945.

Between 1770 and 1870, German identity was shaped by the educated bourgeoisie, placing classical education in the first rank. This was accompanied by Geselligkeit (conviviality, companionship) and Gemütlichkeit (cosiness) promoted by the Vereine (societies, clubs) and by Romantic love as well as Romantic devotion to nature, contributed by the Romantic movement. After 1870 the educated bourgeoisie's influence on society was limited by the rising influence of the Prussian officers' corps, the Prussian bureaucracy, the landowners (Junker) of the Eastern provinces and the large-scale industrialists. The officers' corps promoted the virtues of courage, fearlessness, discipline and obedience in carrying out orders; the civil servants discipline, reliability, obedience and devotion to state service; the landowners commitment to German soil and defending it against enemies;

the large-scale industrialists strategic planning, struggle against competitors and absolute devotion to the goal of success. These virtues grew in the Kaiserreich (empire) so that Germany was not prepared for the Weimar Republic which was unable to bring about a change of character in favour of virtues needed in a free and democratic society. Instead, the Nazi regime turned the German virtues into the virtues of a better race destined to rule the world.

The break in 1945 was deep. The influence of the old classes of the Prussian landowners and the large-scale industrialists was no longer there because of the loss of the Eastern lands and the destruction of the big concerns that had collaborated with the Nazi regime. The educated bourgeoisie and the civil servants remained influential but had to compete with a growing plurality of influences that shaped German identity in the post-war decades: new successful business people, technicians, the mass media, sport idols and global pop stars, particularly from Britain and the USA. The integration of West Germany in Western culture, promoted particularly by the mass media, exerted an enormous long-term effect on German identity. Obedience and discipline diminished as virtues, autonomy and self-realization became the celebrated virtues. The growing confrontation with the plurality of nations, cultures and life-styles made the Germans much more tolerant and respectful of others than before, though to a lesser degree than their change from obedience to autonomy.

The German idea of the nation came under pressure from the various waves of immigration, which have made a great majority much more willing and used to living with foreigners but have also produced xenophobic and violent reactions from a minority of people who feel relatively deprived and see themselves losing in the competition for scarce resources. Acceptance and rejection of foreigners exist side by side because of the different effects of the globalization of life on different strata of the population.

The changes in conception of the nation and in attitudes that took place in the post-war decades indicate that Germany will be able to cope with immigration as well as other European countries if it does not flood the country. This holds true, though the German law of citizenship is still predominantly based on common origin in contrast to other Western countries, and this legislation impedes the practice of naturalization. In the long run, this leads to a growing gap between *de facto* immigration and 'immigrants' who are not naturalized. The fact that up to 26 per cent of city populations are foreigners who are not integrated in the rights and duties of citizenship will cause increasing problems. There is also insufficient contact between natives and foreigners to enhance the integration of a *de facto* pluralized society. Here is a problem area that waits for integrative measures in the coming years.

We can assume that the great majority of the Germans are prepared to live in a pluralized society because of the changes in their mentality that have taken place in the postwar decades. The rejection of National Socialism and its ideology has increased steadily. That development has been complemented by a deepening commitment to the rules of democracy, more tolerance of foreigners and an increased appreciation of freedom and autonomy.

That transformation of the German idea of the nation and of German identity has been further advanced by Germany's integration in the European Union. However, there is a perplexing gap between the German political leadership's promotion of European integration and the attitude of the population towards that process which is only average, or even remarkably below average, in comparison to the other member states of the European Union. Therefore the agenda for deepening Germany's integration in the European Union calls for bringing European matters to the attention of the general public in the mass media and back to the national parliament's participation in European decision-making. And it calls also for programmes of education by giving European matters more space in the curricula of schools, by expanding language courses and by extending exchange programmes. In doing so, the German nation and German identity will be increasingly integrated in a European Union of nations and identities.

NOTES

1. Werner Conze, *Die deutsche Nation. Ergebnis der Geschichte* (Göttingen: Vandenhoeck & Ruprecht, 1963) pp. 17–36.
2. Joseph Rovan, 'Staat und Nation in der deutchen Geschichte', in Werner Weidenfeld (Ed.), *Die Identität der Deutschen* (Bonn: Bundeszentrale für politische Bildung, 1983) pp. 237–240.
3. Johann Gottfried Herder, *Sämtliche Werke*, 33 vols, Ed. Bernhard Suphan (Nachdruck. Hildesheim: Olms, 1877–1913/1967/1968).
4. Wilhelm von Humboldt, *Wilhelm von Humboldts gesammelte Schriften*, vol. 1, Ed. Albert Leitzmann (Berlin: Walter de Gruyter, 1903/1968a). Wilhelm von Humboldt. *Wilhelm von Humboldts gesammelte Schriften*, vol. 2, Ed. Albert Leitzmann (Berlin: Walter de Gruyter, 1904/1968b) pp. 387–399. Johann Wolfgang von Goethe, *Goethes Werke*, vol. 12, Ed. Werner Weber and Hans J. Schrimpf (Hamburg: Christian Wegner Verlag, 1953) p. 269, pp. 361–364. Johann Wolfgang von Goethe, *Goethes Werke*, vol. 45, Ed. by appointment of the Großherzogin Sophie von Sachsen (Weimar: Böhlau, 1900) p. 344. Franz T. Bratranek, *Goethes Briefwechsel mit den Gebrüdern von Humboldt (1795– 1832)* (Leipzig: Brockhaus, 1876). Hans J. Schrimpf, *Goethes Begriff der Weltliteratur* (Stuttgart: Metzler, 1968). Günter Oesterle, 'Kulturelle Identität und Klassizismus. Wilhelm von Humboldts Entwurf einer allgemeinen und vergleichenden Literaturerkenntnis als Teil einer vergleichenden Anthropologie', in Bernhard Giesen (Ed.), *Nationale und kulturelle Identität* (Frankfurt a.M.: Suhrkamp, 1991) pp. 304–349.
5. Paul Kluckhohn, 'Voraussetzungen und Verlauf der romantischen Bewegung', in Theodor Steinbüchel (Ed.), *Romantik. Ein Zyklus Tübinger Vorlesungen* (Tübingen and Stuttgart: Wunderlich, 1948) pp. 13–26.
6. Friedrich v. Schlegel, 'Über das Studium der griechischen Poesie', in: *Friedrich v. Schlegel. Schriften zur Literatur*, Ed. Wolfdietrich Rasch (München: Deutscher Taschenbuch Verlag, 1972) pp. 84–192.
7. Novalis, *Schriften. Die Werke Friedrich von Hardenbergs*, Ed. Paul Kluckhohn and Richard Samuel (historical and critical edition), vol. 3. Abt. IX, HKA-No. 50 (Darmstadt: Wissenschaftliche Buchgesellschaft, 1977).
8. Bernhard Giesen, *Die Intellektuellen und die Nation* (Frankfurt a.M.: Suhrkamp, 1993) pp. 201–229. Louis L. Snyder, *German Nationalism: The Tragedy of a People* (Port Washington, N.Y.: Kennikat Press, 1952/ 1969) pp. 123–152. Georg G. Iggers, 'Heinrich von Treitschke', in Hans-Ulrich Wehler (Ed.), *Deutsche Historiker*, vol. 2 (Göttingen: Vandenhoeck & Ruprecht, 1971) pp. 120–163. Wolfgang Hardtwig, 'Von Preußens Aufgabe in Deutschland zu Preußens Aufgabe in der Welt. Liberalismus und borussianisches Geschichtsbild zwischen Revolution und Imperialismus', in Wolfgang Hardtwig, *Geschichtskultur und Wissenschaft* (München: Deutscher Taschenbuch Verlag, 1990) pp. 103–160. Hellmut Seier, 'Heinrich von Sybel', in Hans-Ulrich Wehler (Ed.), *Deutsche Historiker*, vol. 2 (Göttingen: Vandenhoeck & Ruprecht, 1971). Jörn Rüsen, 'Johann Gustav Droysen', in Hans-Ulrich Wehler (Ed.), *Deutsche Historiker*, vol. 2 (Göttingen: Vandenhoeck and Ruprecht, 1971).

9. Nobert Elias, *Studien über die Deutschen* (Frankfurt a.M.: Suhrkamp, 1989).

10. Thomas Mann, *Betrachtungen eines Unpolitischen* (Berlin: Fischer, 1918/ 1922).

11. Fritz K. Ringer, *The Decline of the German Mandarins. The German Academic Community, 1890–1933* (Cambridge, Mass.: Harvard University Press, 1969). Ulrich Engelhardt, *'Bildungsbürgertum'. Begriffs- und Dogmengeschichte eines Etiketts* (Stuttgart: Klett-Cotta, 1986). Jürgen Kocka (Ed.), *Bildungsbürgertum im 19. Jahrhundert.* Teil IV: Politischer Einfluß und gesellschaftliche Formation (Stuttgart: Klett-Cotta, 1989). Hermann Glaser, *Bildungsbürgertum und Nationalismus. Politik und Kultur im Wilhelminischen Deutschland* (München: Deutscher Taschenbuch Verlag, 1993).

12. Hans-Jürgen Puhle, *Agrarische Interessenpolitik und preußischer Konservatismus 1893–1914. Ein Beitrag zur Analyse des Nationalismus in Deutschland am Beispiel des Bundes der Landwirte und der Deutschen Konservativen Partei* (Hannover: Verlag für Literatur und Zeitgeschehen, 1967). Hans-Jürgen Puhle, 'Lords and Peasants in the Kaiserreich', in Robert G. Moeller (Ed.), *Peasants and Lords in Modern Germany* (Boston: Allen & Unwin, 1986) pp. 81–109. Robert M. Berdahl, 'Conservative politics and aristocratic landowners in Bismarckian Germany', *Journal of Modern History* 44 (1972) pp. 1–20.

13. Snyder, 1952/1969, pp. 227–254. Norbert Elias, *Studien über die Deutschen* (Frankfurt a.M.: Suhrkamp, 1989) pp. 61–158, 271–273. Martin Kitchen, *The German Officer Corps 1890–1914* (Oxford: Clarendon Press, 1968). John C.G. Röhl, 'Higher Civil Servants in Germany 1890–1900', *Journal of Contemporary History* 2 (1967) pp. 101–121. Fritz K. Ringer, 'Higher Education in Germany in the nineteenth Century', *Journal of Contemporary History* 2 (1967) pp. 123–138.

14. Hartmut Kaelble, *Industrielle Interessenpolitik in der Wilhelminischen Gesellschaft. Der Centralverband Deutscher Industrieller 1895–1914* (Berlin: de Gruyter, 1967). Kenneth D. Barkin, *The Controversy over German Industrialization 1890– 1902* (Chicago and London: University of Chicago Press, 1970). Ralf Dahrendorf, *Gesellschaft und Demokratie in Deutschland* (München: Deutscher Taschenbuch Verlag, 1968/1971) pp. 39–55. Helmut Böhme, *Deutschlands Weg zur Großmacht: Studien zum Verhältnis von Wirtschaft und Staat während der Reichsgründungszeit* (Köln: Kiepenheuer & Witsch, 1966).

15. Ernst Topitsch, *Die Sozialphilosophie Hegels als Heilslehre und Herrschaftsideologie* (Neuwied and Berlin: Luchterhand, 1967).

16. Geoffrey Pridham and Jeremy Noakes (Eds), *Nazism 1919–1945. A Documentary Reader*, 2 vols (Exeter: University of Exeter Press, 1983/ 1984). Karl D. Bracher, *Die deutsche Diktatur* (Köln and Berlin: Kiepenheuer & Witsch, 1969). George L. Mosse, *Nazism* (Oxford: Blackwell, 1978).

17. Ralf Dahrendorf, *Gesellschaft und Demokratie in Deutschland* (München: Deutscher Taschenbuch Verlag, 1968/1971). Bernhard Willms, *Die Deutsche Nation* (Köln: Hohenheim, 1982). Gerd-Klaus Kaltenbrunner (Ed.), *Was ist deutsch? Die Unvermeidlichkeit eine Nation zu sein* (Freiburg i.Br.: Herder, 1980). Eberhard Schultz, *Die deutsche Nation in Europa*

(Bonn: Europa-Union-Verlag, 1982). Werner Weidenfeld (Ed.), *Die Identität der Deutschen* (Bonn: Bundeszentrale für politische Bildung, 1983). Werner Weidenfeld (Ed.), *Politische Kultur und Deutsche Frage* (Köln: Wissenschaft und Politik, 1989). Werner Weidenfeld (Ed.), *Deutschland. Eine Nation – doppelte Geschichte* (Köln: Wissenschaft und Politik, 1993). Werner Weidenfeld and Karl-Rudolf Korte, *Die Deutschen. Profil einer Nation* (Stuttgart: Klett-Cotta, 1991). Elisabeth Noelle-Neumann and Renate Köcher, *Die verletzte Nation. Über den Versuch der Deutschen, ihren Charakter zu ändern* (Stuttgart: Deutsche Verlagsanstalt, 1987). Michael Wolffs, *Patriotismus, Wiedervereinigung und Europäische Gemeinschaft in der Einschätzung der Bevölkerung. Umfragedaten aus den Jahren 1951–1986* (Bonn: Forschungsinstitut der Konrad-Adenauer-Stiftung, 1986). Manfred Hättich, *Deutschland: Eine zu späte Nation* (Mainz and München: von Hase & Köhler, 1990). Erwin K. Scheuch, *Wie deutsch sind die Deutschen? Eine Nation wandelt ihr Gesicht* (Bergisch-Gladbach: Lübbe, 1991). Harold James, *Deutsche Identität 1770–1990* (Frankfurt a.M.: Campus, 1991).

18. *Allensbach Archiv* (1988/1989) IfD-Umfrage 5014, (1990) IfD-Umfrage 9010.

19. Elisabeth Noelle and Erich P. Neumann (Eds), *Jahrbuch der öffentlichen Meinung 1965–1967* (1967) p. 156. Frank Brettschneider, Katja Ahlstich and Bettina Zügel, 'Materialien zu Gesellschaft, Wirtschaft und Politik in den Mitgliedsstaaten der Europäischen Gemeinschaft', in Oscar W. Gabriel (Ed.), *Die EG-Staaten im Vergleich. Strukturen, Prozesse, Politikinhalte* (Opladen: Westdeutscher Verlag, 1992) p. 551. *Der Spiegel,* Nr. 46 vom 12.11.1990, p. 114.

20. Rudolf Augstein (Ed.), *Historikerstreit* (München: Piper, 1987). Bernd Faulenbach, 'Eine neue Sicht der Geschichte? Zur Diskussion über die deutsche Vergangenheit', *Blätter für deutsche und internationale Politik* 37 (1992, 1993). Dan Diner (Ed.), *Ist der Nationalsozialismus Geschichte?* (Frankfurt a.M.: Fischer, 1987). Thomas Lillig, Beatrice Mack, Eric Natter and Barbara Rheinbay, 'Deutschland im Einigungsprozeß: Eine Literaturübersicht', in Werner Weidenfeld (Ed.), *Deutschland. Eine Nation – doppelte Geschichte* (Köln: Wissenschaft und Politik, 1993) pp. 354–360. Jürgen Habermas, *Eine Art Schadensabwicklung. Kleine politische Schriften VI* (Frankfurt a.M.: Suhrkamp, 1987, 1990). Rainer Zitelmann, 'Wiedervereinigung und deutscher Selbsthaß: Probleme mit dem eigenen Volk', in Werner Weidenfeld (Ed.), *Deutschland. Eine Nation – doppelte Geschichte* (Köln: Wissenschaft und Politik, 1993).

21. Statistisches Bundesamt (Ed.), *Statistisches Jahrbuch für die Bundesrepublik Deutschland* (Wiesbaden: Metzler-Poeschel, 1993) p. 73.

22. Statistisches Bundesamt (Ed.), 1993, p. 169. Manfred Küchler, 'Germans and "Others": Racism, Xenophobia, or "Legitimate Conservatism"?', *German Politics* 3 (1994) p. 47.

23. Deutscher Städtetag, *Statistisches Jahrbuch Deutscher Gemeinden* (Köln: J. P. Bachem, 1992) p. 26.

24. ZA. ALLBUS (Köln: Zentralarchiv für empirische Sozialforschung), 1980, *ZA-No. 1000*; 1984, *ZA-No. 1340*; 1988, *ZA-No. 1670*; 1990, *ZA-No. 1800*. Küchler, 1994, p. 56.

25. Richard Münch, *Das Projekt Europa. Zwischen Nationalstaat, regionaler Autonomie und Weltgesellschaft* (Frankfurt a.M.: Suhrkamp, 1993) pp. 230–232. European Commission, *Eurobarometer* No. 42 (Brussels, 1995) p. B54. Scheuch, 1991, pp. 162–163.

26. Küchler, 1994, pp. 59–63, 68–69; see also Helmut Willems, *Fremdenfeindliche Gewalt* (Düsseldorf: Leske & Budrich, 1993) pp. 247–267.

27. Edgar Piel, 'Meinungen von Nachbarn über die Deutschen im Spiegel der Demoskopie', in Heinz Duchhardt (Ed.), *In Europas Mitte. Deutschland und seine Nachbarn* (Bonn: Europa-Verlag-Union, 1988), p. 180.

28. *Allensbacher Archiv* (1991) IfD-Umfrage 5047.

29. *Allensbacher Archiv* (1988/89) IfD-Umfrage 5014, (1990) IfD-Umfrage 9010.

30. Heiner Meulemann, *Wertwandel und kulturelle Teilhabe* (Hagen: Fernuniversität, 1989) p. 62. Helmut Klages and Thomas Gensicke, 'Geteilte Werte? Ein Deutscher Ost-West-Vergleich', in Werner Weidenfeld (Ed.), *Deutschland. Eine Nation – doppelte Geschichte* (Köln: Wissenschaft und Politik, 1993) p. 49. *Emnid-Informationen 1951–1989* (Bielefeld. Emnid, 1990). Frank Brettschneider, Katja Ahlstich and Bettina Zügel, 'Materialien zu Gesellschaft, Wirtschaft und Politik in den Mitgliedsstaaten der Europäischen Gemeinschaft', in Oscar W. Gabriel (Ed.), *Die EG-Staaten im Vergleich. Strukturen, Prozesse, Politikinhalte* (Opladen: Westdeutscher Verlag, 1992) pp. 566–567.

31. Meulemann, 1989, p. 62. Klages and Gensicke, 1993, p. 49, based on *Emnid-Informationen 1951–1989* (Bielefeld).

32. Max Kaase, 'Partizipatorische Revolution – Ende der Parteien?', in Joachim Raschke (Ed.), *Bürger und Parteien – Ansichten und Analysen einer schwierigen Beziehung* (Opladen: Westdeutscher Verlag, 1982).

33. Elisabeth Noelle-Neumann and Gerhard Herdegen, 'Die Öffentliche Meinung', in Werner Weidenfeld and Wolfgang Wessels (Eds), *Jahrbuch der Europäischen Integration 1986/87* (1986/1987) pp. 302–304. Werner Weidenfeld and Karl-Rudolf Korte, *Die Deutschen. Profil einer Nation* (Stuttgart: Klett-Cotta, 1991) p. 209.

34. Noelle-Neumann and Herdegen, 1989/1990, p. 282. Weidenfeld and Korte, 1991, p. 220.

35. European Commission 1994, *Eurobarometer* No. 41 (Brussels), p. 30.

36. European Commission 1992b, *Eurobarometer* No. 38 (Brussels), A38–A39.

37. European Commission 1993b, *Eurobarometer* No. 40 (Brussels); p. 68. European Commission 1994, *Eurobarometer* No. 41 (Brussels), A32.

38. European Commission 1993b, *Eurobarometer* No. 40 (Brussels), p. 39. European Commission 1994, *Eurobarometer* No. 41 (Brussels), A20. European Commission 1993a, *Eurobarometer* No. 39 (Brussels), pp. 30, 56, 60. European Commission 1994, *Eurobarometer* No. 41 (Brussels), A22.

39. European Commission 1992a, *Eurobarometer* No. 37 (Brussels), A33–34.

40. European Commission 1992b, *Eurobarometer* No. 38 (Brussels), A46–A47.

BIBLIOGRAPHY

Allensbach Archiv. IfD-Umfrage 5014. 1988/1989.

Allensbach Archiv. IfD-Umfrage 9010. 1990.

Augstein, Rudolf (Ed.). *'Historikerstreit'.* (München: Piper, 1987).

Barkin, Kenneth D. *The Controversy over German Industrialization 1890–1902.* (Chicago and London: University of Chicago Press, 1970).

Berdahl, Robert M. Conservative politics and aristocratic landowners in Bismarckian Germany. *Journal of Modern History* 44, (1972) pp. 1–20.

Binder, Julius. *Der deutsche Volksstaat.* (Tübingen: Mohr Siebeck, 1934).

Böhme, Helmut. *Deutschlands Weg zur Großmacht: Studien zum Verhältnis von Wirtschaft und Staat während der Reichsgründungszeit.* (Köln: Kiepenheuer & Witsch, 1966).

Bracher, Karl D. *Die deutsche Diktatur.* (Köln and Berlin: Kiepenheuer & Witsch, 1969).

Bratranek, Franz T. *Goethes Briefwechsel mit den Gebrüdern von Humboldt (1795–1832).* (Leipzig: Brockhaus, 1876).

Brettschneider, Frank, Katja Ahlstich and Bettina Zügel. Materialien zu Gesellschaft, Wirtschaft und Politik in den Mitgliedsstaaten der Europäischen Gemeinschaft. In: Oscar W. Gabriel (Ed.). *Die EG-Staaten im Vergleich. Strukturen, Prozesse, Politikinhalte.* (Opladen: Westdeutscher Verlag, 1992) pp. 433–625.

Conze, Werner. *Die deutsche Nation. Ergebnis der Geschichte.* (Göttingen: Vandenhoeck & Ruprecht, 1963).

Dahrendorf, Ralf. *Gesellschaft und Demokratie in Deutschland.* (München: Deutscher Taschenbuch Verlag, 1968/1971).

Deutscher Städtetag. *Statistisches Jahrbuch Deutscher Gemeinden.* (Köln: J. P. Bachem, 1992).

Diner, Dan (Ed.), *Ist der Nationalsozialismus Geschichte?.* (Frankfurt a.M.: Fischer, 1987).

Elias, Norbert. *Über den Prozeß der Zivilisation.* 2 vols. (Frankfurt a.M.: Suhrkamp, 1939/1976).

Elias, Norbert. *Studien über die Deutschen.* (Frankfurt a.M.: Suhrkamp, 1989).

Emnid-Informationen 1951–1989. (Bielefeld: Emnid, 1990).

Engelhardt, Ulrich. *'Bildungsbürgertum'. Begriffs- und Dogmengeschichte eines Etiketts.* (Stuttgart: Klett-Cotta, 1986).

European Commission 1992a. *Eurobarometer* No. 37. (Brussels).

European Commission 1992b. *Eurobarometer* No. 38. (Brussels).

European Commission 1993a. *Eurobarometer* No. 39. (Brussels).

European Commission 1993b. *Eurobarometer* No. 40. (Brussels).

European Commission 1994. *Eurobarometer* No. 41. (Brussels).

European Commission 1995. *Eurobarometer* No. 42. (Brussels).

Faulenbach, Bernd. Eine neue Sicht der Geschichte? Zur Diskussion über die deutsche Vergangenheit. *Blätter für deutsche und internationale Politik* 37, (1992) pp. 809–817.

Giesen, Bernhard. *Die Intellektuellen und die Nation.* (Frankfurt a.M.: Suhrkamp, 1993).

Glaser, Hermann. *Bildungsbürgertum und Nationalismus. Politik und Kultur im Wilhelminischen Deutschland.* (München: Deutscher Taschenbuch Verlag, 1993).

Goethe, Johann Wolfgang von. *Goethes Werke.* vol. 45. Ed. by appointment of the Großherzogin Sophie von Sachsen. (Weimar: Böhlau, 1900).

Goethe, Johann Wolfgang von. *Goethes Werke.* vol. 12. Ed. Werner Weber and Hans J. Schrimpf. (Hamburg: Christian Wegner Verlag, 1953).

Habermas, Jürgen. *Eine Art Schadensabwicklung. Kleine politische Schriften VI.* (Frankfurt a.M.: Suhrkamp, 1987).

Hardtwig, Wolfgang. Von Preußens Aufgabe in Deutschland zu Preußens Aufgabe in der Welt. Liberalismus und borussianisches Geschichtsbild zwischen Revolution und Imperialismus. In: Wolfgang Hardtwig. *Geschichtskultur und Wissenschaft.* (München: Deutscher Taschenbuch Verlag, 1990) pp. 103–160.

Hättich, Manfred. *Deutschland: Eine zu späte Nation.* (Mainz and München: von Hase & Köhler, 1990).

Herder, Johann Gottfried. *Sämtliche Werke.* 33 Vols. Ed. Bernhard Suphan. Nachdruck. (Hildesheim: Olms, 1877–1913/1967/68).

Humboldt, Wilhelm von. *Wilhelm von Humboldts gesammelte Schriften.* vol. 1. Ed. Albert Leitzmann. (Berlin: Walter de Gruyter, 1903/1968).

Humboldt, Wilhelm von. *Wilhelm von Humboldts gesammelte Schriften.* vol. 2. Ed. Albert Leitzmann. (Berlin: Walter de Gruyter, 1904/1968).

Iggers, Georg G. Heinrich von Treitschke. In: Hans-Ulrich Wehler (Ed.), *Deutsche Historiker.* vol. 2. (Göttingen: Vandenhoeck & Ruprecht, 1971) pp. 66–80.

James, Harold. *Deutsche Identität 1770–1990.* (Frankfurt a.M.: Campus, 1991).

Kaase, Max. Partizipatorische Revolution – Ende der Parteien? In: Joachim Raschke (Ed.). *Bürger und Parteien – Ansichten und Analysen einer schwierigen Beziehung.* (Opladen: Westdeutscher Verlag, 1982) pp. 173–189.

Kaelble, Hartmut. *Industrielle Interessenpolitik in der Wilhelminischen Gesellschaft. Der Centralverband Deutscher Industrieller 1895–1914.* (Berlin: de Gruyter, 1967).

Kaltenbrunner, Gerd-Klaus (Ed.). *Was ist deutsch? Die Unvermeidlichkeit eine Nation zu sein.* (Freiburg i.Br.: Herder, 1980).

Kitchen, Martin. *The German Officer Corps 1890–1914.* (Oxford: Clarendon Press, 1968).

Klages, Helmut and Thomas Gensicke. Geteilte Werte? Ein Deutscher Ost-West-Vergleich. In: Werner Weidenfeld (Ed.). *Deutschland. Eine Nation – doppelte Geschichte.* (Köln: Wissenschaft und Politik, 1993) pp. 47–59.

Kluckhohn, Paul. Voraussetzungen und Verlauf der romantischen Bewegung. In: Theodor Steinbüchel (Ed.). *Romantik. Ein Zyklus Tübinger Vorlesungen.* (Tübingen and Stuttgart: Wunderlich, 1948) pp. 13–26.

Kocka, Jürgen (Ed.). *Bildungsbürgertum im 19. Jahrhundert.* Teil IV: Politischer Einfluß und gesellschaftliche Formation. (Stuttgart: Klett-Cotta, 1989).

Küchler, Manfred. Germans and 'Others': Racism, Xenophobia, or 'Legitimate Conservatism'? *German Politics* 3, (1994) pp. 47–74.

Larenz, Karl. *Rechts- und Staatsphilosophie der Gegenwart.* (Berlin: Junker & Dünnhaupt, 1935).

Lillig, Thomas, Beatrice Mack, Eric Natter and Barbara Rheinbay. Deutschland im Einigungsprozeß: Eine Literaturübersicht. In: Werner Weidenfeld (Ed.). *Deutschland. Eine Nation – doppelte Geschichte.* (Köln: Wissenschaft und Politik, 1993) pp. 337–366.

Mann, Thomas. *Betrachtungen eines Unpolitischen.* (Berlin: Fischer, 1918/ 1922).

Meulemann, Heiner. *Wertwandel und kulturelle Teilhabe.* (Hagen: Fernuniversität, 1989).

Mosse, George L. *Nazism.* (Oxford: Blackwell, 1978).

Münch, Richard. *Das Projekt Europa. Zwischen Nationalstaat, regionaler Autonomie und Weltgesellschaft.* (Frankfurt a.M.: Suhrkamp, 1993b).

Noelle, Elisabeth and Erich P. Neumann (Eds). *Jahrbuch der öffentlichen Meinung 1965–1967.* (1967) p. 156.

Noelle-Neumann, Elisabeth and Gerhard Herdegen. Die Öffentliche Meinung. In: Werner Weidenfeld and Wolfgang Wessels (Eds). *Jahrbuch der Europäischen Integration 1986/87,* (1986/1987) pp. 302–318.

Noelle-Neumann, Elisabeth and Gerhard Herdegen. Die Öffentliche Meinung. In: Werner Weidenfeld and Wolfgang Wessels (Eds.). *Jahrbuch der Europäischen Integration 1989/90,* (1989/1990) pp. 277–287.

Noelle-Neumann, Elisabeth and Renate Köcher. *Die verletzte Nation. Über den Versuch der Deutschen, ihren Charakter zu ändern.* (Stuttgart: Deutsche Verlagsanstalt, 1987).

Novalis. *Schriften. Die Werke Friedrich von Hardenbergs.* Ed. Paul Kluckhohn and Richard Samuel (historical and critical edition). vol. 3. Abt. IX, HKA-No. 50. (Darmstadt: Wissenschaftliche Buchgesellschaft, 1973).

Oesterle, Günter. Kulturelle Identität und Klassizismus. Wilhelm von Humboldts Entwurf einer allgemeinen und vergleichenden Literaturerkenntnis als Teil einer vergleichenden Anthropologie. In: Bernhard Giesen (Ed.). *Nationale und kulturelle Identität.* (Frankfurt a.M.: Suhrkamp, 1991) pp. 304–349.

Piel, Edgar. Meinungen von Nachbarn über die Deutschen im Spiegel der Demoskopie. In: Heinz Duchhardt (Ed.). *In Europas Mitte. Deutschland und seine Nachbarn.* (Bonn: Europa-Verlag-Union, 1988) pp. 179–186.

Pridham, Geoffrey and Jeremy Noakes (Eds). *Nazism 1919–1945. A Documentary Reader.* 2 vols. (Exeter: University of Exeter Press, 1983/1984).

Puhle, Hans-Jürgen. *Agrarische Interessenpolitik und preußischer Konservatismus 1893–1914. Ein Beitrag zur Analyse des Nationalismus in Deutschland am Beispiel des Bundes der Landwirte und der Deutschen Konservativen Partei.* (Hannover: Verlag für Literatur und Zeitgeschehen, 1967).

Puhle, Hans-Jürgen. Lords and Peasants in the Kaiserreich. In: Robert G. Moeller (Ed.). *Peasants and Lords in Modern Germany.* (Boston: Allen & Unwin, 1986) pp. 81–109.

Ringer, Fritz K. Higher Education in Germany in the nineteenth Century. *Journal of Contemporary History* 2, (1967) pp. 123–138.

Ringer, Fritz K. *The Decline of the German Mandarins. The German Academic Community, 1890–1933.* (Cambridge, Mass.: Harvard University Press, 1969).

Röhl, John C.G. Higher Civil Servants in Germany 1890–1900. *Journal of Contemporary History* 2, (1967) pp. 101–121.

Rovan, Joseph. Staat und Nation in der deutschen Geschichte. In: Werner Weidenfeld (Ed.). *Die Identität der Deutschen.* (Bonn: Bundeszentrale für politische Bildung, 1983) pp. 229–247.

Rüsen, Jörn. Johann Gustav Droysen. In: Hans-Ulrich Wehler (Ed.). *Deutsche*

Historiker. vol. 2. (Göttingen: Vandenhoeck and Ruprecht, 1971) pp. 7–23.

Scheuch, Erwin K. *Wie deutsch sind die Deutschen? Eine Nation wandelt ihr Gesicht.* (Bergisch-Gladbach: Lübbe, 1991).

Schlegel, Friedrich v. Über das Studium der griechischen Poesie. In: Friedrich v. Schlegel. *Schriften zur Literatur.* Ed. Wolfdietrich Rasch. (München: Deutscher Taschenbuch Verlag, 1972) pp. 84–192.

Schrimpf, Hans J. *Goethes Begriff der Weltliteratur.* (Stuttgart: Metzler, 1968).

Schultz, Eberhard. *Die deutsche Nation in Europa.* (Bonn: Europa-Union-Verlag, 1982).

Seier, Hellmut. Heinrich von Sybel. In: Hans-Ulrich Wehler (Ed.). *Deutsche Historiker.* vol. 2. (Göttingen: Vandenhoeck & Ruprecht, 1971) pp. 24–38.

Snyder, Louis L. *German Nationalism: The Tragedy of a People.* (Port Washington, N.Y.: Kennikat Press, 1952/1969).

Spiegel, Der. Nr. 46 vom 12.11.1990 (1990).

Statistisches Bundesamt (Ed.). *Statistisches Jahrbuch für die Bundesrepublik Deutschland.* (Wiesbaden: Metzler-Poeschel, 1993).

Topitsch, Ernst. *Die Sozialphilosophie Hegels als Heilslehre und Herrschaftsideologie.* (Neuwied and Berlin: Luchterhand, 1967).

Weidenfeld, Werner (Ed.). *Die Identität der Deutschen.* (Bonn: Bundeszentrale für politische Bildung, 1983).

Weidenfeld, Werner (Ed.). *Politische Kultur und Deutsche Frage.* (Köln: Wissenschaft und Politik, 1989).

Weidenfeld, Werner (Ed.). *Deutschland. Eine Nation – doppelte Geschichte.* (Köln: Wissenschaft und Politik, 1993).

Weidenfeld, Werner and Karl-Rudolf Korte. *Die Deutschen. Profil einer Nation.* (Stuttgart: Klett-Cotta, 1991).

Willems, Helmut. *Fremdenfeindliche Gewalt.* (Düsseldorf: Leske & Budrich, 1993).

Willms, Bernhard. *Die Deutsche Nation.* (Köln: Hohenheim, 1982).

Wolffs, Michael. *Patriotismus, Wiedervereinigung und Europäische Gemeinschaft in der Einschätzung der Bevölkerung. Umfragedaten aus den Jahren 1951–1986.* (Bonn: Forschungsinstitut der Konrad-Adenauer-Stiftung, 1986).

ZA. ALLBUS 1980. *ZA-No. 1000.* (Köln: Zentralarchiv für empirische Sozialforschung, 1980).

ZA. ALLBUS 1984. *ZA-No. 1340.* (Köln: Zentralarchiv für empirische Sozialforschung, 1984).

ZA. ALLBUS 1988. *ZA-No. 1670.* (Köln: Zentralarchiv für empirische Sozialforschung, 1988).

ZA. ALLBUS 1990. *ZA-No. 1800.* (Köln: Zentralarchiv für empirische Sozialforschung, 1990).

Zitelmann, Rainer. Wiedervereinigung und deutscher Selbsthaß: Probleme mit dem eigenen Volk. In: Werner Weidenfeld (Ed.). *Deutschland. Eine Nation – doppelte Geschichte.* (Köln: Wissenschaft und Politik, 1993) pp. 235–248.

2 The International Position and the National Interest of Germany in the Nineties

Bertel Heurlin

The Federal Republic of Germany has become a new country. It has swallowed the GDR, the paragon of Soviet socialism, which was considered an influential member of the United Nations, and rated as the tenth richest country in the world.[1] The GDR was bi-polarity's perfect artificial creature and was thus bound to vanish together with bi-polarity itself. Germany is new because Europe is new. And Europe is new because the world is new. The United States is the only remaining superpower. The Soviet Union surrendered voluntarily in the cold war and gave up its superpower status.

The Soviet Union functioned as a dictatorship. But in contrast to Nazi-German dictatorship, the Soviet Union 'liberated' itself. And the same was the case with the GDR. The Eastern German regime had, however, until the very last minute, severe reservations towards the Soviet official glasnost and perestroika signals. The GDR felt no need for glasnost or perestroika, and many of the Soviet 'excesses' were simply forbidden by the East-German authorities. In the last analysis the GDR had to disappear due to the Soviet self-liberation.

The result was a Soviet bandwagon moving in the direction of Western norms and values. For the GDR there appeared to be only one solution: the complete integration into the FRG.

Has the new expanded state, in spite of the formal continuation of the former FRG, acquired new interests, new goals, new capabilities? Basically, yes. Germany has, with its extended capabilities, and with its changed geostrategic political, economical placement and position, a new role in the international system and in the European sub-system.

Germany received maximal gains through the Western victory in the cold war. The fundamental German goals in this war – namely reunification, equality and security – were fulfilled to a degree nobody would have expected. Germany was confronted with no less than a historical wonder. Now there is only one Germany: the occupation forces have been withdrawn and it is a free, fully sovereign state, seemingly as 'normal' as any other unit in the international system.

Germany is also more secure than ever in history. There are no longer any military threats towards it.

CONTRADICTIONS – DOUBLETALK

Germany is, according to this assessment, living in the best of all worlds. A recent editorial in *The Economist* stated that 'Germany is a strong, secure country with less to fear from past demons than from modern doubletalk'.[2] Certainly Germany is still haunted by demons – but is Germany more than other countries exposed to, or a victim of, doubletalk? There could be several kinds of doubletalk based on fundamental contradictions.

First, Germany is now formally a normal state and at the same time is not behaving like one, nor is it considering itself as one.[3] Germany is talking normality and no-normality at the same time.

Second, Germany is connecting its destiny to the notion of an ever closer integration – including widening as well as deepening among the European countries using the slogan 'a European Germany and not a German Europe'. Germany is talking about a federal Europe but is certainly not willing to give up Germany as a nation state. In 1989–90 the national unification got first priority.

Third, Germany is downplaying what really counts in international politics: the relative capabilities – namely the resources, the population, the territory, the military and the political coherence. Germany is emphasizing intentions, such as peace, freedom, stability and human rights. But at the same time Germany is more or less discreetly hinting at

Germany's new relative position in terms of capabilities. An example was the – fully justified – claim for an increased number of seats in the European Parliament.

Fourth, and finally, Germany seems to imagine that it does not have any explicit national interests. If this really is the case we would have invented quite a new kind of unit in the international system. Germany emphasizes that its vital interest is 'stability for all Europe'. The former German president expressed it in this way: 'Germany's central interest is – after having defeated the partition of Germany – to defeat Europe's'.[4] And on the other hand it is of course possible to identify German national interests. Indeed they have been demonstrated in the Slovenia–Croatia recognition case in 1991 and the very active policy regarding the widening of Europe in 1994. The formulation of national interests has, however, been rather vague.

Following up one could ask: Does Germany have an independent foreign policy or an independent security policy? Or is the main interest of Germany primarily to remove or reduce itself as a security problem for Europe through a policy of convincing Europe that Germany will remain a non-threat?

Maybe the reason for the doubletalk is the fact that everybody recognizes, but very few state officially, that Germany in its new shape is too big for an equal cooperation with the former more or less equal partners, but luckily still too small to exert hegemony.

There may be another reason for the doubletalk: Germany is much more exposed and much more sensible to criticism that any other country in the world. The United States can identify its national interest with global interest. Great Britain and France can allow themselves to refer to specific national strategies and conditions and act accordingly. France can have projects of a Europe operating as an expanded France. Great Britain can operate with concepts of a European Union covering all Europe based on the nation states, and at the same time refer to England as a unit on a par with Continental Europe. Both can talk convincingly of vital national interests and act accordingly. Germany cannot.

The Unique Germany

The reasons for Germany's inability to act in the same way as other countries are, among others, geopolitical and historical.

First, the new Germany cannot, due to her geographical position, do without Europe. No other country has common borders with so many countries. Germany needs – as it is officially emphasized – Europe more than any other country. This implies that Germany can expose itself – politically, economically, militarily – only embedded in European and transatlantic institutions.

Second, Germany is, for historical reasons, responsible for the international negative attitude to hypernationalism. This implies that Germany has a greater need for being accepted internationally and regionally – even a need to be loved! The tool to be accepted is the political will to be embedded. The slogan could be 'Bind me, love me!'

Chancellor Kohl has – in a less elegant way – conveyed this as follows: 'Because Germany has most neighbours, has most inhabitants, has the strongest economy, has the most industrious people [the strongest Arbeitswut, a characteristic which Kohl, hovever, is seriously doubting!] and further is best organized', then Germany is 'nicht unbedingt beliebt. Als Land der Romantik haben wir aber eine tiefe Sehnsuch . . . beliebt zu sein!'[5] (We are not wholeheartedly loved. As the Land of Romanticism we do, however, have a deep yearning to be loved!)

This is the main problem for Germany. The world is supervising Germany with the eyes of Argus. Every political move, domestically as well as internationally, every painted swastika, every racist remark, all hypernationalistic excesses, all political attempts to keep away from, or to participate in, peacekeeping/peacemaking operations are followed most closely by the surrounding states and world opinion.

The question then is: Will Germany be a normal state – or will it attempt to set up new international standards for 'normality'? Will the optimal situation for Germany be a world where the states are 'mutually penetrated', to use the concept of Wolfram Hanrieder, referring to the process of external societal, political, economic and military penetration of Germany after the Second World War.[6]

Another scenario would be that Germany now – free and totally independent – would formulate narrow, specific German national security interests and goals and pursue them rigorously. For reasons to be further explored this scenario is not considered probable.

Security Formulation

In German self-understanding, four security interests can be identified for Germany according to the 1994 Defense Whitebook (Verteidigung Weissbuch): (1) Freedom, (2) Security, (3) Welfare and (4) Integration with European democracies.[7]

This indicates that Germany is no 'normal' state. The norm among states would be to emphasize sovereignty. Here sovereignty is replaced with integration. As concerns security there are, as we have noted, no threats of aggression against Germany. To Germany it is a new experience to be surrounded by democracies, partners, allies and friends. Also new is the fact that Germany now considers itself as 'eine gestaltende Kraft für Frieden und Fortschritt in der Staatsgemeinschaft'; that the nuclear dilemma from the cold war – that of being the nuclear arsenal of Europe – is solved; that German soldiers highly prepared for war are no longer facing German soldiers in what used to be the most militarized centre of the world; that Russia is now a partner and that the Eastern European states are closely related to Germany.

There seems to be a fair possibility that the goal for the German security and foreign policy stated in the German constitution can be met: 'As an equal part of a united Europe to serve World Peace'.

Germany is like any other state occupied not exclusively by absolute gains – but also by relative gains. A serious problem is 'Standort Deutschland zukunftfähig', meaning 'how to maintain Germany as a strong competitor also in the future'. The crucial factor seems to be that Germany in economic-productive terms is not weakened, but that other countries have improved substantially.

But there are limits which Germany is not interested in crossing. The restraints are to be found on all levels: politically and economically as well as militarily. Officially expressed: 'Europa braucht Deutschlands Kraft, aber keine ungebührliche Stärke', meaning that 'Europe needs the strength of Germany but no improper power'.

Therefore the notion of stability is the proper point of departure for Germany. Instability and excesses, political, economic or societal, are the greatest threats to Germany. Germany thrives – as a civilian power – in a stable, dynamic environment. And, in order to secure stability, Germany has protected itself against the excesses of democracy by forbidding Nazism and communism, against the excesses of the market by promoting the so-called 'soziale Marktwirtschaft', against the excesses of the principle of self-determination of people by accepting the reduced size of the territory of Germany following the Second World War, and finally against the excesses of the freedom of speech by a remarkable self-censorship in international affairs.

Stability is also attached to the geopolitical fact that the European Centre – 'Die Mitte Europas' – has been re-established in economic terms, as well as in political, communicational, societal, cultural and military terms. The Centre of Europe has to be stable in order to have a stable Europe. Germany here has a heavy responsibility.

Why does Germany act as it does? Why does it have the role it has in European affairs? Some simple theoretical considerations could add to our understanding.

THEORY

The theoretical point of departure will be a conception of the international system which will postulate that the main conditions for the German position and interests are to be found in what broadly will be called the structure of the international system.

More than any other state, Germany is dependent – in its domestic as well as in its foreign policy – on the structure and the processes of the international system. The reason is that Germany has been, and is, an important part of this structure due to German capabilities, relatively speaking. These capabilities have implied that Germany has been in the position of being a potential superpower, striving for superpower status twice in this century. Each time it failed and was punished. These punishments have had an immediate influence upon the structure of the system.

These remarks indicate a neo-realist theoretical framework which could be characterized as modified neo-realism. This framework will refer to the international system as a theoretical construction consisting of three parts, each having its unique importance: structure, processes and units. Structure is considered as setting up fundamental restraints and possibilities and propelling units and processes in certain directions.

It is fundamental, however, that there is a clear distinction between the three parts. Structure will be considered exclusively as the organizing principle for the system, but this organizing principle depends on the relative capabilities (stratification, position) of the units. In this way Germany – like any other unit – theoretically is affected by the structure, but not part of it.

A Modified Neo-Realism

The construction is based on the allegation of the existence of an international system having political, economic, military, technological and societal dimensions. This system consists of:

1. Strucure (the organizing principle of the units involved). Structure in the international system is:
   a. Anarchy (the deep structure).
   b. Stratification of the units which implies a dominating realm (poles). Stratification refers to distribution of capabilities across units.
   c. Structural rules having to do with the survival of the system.
2. Processes, which are general patterns of behaviour and the changing of positions of the units. Here they can be identified as:
   a. The relative rise and fall of units as concerns the combined capabilities of the units. This also involves the sudden changes in unit capabilities – such as fusion and fission of units (integration and disintegration).

b. The pattern of conflict/cooperation including the dependence, interdependence and independence relations.

c. 'Deep processes' dealing with the degree of density in the relations, which is attached to the technological development. This density implies the following trends:
   – globalizing of common problems (resources, environment etc.);
   – globalizing of international norms (democracy, human rights, protection of minorities, condemnation of racism, facism, Nazism and genocide).

3. Actors, the most important of which are states. Actors can also be international organizations or other institutions/organizations acting as states. State actors will, according to the theory, have structurally determined goals – logically also due to their relative capabilities. Capabilities and positions will be the preconditions for their strategies, doctrines and actual policies. The structurally determined goals will be identified below.

The Transformation of the International System

Crucial for this essay is the allegation of the emergence of a fundamentally new international system after 1989–90, where the analysis commences. The system is transformed from a bi-polar system into a uni-polar system with tendencies in the direction of multi-polarity. Uni-polarity does not necessarily nullify the basic balance-of-power assertion. The point is that the United States *p.t.* is the only superpower – i.e. the only power having the aggregated capabilities second to none enabling it to be the only pole, the only reliable organizer – politically, militarily and economically – of the system.

A uni-pole having this relatively high amount of superior aggregated capabilities and the position of a 'primus inter pares', or system-organizer, will provoke a reaction from the other units which will be partly bandwagoning and partly balancing. The counterbalancing will take place in a fragmented pattern, and will therefore impact much less upon the structure and be less threatening to the only superpower.[8]

This means that Germany (often identified with or including the EC/EU) and Japan will be able to counterbalance economically (but they still display a bandwagoning behaviour towards the American uni-pole – politically/normatively/ diplomatically and militarily). Furthermore it means that Russia can balance geostrategically (as the second global nuclear power) – but still there is a bandwagoning behaviour, economically and partly politically. Finally China can balance geopolitically – but still there is a partly bandwagoning behaviour economically and militarily.

In this general structural context Germany will be positioned and analysed.

The European Context

Germany will be examined as an integrated part of the European sub–system. This European sub-system will be defined as the geographical Europe – ATTU, from the Atlantic To The Urals. The ATTU notion was formulated by Adenauer and by de Gaulle – and has been realized politically and militarily through the CFE treaties (the conventional disarmament agreements in Europe). Furthermore it has been revitalized politically through the different European Confederation Concepts and ideas of France, including the latest organizational invention, the Stability Pact.

Before the structural transformation there was no functioning European sub-system. Bi-polarity operated structurally by maintaining a clear-cut division of Europe. There were even very physical manifestations of this division such as walls and 'curtains', almost impenetrable due to heavy military presence.

Now Germany is positioned in a European sub-system – still having a certain American 'overlay', to use Barry Buzan's term, due to uni-polarity.[9] Germany has changed position from a block-periphery to the European centre. The core of the sub-system is the French–German axis, surrounded by the EU, countries about to join the EU and longer-term potential EU countries.

OBSERVATIONS IN RELATION TO THEORETICAL CONCEPTS

The following observations concerning Germany can be derived from the theoretical framework:

Structure

As already mentioned, Germany has in the last centuries been part of the dominating realm of great powers. And twice in this century it could be characterized as a potential superpower. Two world wars changed this status, and a third substitute 'World War' between the East (the Soviet empire) and the West (the 'free world' led by the USA) has now come to an end due to the voluntary surrender of the Soviet Union. In this new context Germany was unified and, not least due to its increased relative combined capabilities, there is the possibility of its regaining its former status as a potential superpower. This has changed the potential dominating realm. It is important to emphasize, however, the 'potential' nature of this status. After all, Germany will probably not in any foreseeable future develop into a superpower, due to exactly the structural and processual restraints to be mentioned below.

One of the ideas of the modified neo-realism to be used here is that the deep structure of anarchy in this century has been moderated by one ruling principle – the prospect of the threat to the survival of the international system as such.

The ruling principle is based on the position of nuclear weapons. This position can be considered part of the organizing conception of the system. I will argue that the international system underwent a fundamental transformation in the late 1940s. It changed from multi-polarism to bi-polarism and its anarchical deep structure was modified due to a new generally accepted ruling principle which can be stated as follows: a global nuclear war is not accepted and will not take place due to threat to the physical survival of the system. Although the notion of the international system is a theoretical construction one can speak of its physical survival, as the construction would be of no interest if its components, the units, did not exist.

This ruling principle is so strong that, although Germany has all the potential necessary and all the strategic reasons to develop an independent national nuclear strike-force, it will meet a massive reaction from the rest of the international system if it officially strives for such an option.

Processes

Concerning the processes in the international system Germany will also have a specific standing and status. In the long run it is characterized by a relative increase in its processual capabilities. The current German economic weaknesses are transient: it will see 'blooming landscapes' in the Eastern part in the long run. Germany has, more than any other state, been profiting from the removal of the global bi-polar confrontation. It is in a 'rising' position, relatively and absolutely as concerns combined capabilities. Safely embedded in the EU and in NATO with the USA to take care of its security, Germany has chosen wisely, by emphasizing the area where it is strong – the economy.

Concerning the war–peace process dimensions Germany is again enjoying a relative advantage as it leaves behind it a placement in the midst of the most militarized area in the cold war period – central Europe. Now it is envisaging a very peaceful neighbourhood.

The dependence processes are ambiguous.There are two tendencies: partly towards interdependence, partly towards independence. Germany as part of the process patterns is characterized by both tendencies: in the direction of increased integration and in the direction of renationalization.

As regards international norms, the situation is as follows: new common globally dispersed international norms based on Western values are very close to official German internal and external norms but international norms in another context will still have a fundamental influence upon the German role in the international processes – and certainly a very restrictive one.

As a result of the Second World War a new international norm was set up. This norm, very close to being recognized as a structural principal rule was a general condemnation of the fundamental principles of Nazism. More precisely it

was a condemnation of policies based on biological principles aiming at the destruction of individuals because of their
biological characteristics (Nazism, racism, ethnic cleansing
etc.). The reason for this norm is that national or international 'biological policies' are considered a threat to the
survival of the system as a multi-racial system, which seems
to be a precondition for the present international system.

Germany – as the emerging superpower in the Second
World War, resulting in 50 million victims – was the main
reason for this new international norm. This fact will stig-
matize Germany for some time to come, especially due to
its exposed geographical position in the regional European
system.

All in all, Germany is processually restrained in a way which
is not the case for other units. This means that Germany
will not be a fully 'normal' state for some time. This will set
certain limits and constitute a restraining setting for the
German domestic and foreign policy.

Actor

This part of the theoretical framework deals with Germany
as a unit in the international system. I shall identify and
analyse the national interests (the general goals of the state),
the capabilties, the placement/position and finally actual
policy.

Six theoretically generated national interests can be listed:

1. Existence as a unit in the international system
This is the superior goal. Does Germany want to exist as a
unit on a par with like-minded states? No doubt. But Germany does not want this unit to be a 'normal' nation state
in the tradition of the 19th and 20th centuries, despite the
socializing pressure from the international structure for it
to perform as a normal nation state. Exactly this kind of
nation created the conditions for two world wars. Exactly
this kind of a German nation became hated and considered as a threat to the national security of almost all the
neighbour states. Germany has to invent a new kind of nation – a federal nation in a federal European regional unit.

This means a three-level identity: 'Land' (sub-region),

nation, Europe (region). Still there is a preference for the nation. The German nation is a coherent unit with no inherent dominating fusion or fission factors at work.

Translated into the case of Germany: first, the Länder units are not interested enough, strong enough or persistent enough to stand up against the Bund in a possible wish or attempt to be accepted as fully sovereign units; second, Germany – and with Germany the other EU countries – are not interested enough in creating a fully sovereign new international unit, the United States of Europe, and thereby giving up their status as sovereign states.

Germany's existence goal is primarily attached to the notion of absence of military threats against Germany. The transformation of the international system in 1989–90 has materially enhanced the situation in this field. Germany is attempting to solve the problem in the longer run through integration – militarily, politically, economically and societally – primarily based on transatlanticism (NATO) and Europeanization (EU and WEU).

Also partnership with Central and Eastern Europe, including Russia, are options and possible ways to achieve this goal. The existence of Germany has thus evidently two dimensions: the European dimension as part of and positioned in the centre of the European sub-system, and the transatlantic dimension due to the US uni-polar position.

2. Integrity/identification

Here Germany is again in a special situation. Germany succeeded in 1990 in fulfilling its fundamental goal as regards geographical integrity, namely reunification. This had became a fundamental problem after the creation of two German states in 1949.

Unification must be characterized as an entirely unique event. Germany has hereby increased its general capabilities, in absolute and in relative terms. In terms of general capabilities Russia is the stronger state in Europe. In specific economic terms Germany is stronger.

But still Germany has integrity problems. Border questions and minority problems are emerging and occasionally politicized – if only at a low-key level. And the general questions, What is Germany? Who are Germans?, are constantly in focus.

Three aspects of the integrity/identification goal particularly stand out. First there is the integration between East and West Germany – which is a painful process. Second is the integration of the large number of immigrants and refugees moving to Germany as the land of welfare and opportunities and – for historical reasons – as a country with relatively liberal immigration and refugee legislation. Third, and finally, is the prospect of a triple identity.

The first identity is the sub-regional (Länder) identity, which exists as a real possibility, although the construction of the Länder borders was more or less random or at least took into consideration other factors than historically determined borders of identification. The borderlines were generally determined by the occupation forces in the years after the Second World War.

The second identification point is the national German identity, which is still underplayed.

The third is the European identity which lately has been promoted in a manifest way through the Maastricht Treaty, introducing the notion of a European citizenship.

3. Autonomy

Autonomy means the evident strive for internal independence for the state. Autonomy is considered a specific category and is not just seen as being part of the concept of sovereignty. This autonomy goal has particular relevance for Germany.

After the Second World War Germany had no choice. It had to accept the conditions of the conquerors: de-Nazification, democracy, demilitarization, decentralization. The German autonomy was to a certain degree internationally penetrated. One way to overcome this problem, to regain autonomy, was to internationalize the surroundings – which in the specific German situation would mean integration with the Western European countries within a more general Atlantic framework.

But still the particular role and background for German autonomy implies a certain German sensitivity in connection with societal balance and stability. The prospects of neo-Nazism and German hypernationalism make Germany vulnerable in a European context, *vis-à-vis* its neighbours.

This involves a certain restraint concerning full autonomy in comparison with, for example, England and France. These two countries can allow themselves domestically – and also externally – to behave nationalistically, to practise nationalism. Germany cannot. The maintenance of German internal stability and the status of German democracy is not considered just a German problem, but a European and also an international problem.

4. *Sovereignty*

This concept is here understood as the unlimited power of the state, its freedom of action as a unit in the international system. To Germany the sovereignty goal has the same high standing as to any other unit, but again the German situation is unique. It was not until the reunification that Germany regained its full sovereignty. Now the last features of occupation have disappeared.

But Germany still recognizes its interest in having its sovereignty 'embedded' in some sort of European organization. It accentuates this position in its Euro-political doctrine – which underlines that 'Germany needs Europe more than any other state'. Of course Germany is constantly striving to secure sovereignty and of course Germany does not want 'singularization' – having a restrained status different from other states. On the other hand – and this is furthermore underscored in connection with the general goal of having peaceful surrroundings which can be counted on and possibly influenced – Germany still is, tacitly, restrained and is restraining itself.

Germany is aware of its size and influence through its general political, geopolitical, strategic, territorial, demographic, societal and economic position. This awareness is mirrored in attempts not to use this position and not to exploit fully its sovereignty to exert hegemony. Such a behaviour would, in the last analysis, have negative effects on the general position of Germany. The result could very well be a balancing comprehensive counter-alliance against Germany. Such an alliance could be a catastrophy for Germany as it would weaken other vital goals such as the securing and increasing of material status and welfare.

As it has been stated, Germany is fully aware that it is too big for a European sub-system consisting of relatively equal states in terms of capabilities – and too small for exerting a 'natural' hegemony in this under-system. One way to solve this problem, together with the problem of structural restraints, is a policy of being embedded in integrative institutions like the EC, WEU and NATO. Germany wants to be accepted in its new position. It wants to emphasize that nobody has to fear Germany. It wants to be 'loved' in order to exist as a unit in the European system. Therefore the notion of 'Bind me, love me' is not so primitive as it appears on the face of it.

5. Economic welfare of the state

This refers to Germany's economic capabilities and to its European and international position with respect to resources, production and finance. Germany is the number three world economic power after the United States and Japan, and number two as regards size of external trade.

Germany is economically strong. But the relative strength is undergoing changes. Germany – before assessed as the centre of economic miracles, high productivity, stability, high quality based on advanced technology – still has these qualities. The problem is that many other states are now in the same position. Much of the German relative strength has gone.[10]

Add to this that Germany, more than the economic giants in terms of production and income per head (the United States, Japan and other strong economic powers), is dependent on external trade. Therefore the EU and the European Economic Area are of vital importance to the German home market.

As Germany – for the afore-mentioned reasons – has more than any other countries to exploit its economic position as the fundamental national asset, it is no wonder that economic stability and strength are assigned vital importance, domestically as well as internationally.

But here also Germany is willing to give up its national interest (the independent, strong D-Mark) through the EMU (Economic and Monetary Union). The proviso is, however, that a strong political and military integration is developed in parallel.

6. Influence upon the international system in order to establish
peaceful and perceptive surroundings
Each unit will want to have its own values and norms inter-
nationalized. For Germany it is important to have peaceful
surroundings. Only with a peaceful setting can Germany flourish and avoid being considered the threatening trouble-maker
in the European sub-system.

The dissemination of common, global values in Europe
and in the rest of the world – values originated in the United
States (and Western Europe) but entirely adhered to and
overtaken by Germany – are thus very beneficial to Germany. They support intensively the goal of peaceful surroundings. In the cases where this policy of exerting influence on
common values has failed – for example, in Yugoslavia –
Germany suffers immense problems.

Questions

This brief analysis has attempted to outline some fundamental
characteristics of German goals, positions and capabilities.
On this basis the following questions are put forward:

1. The problem of 'normality' and 'Sonderweg'
Is Germany going to become a normal state – striving for
goals theoretically derived from a neo-realistic interpretation of the international system based on anarchy – or are
we envisaging a 'post-sovereign' state – renouncing nationalism and sovereignty as the organizing principles and seeking a new position in a federal Europe? Will this new state
be what has been characterized as 'Der neue Handelsstaat'
(Richard Rosecrance, 1987)?

The preliminary answer seems to be that Germany will
not give up the idea of 'nation' as an important organizing
principle for the country, but that the vision of a pooling
of sovereignties on vital, selected issues among the nations
of Europe still leaves room for a core Europe based on the
French–German special relationship which encompasses two
contrasting Europe-projects. This core will, however, still be
dependent on the American uni-pole.

2. The problem of 'Einbindung' (embedding)

This reflects the possibility of a 'post-sovereign' Germany: Will this Germany continue to use the embedding concept as a tool to be accepted in a new Europe where the geopolitical positions and the relative capabilities among the units have entirely changed the role of Germany? If so, for how long – and what are the conditions?

The embedding concept – which covers political (UN, EU), economic (EU) as well as military (WEU, NATO) dimensions – is very close to the concept of integration.

The preliminary answer is that Germany will continue to be cautious in relation to every move which could be interpreted by the political environment as a renationalization of the German European or international position through security or foreign policy.

The embedding concept is, however, emphasizing more the 'specific' role of Germany, demonstrated in the doctrine of 'Germany needs Europe more than other states'. Embedding leads to the policy notion of reducing Germany's possibilities and capabilities through multilateralism and thereby reducing the fears of the other countries of Europe towards Germany. In this way Germany hopes to be accepted by its surroundings. Or, as it has been expressed before more simply and primitively, 'Bind me, love me'.

3. The specific features of 'anti-biological' policies (racism)

What is the impact of the Nazi-racism heritage? For historical reasons racism policies will still be more restrictive to Germany than to any other states. They will facilitate the internationalization of German domestic politics and will probably be a specific condition for Germany for some time to come, unless Germany emerges into superpower status, which is not probable.

So Germany will, in the forseeable future, continue to be specifically exposed and sensitive in relation to internal, domestic excessive developments, which will in turn provoke reactions from the surroundings.

4. The main problem: foreign and security policy

Given the structural restraints and possibilities, given the 'deep processes' and the specific conditions for the units in Europe, what will be the most likely broad development in the formulating of German foreign and security policy interests in the coming years? What will be the perspectives?

Again the answer is that there probably will emerge no substantial changes in the German foreign or security policy. Germany will stay cautious and follow the logic of latent vulnerability. Germany will pursue and secure its interests through multilateralism, integration and economic structural power. It will remain a potential nuclear power and a potential superpower. But the border between the potential and reality will not be crossed.

NOTES

1. According to UN publications.
2. *The Economist*, 20.11.1993.
3. Representative Social Democrat Günter Verheugen is e.g. arguing for Germany staying an 'un-normal' country, in 'Vor-wärts', cit. in *Politiken* (12.8.1995), II, 5.
4. *Bulletin, Presse- und Informationsamt der Bundesregierung*, no. 53 (3.6.1994), p. 498. From a speech by the then German president Weizsäcker.
5. *Bulletin*, no. 54 (7.6.1994), p. 507.
6. Wolfram Hanrieder, *West German Foreign Policy 1949–1963* (Stanford, 1967).
7. 'Das Deutsche Verteidigungsweissbuch 1994', in *Europa Archiv*, Folge 10 (1994), pp. D. 325–348.
8. See Bertel Heurlin, *From Two to One Superpower* (1996).
9. Barry Buzan, *People, States and Fear* (2nd Ed., London, 1991).
10. An investigation by the Swiss Bank Society (SBG) from 1994 indicates that in the year 2000 South Korea will be the leading country as regards ability to compete (with the index of 100, Japan will have an index of 76, Germany and the USA – after the Nordic countries, Spain and France – will score as low as 62). From *Die Welt*, 9.3.1994, p. 13.

BIBLIOGRAPHY

Bulletin, Presse- und Informationsamt der Bundesregierung, no. 53 (3.6.1994,
    p. 498).
Bulletin, no. 54 (7.6.1994, p. 507).
Buzan, Barry, *People, States and Fear* (2nd Ed., London, 1991).
Europa Archiv, 'Das Deutsche Verteidigungsweissbuch 1994' (Folge 10,
    1994, pp. D. 325–348).
Hanrieder, Wolfram, *West German Foreign Policy 1949–1963* (Stanford, 1967).
Heurlin, Bertel, *From Two to One Superpower* (1996).
The Economist, 20.11.1993.
Verheugen, Günter, 'Vor-wärts', cit. in. *Politiken* (12.8.1995, II, 5).

3 Germany as a World Power and as a European Power

Ekkehart Krippendorff

'Germany as a world power' is a somewhat problematic concept. It states as a fact something which is far from certain and would need careful analysis and terminological clarification before being acceptable *tout court*. To be a power in this world of nation states (and others) and, because of its economic performance and weight (more than its territorial size or population), a not insignificant power does not make Germany already a world power as the term is currently used. We have to look into that more carefully. We probably have fewer problems in agreeing on 'Germany as a European power' – but even there a closer look at the context reveals uncertainties and both historical and current ambiguities. Which Europe are we talking about? If we mean the European Community and its 'hard core', i.e. the founding members, then Germany no doubt has for years had a dominant, 'powerful' role. But if by Europe we mean Northern and particularly Eastern Europe as well, which should include even Russia, then Germany's role and relative weight appears in many respects reduced and more counterbalanced.

FROM TWO TO ONE GERMANY

However, behind the affirmative wording a much more important question mark seems to be lurking. For more than four decades after the Second World War, when we talked about Germany here in the West, we meant West Germany, the FRG, as distinct from East Germany, the DDR. Being only half – or rather two thirds – of the two Germany, even though always considered the only really legitimate part, its

64

wings were clipped by both the division and the firm integration into Western Europe and American-dominated NATO. It was not too long ago, in 1986, that one of the most experienced European statesmen, Giulio Andreotti of Italy, said in public what most of his colleagues and almost the whole European political class held as their private opinion – that it was better for peace in Europe to have two Germany rather than only one. And when, after the fall of the Wall, the fate of the DDR was still open, it was François Mitterand who paid an official state visit to East Berlin with the barely concealed purpose of strengthening the identity of the DDR against absorption by West Germany. All this is history now – but it should not be forgotten when we deal with the underlying fear and concern about the role of a unified Germany in Europe and beyond.

As late as August 1994 the last Allied troops left Germany. This date marks the real end of the Second World War and, therefore, the restoration of Germany to normalcy, to its place as a regular nation state in the 'family of states'. But all those concerned with international relations, with the possible future of the international system, ask themselves which role Germany is going to play from now on. In this moment of uncertainty, most analysts resort to history for answers. It is a rather strange fact that history is invoked to find clues for understanding Germany's foreign policy future much more so than it is for, let us say, France, or England, or any of the Scandinavian countries. It is an undeniable fact that German politics have in the past been not only a threat but a veritable disaster to its neighbours. This very past haunts public opinion in most European countries, including ordinary common people normally unconcerned with foreign policy issues. But this does not explain sufficiently the analytical use of history as a salient clue to the future in the case of Germany.

WILL THE GERMAN EAGLE FLY AGAIN?

There seems to be a deep-seated fear that the German eagle, now that its feathers have grown back, might spread its wings again and fly over Europe, menacing Germany's neighbours with revived hegemonic ambitions. After all, this eagle is still the heraldic figure of the German state and seems to stand for continuity – exactly the continuity that many are afraid of. Those who look for patterns in Germany's international strategies in the past, will recall not only the Second World War, but the First World War as well. They point out that even Bismarck's Germany was too strong and powerful to be integrated into the European state system and that German aggressiveness, materially supported by its socio-economic strengh, can be traced back even further to the militarism of Prussia, to that very state which made the eagle the symbol of Germany. And if one wants to continue this line of historical reasoning, one will discover that in 1250 this eagle was given by the Emperor Frederick II to an order of crusading knights, whose military energies, after being defeated in the Holy Land and in Hungary, were directed towards the colonization and conquest of the East (of the Slavs in what then became Prussia). So there is a lot to be learned and to be concerned about within historical continuity – if one wants to look for such patterns.

REGIONAL POLICY?

But the doubts and the objections to this approach are stronger than such all too easy evidence. And for one very basic reason this brings us back to the present time and to our problem of Germany today. Time and space do not permit me to elaborate on this point, but I would insist on the proposition that the various power holders – dynastic rulers, foreign policy élites and political classes – governing Prussia and Germany during the last centuries behaved no differently from their French, Habsburg, English etc. colleagues. All seized their opportunities to aggrandize their respective power positions in competition with each other. That was – and to some extent still is – the rule of the game of state politics on the international stage: a zero-sum game that has seen winners and losers, risk-takers and cautious statesmen, irresponsible aggressors and prudent diplomats at the helm of their states at any given time. A.J.P. Taylor provoked us some 20 years ago with the reminder that even the most sinister of all the black sheep among statesmen, Hitler, played a quite reasonable, normal political game by the established standards of statesmanship until 1939 – only then did he miscalculate. But miscalculation is part of the foreign policy game and no German speciality. After all, everybody did business with Nazi Germany, some even to the very end (like Sweden, Switzerland or Spain), and nobody broke off diplomatic relations after 1933, the year in which – from a German historical and moral point of view – the catastrophe of the Second World War began. A critique of Hitler's foreign policy, carried to its politico-logical conclusion, should arrive at a critique of international statesmanship – or rather 'gamesmanship' as it was called, with positive connotations, during the years of the cold war. If you are good at gamesmanship, you might even win elections that way. If you play the game badly – as in the recent spectacular case of Saddam Hussein with regard to Kuwait – you are ostracized by your statesmen–colleagues. The stakes are particularly high here – you either win big or lose big. To play the foreign policy game of your country carries the highest prestige everywhere.

GERMANY – A NORMAL STATE

Why do I go into all of this? The reason is that I do think that Germany, the Germany of the Second Federal Republic, is right now at the threshold of re-entering the international stage as a regular and fully equal member of the international community of states, something it has not been as the First Federal Republic, i.e. as a divided country. I will not discuss the foreign policy of East Germany because, as remarkably successful as it was with regard to its prime objective – international recognition as a state – with the disappearance of the DDR this left no trace, charted no new tradition to become part of the unified country. As a matter of fact, more than any other professional category of the DDR, her diplomats are the most systematically purged group – second only to the members of the state security apparatus. But as far as the Federal Republic is concerned, the proposition that only from now on shall we be able to speak of a genuine, autonomous foreign policy certainly needs considerable qualification. It would be absolutely wrong and misleading to maintain – as in retrospect many analysts and not least certain politicians claim – that West Germany has been basically powerless and weak and has had hardly any foreign policy worthy of the name. This is a myth being created right now in the process of historicizing its 40 years of existence. Many, if not most, political comments on the historical decision of the constitutional court in July 1994, which gave the government a free hand to use the federal army 'out of area' within the context and framework of international peacekeeping operations, promoted exactly this myth. Only now was Germany presumably free to have her own, sovereign foreign policy, as opposed to the years of the 'old' Federal Republic which, in Willy Brandt's definition, was economically a giant but politically a dwarf. Now, after that extremely important, although absolutely foreseeable, court decision, we will have to come back to it – Germany's previous role in international affairs was interpreted as 'idyllic', 'tame', 'lame' and all too comfortable in the shadow of the Western allies, the USA above all, who took care of Germany's security and in turn obtained a loyal junior partner on all cold war issues.

To counter this legend – at least very briefly – we should remind ourselves that even the decision made during the early years of the FRG to opt for an almost unconditional West European integration was everything but uncontroversial and constituted a real foreign policy decision. The same is true of Adenauer's decision in favour of West Germany's rearmament, certainly no secondary matter, carried through against considerable obstacles and particularly against a largely hostile public opinion. All through the 1960s and 1970s, West Germany followed a deliberately tough cold war foreign policy, particularly in the Third World. It was certainly second to none in the West when it came to support repressive regimes like the Shah's Iran. To the UN-recommended boycott of South Africa it paid lip service only and in so far as the active participation in arms exports is a foreign policy decision, West Germany went as far as it possibly could. Even the 'positive side' of the picture, the historic 'Ostpolitik' of Willy Brandt (as foreign minister first and chancellor later) – a policy to be continued by all German governments since then until the 'turn', 'die Wende' – was by any measure a genuine German foreign policy decision, observed with great scepticism if not suspicion on the part of its Western allies, the USA in particular. In other words, West Germany did have a foreign policy of its own, it had its options, and its decision-makers did make real decisions – consistently in favour of increasing and deepening West European integration.

LOW-PROFILE POLICY

And yet, there is some important truth in the claim that the foreign policy of the 'old' Federal Republic has been low key and low profile. The history of the West German Federal Republic, as far as its foreign policy is concerned, is a history of tensions and contradictions that are approaching a rather dramatic climax right now. The government formed after the elections of 16 October 1994 has set the pattern of Germany's foreign policy far beyond its own term of office. What are these contradictions and tensions that will be resolved, one way or the other, during this coming legislature?

From the first Adenauer government to the present, we find a basic tension between a widespread 'anti-foreign-policy' attitude on the part of the (West) German people and the 'responsible', 'far sighted' political class. This became manifest for the first time when Adenauer decided on West German rearmament in order to obtain a higher degree of sovereignty for the newly formed state, despite the widespread opposition this policy provoked. 'The Germans' seemed to have learned the lesson of the Second World War, that militarism and power politics are dangerous and counter-productive and should not be revived. The new Germany should be a peaceful, disarmed Germany. Only the so-called 'economic miracle' pushed the rearmament issue into the background during the second parliamentary elections of 1953. The people voted with their wallets and swallowed the new army as the bitter price to be paid for economic recovery.

This set the pattern for the future: foreign policy issues were played down as much as possible, and the performance of the economy became the corner-stone of electoral approval or disapproval of governmental policy. But this also meant that the German government – independent of party political composition – tried to be extremely careful in foreign policy matters. Or, put it to differently, foreign policy became a non-issue in West German political debates and in the political culture in general. Any attempt on the part of the government to assert 'national interests', to play an active role on the international stage, was heavily criticized by the opposition and/or concerned public. German public opinion watched carefully and suspiciously any move that could be interpreted as a revival of traditional patterns of national, hegemonic ambitions. German history, the history of Wilhelminian imperialism and Nazi expansionism were all invoked as warnings against any reassertion of German power politics in Europe and beyond – but not only in the field of foreign policy itself. When, in the 1970s, internal repression of the radical, terrorist left seemed to threaten German democratic structures and when West Germany projected herself as a model of conservative order to other West European countries faced with similar movements and activities, German radical democrats tried to alert the West to the danger of a new German political hegemony in the guise of law and order. Chancellor Helmut Schmidt was quoted as threatening to send German tanks into Italy in the event that the Communist Party should legally assume power there.

This sounds all rather far-fetched today and more like political science fiction, but the point is that it was West Germany's left-leaning public opinion and spokespersons who raised their voices to such imagined dangers, thereby conditioning the government to a more cautious line of conduct (even if this tough line was very much in agreement with the American approach to the seemingly imminent threat of democratic left-wing victories of Eurocommunism in the mid-seventies). In 1977, the prestigious Russell Tribunal held its hearings on the case of West Germany as a threat to democracy in other parts of Europe.

THE SENSITIVE GERMANY

Inasmuch as political classes in Western democratic countries are responsive at all to internal pressures and concerns on vital issues, German politicians have been extremely sensitive to avoid the impression of being nationalistic, 'imperialistic' or in any way following in the footsteps of the hegemonial power ambitions of Germany's terrible past. One might argue that it did not take much to opt for this low profile and for the policy of unconditional West European integration since that is what its Western allies expected from West Germany anyway. Maybe. But for the Federal Republic to become even the locomotive of 'Europeanism', to insist on the strengthening of community institutions and to renounce actively part of its sovereignty to European institutions so that at times it looked as if Germany was even anxious to 'Europeanize' itself, was by no means predictable and to be taken for granted. Certainly, it did correspond to German economic interests and served them more than well. But it also corresponded to a genuine belief of the first two or three generations of Germany's political leadership for whom Europe, meaning Western Europe, constituted a new and larger political home than the discredited and divided 'nation'. The German political class was, for almost 40 years, genuinely European in outlook and orientation.

Moreover, and this is what I would like to stress, this political orientation reflected an even stronger 'a-national' outlook on the part of the general public. Throughout the 1970s and 1980s, various comparative opinion polls showed the Germans in the lowest position when it came to 'pride in one's country', or 'willingness to serve in the army', but very high when asked about 'trust in one's institutions' or 'willingness to relinquish national prerogatives in favour of a United Europe'. And certainly any government complicity, real or assumed, with active, interventionist or militant foreign policies of Germany's allies would and did meet the strongest possible resistance from public opinion. Evidence of this is legion, from the Algeria and Vietnam protests (the latter contributing in no small measure to the electoral success of the opposition Social Democrats) to the mass protests against NATO's arms race policy in the early 1980s to the widespread refusal to side with the USA in the second Gulf War. The constitutional proviso that the federal army had only territorial defensive functions was genuinely believed and 'internalized', so to speak, in German political culture. Nowhere else in Europe and beyond (with the possible exception of Switzerland) did the fall of the Wall (i.e. the end of the communist regimes) lead to widespread initiatives for the abolition of the army altogether. This led to a crisis of purpose and identity within the army itself, which has not been overcome to this very day (it was Saddam Hussein's aggression and the violent break-up of Yugoslavia which 'saved' the military and gave it back some political credibility). With 28 per cent conscientious objectors, Germany may hold the world record.

POWER OBLIVION?

All this might be coming to an end. We are right now witness to and/or active participants in a public debate on reorientation. This had already started in the mid-eighties, i.e. even before the 'turn' of 1989, but it has accelerated and become more focussed since then. At least half a dozen influential or at least widely discussed books by liberal-conservative academic authors have appeared during the last few years which lament in various ways the deplorable lack of a sense of power on the part of 'the Germans'. 'Macht-vergessenheit' has become a key word and an almost common denominator when it comes to the description of the general attitude towards international politics: 'power oblivion'. They write in the worst tradition of Max Weber (it was the Weber of the 1890s who looked with envy to the British political class because it had successfully accomplished, as he saw it, the education of its people to an imperial, i.e. world, outlook, while the Germans were presumably all too self-satisfied with the pure achievement of their national unity). These analysts claim that the Germans are, as far as the international role of their country is concerned, naive, badly educated, unwilling to face reality, shirking responsibility, and concerned only with economic matters and private careers. They are pro-Europe or pro-UN, but believe that others should do the hard work of international politics. At most they are willing to share some of the costs. From being extremists in nationalism and world power ambitions in the past, they now have become extremists of the opposite – one more sign of a lack of equilibrium and balanced, 'realistic' political judgement in world affairs. From priding themselves on their military virtues they have become soft, cowardly (this was a very frequently used term in criticizing the Gulf War protesters) and tendentiously pacifist. The general conclusion is that something has to be done about this. A serious educational effort is required, so that the German political class can shoulder the new responsibilities in a changed world and can live up to the expectations of the international community.

The fact of the matter is – and here is the drama – that the present generation of Germany's political leaders – call them 'élite' if you wish – has been trying for some time now to overcome these domestic restrictions to its more activist ambitions on the international stage. What once was considered almost a statement of virtue – the economic giant as a dwarf in international politics – is now seen and experienced as an unnatural and absurd situation not to be tolerated any longer. This new generation, politically grown up and socialized internationally during the seventies and eighties, does not feel burdened any more by the nationalistic past. Being good Europeans, they feel every right to be treated not only as equals but according to the real weight Germany represents economically and even militarily – which means, in the European context at least, to be 'more equal than others'. They are not necessarily arrogant, but they are self-assured, self-confident and in no small measure proud of Germany's achievements in economic performance, administrative efficiency and socio-political stability. They feel that they have something to teach their neighbours and partners about how to run a country, how to put your house in order. The German interest and initiatives in European integration no doubt have their economic foundation in Europe as the most important market place for Germany's economy. But there is also the political dimension. With 80 million people as the largest single electorate and producing about 30 per cent of the Common Market's GNP, its weight and influence in a united, or at least more centrally administered, Europe would be infinitely greater than it is now. And by 'influence' I mean that Germany's industrialists, managers and politicians see the chance to organize the European economies and state structures in a way that allows for maximum interdependence and mutual penetration. They are convinced that such mutuality and interdependence would serve German interests more than those of other member states, given their competitiveness and the quality and efficiency of the German service sector as well.

The political dimension of this expectation of Germany's 'natural' strength and weight rests on a higher degree of national cohesiveness and solidarity than is now the case with the German electorate – at least from the point of view of the national conservative ideologists. Only a nation proud of itself and centred around such values as 'national solidarity', 'patriotism' and even cultural–ethnic homogeneity – as opposed to the concept of a 'multicultural society' – will enable the construction of a political force to complement and assist the economic interests which always need a 'voice' in order to realize their potential. Thus, besides the exhortations of those who call upon the German people to 'wake up' and become 'responsible', we see another ideological operation on the move right now with the call for a greater national identity and identification. This is obviously not intended to be anti-European – quite the contrary. It involves the strategy of giving Europe, the Europe of the Common Market, a political shape in the image and according to the concept or the 'recipe' of Germany's vision of socio-economic stability. And it has to be admitted that this can have legitimate claims to being a successful recipe.

GERMAN HEGEMONY IN EUROPE?

Europe, i.e. the policy of European integration, has been and will remain the absolute priority of Germany's foreign policy. But that by itself does not mean very much. Within that option there are variations, different tactical moves in order to achieve the long-range goals. The recent proposition of a Europe in two tiers or in two speeds is more than a pure exercise in political speculation. Both the chancellor and his foreign minister have played down the contents of a paper circulated at the recent CDU party conference which advocated this. Academic analysts quite some time before had discussed this possibility as a way out of the showdown of the integration process. The Bonn–Paris axis has always been the real corner-stone of the Common Market, a 'special relationship' that one might now call historical, i.e. hardly reversible. In the past, France had lent Germany her political credibility in exchange for considerable economic benefits. This has created a structural dependence of important sectors of the French economy on German counterparts, and the German leadership seems to be aiming at using this 'special relationship' for creating – together with Benelux – a Western Europe within Western Europe, i.e. a hegemonial hard core within which Germany has the leading role.

'Hegemony' is a term loaded with many ambiguous meanings. But if we strip it of its political connotations, then Germany has achieved, for all practical purposes, a new form of hegemony in Europe. The strategy of forming a 'hard core' of a 'faster Europe' would increase and *strengthen* this type of hegemony by giving it a managerial directorate, however institutionally formalized, which Germany alone would never have been able to establish in its own right. And I think it is only fair to add that this new German leadership does not even have the ambition of becoming the hegemonial political power of Europe: it is far too sophisticated and modern to take such an atavistic approach. A hegemony without the political power dimension, however, is qualitatively different from previous forms of (German) attempts to dominate. Controlling and exploiting by means of physical violence, i.e. by military means, by war and occupation, is quite different from dominating by way of greater efficiency, a better-functioning administration, the quality of your products, the greater reliability of your service systems etc. After all, this is the world of capitalism which most people in Europe now seem to want.

The new German hegemony, if it makes sense at all to use this term, is certainly infinitely more benevolent than all previous attempts in that direction. But above all,

Germany's powerful position is largely a function of the weakness of its partners and not the result of a systematic and strategically conceived power plan or grand design. Take the case of Italy, the other founding member of the EEC which is to be excluded form the 'hard core'. There was an outcry of protest and indignation on the part of prominent spokesmen of the Italian government when the existence of such a plan, or rather study, became known. The prime minister and his foreign minister as well felt obliged to ask for reassuring clarifications to the contrary of what had been reported in the press – and they were told what they wanted to hear for the benefit of an embarrassed public opinion. But there were quite a few prominent Italian politicians and analysts who sided with the German position. They reminded their fellow citizens that it was, after all, the result of the catastrophic policies of *Italian regimes* – characterized by corruption, administrative inefficiency and unproductive waste on every level of society – which had created the dangerous gap in overall performance between the 'core group' (Germany in particular) and Italy itself. And for this, Italian society had only itself to blame. 'If I were German, I would do the same', one minister was quoted as saying. 'Predominance by default' is how one might define Germany's position in Western Europe.

And the same holds true, obviously, with regard to its position *vis-à-vis* the former East European countries. During the first dramatic years after 1989 when the books were opened on the disastrous state of their economies, not a few East European voices could be heard saying that the Germans should take over the whole show directly. Needless to say, West Germany had and still has enough of a burden to carry with the integration of the Länder of the former DDR. On the level of political diplomacy, German politicians have demonstrated a rather remarkable degree of psychological sensitivity, particularly in Poland, which seems to contradict the general pattern of normalization as it has evolved during the last few years.

NORMALIZATION

'Normalization' then seems to be a key word in characterizing a rather dramatic period of reorientation and possible change in German attitudes towards the outside world, towards Europe and beyond. This reorientation is taking place on two levels: at the level of the governmental élites on the one side (this includes the Social Democratic leadership and most established opinion leaders), and at the level of liberal public opinion on the other side (which has, with the exception of the Greens, no political representation and very few prominent spokespersons). As far as the first group is concerned, almost everybody active in foreign policy is convinced that the time has come to turn over a new leaf. By that the political establishment means that reunified Germany should not claim any special 'non-responsibility' in international politics because of its Nazi or Wilhelminian past for that matter. They feel that it is time for Germany to play its role alongside the other major industrial powers and not to be ashamed of, or embarrassed by, its political weight and economic strength. They feel annoyingly restricted by a diffuse liberal public opinion which feels obliged to warn continually against any signs of the arrogance of power. The constitutional court's decision of July 1994, declaring the constitutional compatibility of the federal army to be employed 'out of area' is a significant case in point. Because of the widespread suspicion of public opinion on this matter, which includes a large majority of the Social Democratic Party membership in open conflict with the party leadership (the small Liberal Party had similar internal problems), the parties did not dare to debate a change of the constitution itself which would have been the most honest and correct move to make. Instead, they all resorted to the court and – in different degree – they were all only too relieved about a decision which saved everybody's face and effectively silenced any further discussion of the principle of this important issue. It was a victory of the political class as a whole over a public opinion deprived of any articulate voice or political representation – with the exception of the Green Party, of course. In a way this was a replay of the way German rearmament had been imposed on a population weary of war and the military in the early 1950s under Konrad Adenauer.

While there is hardly any prominent politician – or opinion-maker for that matter – who is not convinced of the legitimacy of Germany playing a more active foreign policy role (you could hardly hear a dissenting voice to that historical court decision), 'the people' are far from being convinced, let alone enthusiastic. The general line of the news analysts and commentators was: 'Germans, wake up! The time for being morally self-righteous bystanders has come to an end.' But the exhortatory tone of politicians and journalists itself reflects a basic scepticism on the part of a significant and *engagé* segment of the population towards possible foreign adventures. It is the last residue of the attempt to 'learn the lesson of history', or at least to learn the lesson of German history, that is at stake in the fight over the orientation of this second group as identified very crudely above. Those who maintain that Auschwitz should never be forgotten and for whom such rememberance is not an empty phrase, and who, moreover, insist on the singularity of Auschwitz and the whole Nazi experience, feel that Germany is in a certain sense morally obliged not to become a 'normal power' like her major foreign policy partners and allies. From the perspective of these people, 'normalization' has only negative connotations and means the loss of a crucially important historical chance: to renounce any form of militarily based power politics and interventionism even under the guise of multinationalism. They suspect – and not without good reasons – that since 1990 the government's piecemeal approach to gaining acceptance for the German army as an instrument for the defence of 'national interests' (defined, among others, as access to vital raw materials, to open seas and open markets), conceals only more ambitious strategies. These could eventually emancipate themselves from current restrictions and open the doors to a 'Germany alone' interventionist foreign policy. In other words, they suspect that the eagle will be flying.again and that now is the last chance to stop it. It might very well be so.

THE MILITARY DIMENSION

If one looks into military planning alone, it gives reason for concern, if not even alarm. The newly formulated 'defence policy guidelines', drafted by the army's chief of staff and officially adopted and proclaimed by the minister of defence, state with a remarkable clarity, impossible only a few years ago: 'The overall national interest is the cornerstone of the security policy of a sovereign state.' This security is then defined in the widest possible terms as 'containment and the termination of crises and conflicts which might compromise Germany's integrity and stability'. By this is meant 'the maintenance of free world trade and unobstructed access to markets and raw materials all over the world in the framework of a just world economic order'. It is no accident that the maintenance of 'peace' does not appear as a top priority in these guidelines. As a leading army general put it bluntly: 'The constitutional task of the federal army is defence without any qualifications, but not peace.' Presently a special unit, the so-called 'crisis reaction force' is being organized for which a new central command structure is required. For the first time since the Second World War, the German army will have again a supreme command. Its specific purpose is to allow German military interventions 'outside the alliance structures'. Thus the intentionally restrictive decision of the constitutional court is being given a dangerously wide interpretation and application. All of this might not have to be taken too seriously. The self-inflated and aggressive strategic language of the generals and their political spokesmen might reflect a deep-seated insecurity and a desperate attempt to regain not only public acceptance but also a sense of purpose and importance. Various enquiries among soldiers and junior officers have shown that a service as peacekeepers (or peacemakers, which includes the possibility of combat) under UN auspices in remote parts of the globe is not greeted with any enthusiasm. The quite unexpected decision of the constitutional court of September 1994 – declaring that 'all soldiers are potential murderers' is protected by the constitutional guarantee of freedom of opinion and, therefore, not punishable – has undermined the self-confidence of the army even more.

And yet, in whichever form the Bundeswehr survives (we are likely to see eventually the abolition of the draft and the creation of a professional army which will give reason for concern on a different level), the government will have its military instrument and will use it. Where, how, and for what purposes – in which specific contexts – is a matter of speculation and to my mind not even terribly important. Students of international relations (just like political scientists in general) very rarely look at political strategies in psychological terms. However, it seems that the stubbornness and perseverence with which the German government has pursued the goal of having the army recognized, and hopefully used, by international organizations – above all in the service of the UN – should be explained not in terms of the political economy of Germany as a 'world power' but rather in psychological terms.

For 40 years, Germany had to operate under specific restrictions and, much as everybody respected the German economic performance, political stability etc., its representatives were still not full 'club members' like the French or the British. Certainly France and Britain are no longer the world powers that they used to be, but they own atomic weapons, they are members of the Security Council, and they can and do play the game of international power politics, even if that game looks today more like a caricature of what it used to be in the days of their glory (e.g. the pathetic Falkland War or the French interventions in her former colonies). The German political class has very little of that sort to show for itself. The chance, opened up all of a sudden in 1989, to participate in spectacular international actions, particularly when they can be interpreted as being in the service of just causes – like peacekeeping or the punishment of an aggressor – was not to be missed. Offering German troops to the international community (which, in reality, was and is the rich men's club of the G7) was tantamount to saying to the whole world: 'We are again somebody, we belong.'

For the reasons discussed earlier, this strategy had to be sold domestically as the result of the pressing demands of the allies and of the UN as well. Boutros Ghali, for example, was promised more German financial contributions if he in turn would, during his visit to Bonn and while the constitutional court was debating the issue, publicly express the need and desire of the UN for a German military contribution (this, at least, is my interpretation of this episode).

The world of international political diplomacy is a relatively small world where most relevant actors know each other, know the internal restrictions or freedoms of action they all have, and evaluate their mutual political performance accordingly. Who is capable of delivering which goods when and how (to paraphrase a famous title of Harold Lasswell)? And the military, and military intervention capabilities, are one of these goods – an important currency in international politics. That is, obviously, the only reason why so many 'third-rate' countries and dictatorial regimes are so anxious to acquire an atomic bomb: they also want 'to be somebody' ('they' meaning their ruling groups or élites). 'The bomb' is out of the question for Germany (probably the one and only remaining sign of earlier discrimination), but its leaders try to acquire everything else. This includes permanent membership of the Security Council – for the very banal and yet politically quite powerful reason that it wants recognition, to become *de facto* and *de jure,* a full member of the world's governing bodies. The military is the entré-billet for that purpose. Germany as a whole, the 'German people' or German 'national interests' (whatever they might be specifically) are not in the least being served by that accomplishment. But what is being served is the vanity and the lust for glory of the collective protagonists of this strategy. Older élites like the British and the French, for whom acting on the world stage has been something much more natural, don't have this problem of recognition: they are there by historical right (or at least they are convinced of such rights).

GERMANY – A WORLD POWER?

Does that strategy make Germany a potential world power as our topic suggests? I do not think so. First of all, what is a 'world power'? World power, superpower, regional power – all these and others are rather superficial categories, useful

for popular consumption and easy discourses but rather
hollow and of very little analytical value when you look closely
at the reality they are meant to describe. However, if we
define a 'world power' as fulfilling at least one of three
conditions –

– to be able to conduct at least two wars or military interventions in different regions of the world simultaneously;
– to own and/or protect islands of property outside of the
country proper and to be able to defend them militarily;
– to own nuclear weapons –

then Germany does not qualifies for this status. The USA
does, obviously, so do Russia, China, France and Great Britain, possibly Israel as well (which would indicate of how
little systematic value these categories are) but not Japan,
for example. To those three categories, often used by analysts of the international system, I would add a fourth one
which seems to me at least as important as the more narrowly political ones, if not in the last analysis even the most
important one (and one which would again and even more
clearly exclude Germany): a country or state qualifies as a
world power if, with or without direct governmental support, its life-style, tastes, way of life and popular as well as
'high' culture (the former definitely more so than the latter) become a model for other societies and cultures, a standard by which others measure themselves, a set of images
others try to emulate, an ensemble of values people in other
parts of the world try to adopt. Thus England certainly was
always more than just an imperial – or imperialistic – country, and to this very day it sets the standards not only for its
former colonies and dominions but well beyond. The same
is true of France and certainly this is a more important base
of power and long-range influence for the USA than its
military strength or its weight in the world economy. The
strength of the Soviet Union rested for many decades on
the loyalty of millions of communists all over the world and,
even though more confined regionally, the identification
of the overseas Chinese with their homeland is a similar
phenomenon.

 All this needs qualification and differentiation – but German socio-political culture, the German life-style and way

of life, has never had the type or the quality of attraction for its European neighbours – let alone for people in other continents – that, for example, Italian society exerted, or 'la civilisation française', or Great Britain whose Beatles revolutionized the imagination and outlook of a whole generation. German culture and society are respected, at times even admired with envy, for their efficiency and the orderliness of the people – but hardly ever loved. Except for specific areas and limited to certain periods, German culture and society as a whole have never been fashionable, trend-setting, making an impact beyond the reach of politics and economics. I suggest this to be the most serious obstacle to any ambition towards being or becoming a world power in the wider and real sense.

THE POSITION OF ÉLITES

It is only fair to add here that the German élites, whatever their shortcomings in other respects, no longer aim for world power status, as was certainly the case for the Wilhelminian period and, again, under the Nazi regime. What they want now is simply political membership to that club of industrialized countries to which they belong already economically. Any substantial independent and autonomous initiative in international politics (notwithstanding the case of the too early recognition of Croatia) is more or less precluded – if for no other reason, because it would be domestically extremely difficult to legitimize. German leadership is fully aware of the historically unique dependence of its economy on the world market. More than 25 per cent of Germany's economy is dependent on exports, and more than half of this goes outside the EC. This means that its political stability is highly vulnerable to factors over which German political and economic managers have only extremely limited control. A cautious, low-profile and moderate position in all international political issues that might involve the world market mechanisms of free trade and access can therefore be expected – despite the more far-reaching ambitions of German military strategists in search of a new role for the army.

And yet, even in this not particularly alarming picture of Germany's forthcoming role on the world stage and its well-known and coherent primary interest in European stability centred on a hard core of 'inner Europe', I see reasons for alarm. It is the very process of normalization, i.e. the possibility, if not probability, of united Germany taking over the role and position it might legitimately claim as its own by the standards and the interests of the international community of states, that should make us reflect. I see Germany, from the point of view of the international system or rather, of the 'global community', at a crossroads. All international politics are constantly at crossroads, but Germany more so because in a certain way it is a newcomer, a new actor on the world stage and one with enormous weight. Let me explain this paradoxical statement.

GERMANY AND THE GLOBAL COMMUNITY

I see the real and urgent need of politically organized humankind to devote all of its energies to tackling four basic socio-economic and two basically political problems. First the socio-economic concerns:

- the rapidly increasing destruction of our natural environment, i.e. the ecological problem;
- the problem of non-renewable resources, particularly in the field of energy;
- the fast-growing economic disequilibrium between North and South, with over-consumption and over-development in the North and under-development and sub-standard mass misery in the South;
- the dramatic population growth, particularly in the poor countries of the South as a function of their socio-cultural disintegration.

And in the field of politics:

- the urgent need to demilitarize inter- and intra-state relations not only because of the enormous social costs involved (which were only marginally reduced in the area of mass destruction arms systems after 1989), but above

all to allow for the development of political solutions to socio-economic problems;
– the devotion of a maximum of our social energies to the creation of better conditions for inter-cultural (inter-religious, inter-ethnic) tolerance in a world society that will become more pluralistic rather than less, that will by necessity experience more cultural intercourse rather than less, and where consequently we will experience more tensions of this kind rather than less.

Against this general background, the prospect of Germany's membership of the power directorate of the international system has to be seen and evaluated. In the face of a widely diffused internal opposition that views such a development with considerable suspicion while insisting on a foreign policy that gives priority to peace, human rights, development aid, protection of the environment (such as the rain forests) and demilitarization after the end of the cold war, the German political class has been pushing to achieve this membership. And, it should be added, Germany has been quite openly invited to join 'the club', particularly by consecutive US governments, independently of particular presidencies. How could any political leadership not be flattered and tempted to accept such an invitation and opportunity, particularly since it coincides with its own inclination and strategies? And what this 'club' – essentially the G7 countries – stands for is quite the opposite of the aforementioned agenda which, in my opinion and in the opinion of many concerned citizens, should have absolute priority and urgency. Together with its partners in power-political management, Germany would then stand for West European, or even 'core European', egotism; for economic growth of the centres at all costs; for military preparedness as the backbone of the hierarchical international order; for military intervention to repress violent conflicts with violence if they threaten the core countries' stability rather than facing the root problems of such conflicts; for paying lip service to the ecological catastrophe, etc.

But that is not all. Other forms of international relations would remain unexplored or neglected or even obstructed. By that I mean, at least as far as European politics is concerned, a Europe of the regions as opposed to a Europe of the Brussels bureaucrats; a political devolution of inter-societal relations to the community level rather than their remaining a state monopoly; the systematic organization and even institutionalization of the collaboration of sectorially concerned citizens' associations across boundaries and cultures, be it in the field of environmental protection by self-help, or as what has been called 'popular diplomacy'. In the tragic case of former Yugoslavia, such European groups trying to establish contacts and a broad cooperation with non-ethnonationalist and anti-military groups in Serbia, Slovenia, Croatia and Bosnia were never given any chance or support. Conventional European and NATO diplomacy monopolized quite successfully the mediation in this war of military warlords against their people – and we know with what results. 'Normalization', the return of Germany to the nuclear family of powerful nations, would mean an end to all these and other options that are in urgent need of exploration.

CONCLUSION: REALPOLITIK IS NO SOLUTION

So far, German international relations experts – academics and non-academics alike – are doing everything to exhort their fellow citizens to grow up to world politics, to shoulder with sobriety and realism their country's new responsibilities and to emancipate themselves from any vision of a foreign policy different in quality from that of other states of its group. This is exactly what Max Weber had urged on the Germans back in 1895, that they should learn to behave and act according to the same rules and interests as other big states. I alluded to this important intellectual heritage earlier. Here, then, is what he said:

> We must realize that the unification of Germany was a youthful prank committed by the nation in her old age and that, because of the costs involved she should have better abstained from – if it were to be the end rather than the beginning of German world politics.

It could have been said today, after the second unification, and it is being said and written today only in more 'sophisticated' terms. As we all know, the Germans then did learn their lesson, they followed the advice of their academic intellectual leaders and claimed their rightful 'place near the sun', as the Wilhelminian slogan put it, and they got very badly burned by this experience, twice. But it wasn't so much that they had 'overdone it', that they had been extremists in pursuing their presumed national interests – it was much more the inner logic of the whole system of international politics that led twice to disaster, the system of 'realpolitik'.

Now we are called upon to continue on this road – the 'realpolitik' being this time the collective egotism of a handful of industrialized nations in a sea of misery, poverty and socioethical degradation. As weak, as confused and as poorly organized in political terms as the inner-German opposition to such a course may have been during the years of the first Federal Republic, it did restrain the German political class and imposed on it a relatively moderate, unaggressive foreign policy. The drama of the present and of the near future will be whether this opposition can be silenced sufficiently to give the leadership of the newly united Germany a free hand in joining the policies of defending the international socio-economic *status quo* of 'one quarter against three quarters of mankind'. We, the intellectuals and international relations experts, are not only observers and academic book-keepers of this drama but active participants. Whether we admit it or not, in the struggle over the education of the public, of public opinion, our own opinions do count and are not irrelevant. We have a responsibility by which future generations will measure us.

Part II: Germany's Policy

4 Gulliver in the Centre of Europe: International Involvement and National Capabilities for Action[1]

Helga Haftendorn

On 3 October 1990, as the jubilation over unification faded away, many Germans asked themselves what consequences the end of the partition of Germany (and of Europe) would have regarding Germany's role in international affairs. With the 'Final Settlement with Regard to Germany',[2] the last legal effects of the war ceased to exist. The military threat from the Soviet Union and the Warsaw Pact had abated and the possibility of setting up in Europe a new peace order seemed to open up.[3] Is Germany still the 'reluctant power' (Franz-Josef Meiers) that it was through the post-war period, cultivating what foreign minister Klaus Kinkel has termed its 'culture of restraint', or will it in the future be more willing to bear the burden of global responsibilities and accept a leadership role in international affairs?

THE TRANSFORMATION OF THE STRUCTURAL FRAMEWORK

The new European political structures have fundamentally changed the conditions under which German foreign policy operates. In the past, as a result of the East–West conflict, the Federal Republic was anchored to the Atlantic Alliance as was the GDR to the Warsaw Pact. The USA as well as the Soviet Union became European powers and thereby guarantors of the stability of this structure upon which the partition of Europe and of Germany was built. The German economy was integrated into the Western European and world markets, and the Federal Republic participated in their regional and global institutions. Various special standards, however, underlined the dominance of the East–West security structure.

Which structures will in the future take the place of the old bi-polar cold war grid? Which consequences will the dismantling of the military confrontation have on the Atlantic Alliance which Alfred Grosser once described as a child of the cold war?[4] Will NATO lose its military mission and will the United States leave Europe when the job 'to keep the Russians out, the Americans in, and the Germans down' has been completed? Which priority will be given to the Central and Eastern European region as well as to Russia, since with the end of the East–West conflict the Soviet Union/Russia has lost its functions as an 'enemy power' and as a watchdog over German partition? Will disintegration in Eastern Europe lead to a new destabilization of the continent and to a potential new security threat for Germany, which was thought to have ceased with the disappearance of the Soviet threat? Will (Western) European or globally orientated economic structures dominate? Will Germany gain a controlling position due to its increased political and economic potential?[5]

Due to its historical experience, an export-orientated economy and geographic location, Germany is dependent upon international structures, yet it builds structures itself.[6] In the past, the Federal Republic has realized its foreign policy priorities primarily through self-constraint, adaptation to demands from its partners, and exploitation of its economic potential.[7] It could best achieve its national interests – protection from outside threat and domestic stability based upon economic prosperity as well as social balance – in a European system which was marked by democracy, a free market economy, and cooperation among its members. Will Germany in the future become a major power in this system, and in doing so, how will it deal with its historical legacies? Can it assume that its positive behaviour over the past 40 years has allowed its historical debt to lapse? Will Germany gain new international options which differ from those in the post-war period? Are Germany's allies and partners prepared to tolerate an international activist and assertive power in the centre of Europe? Which new demands will be made on united Germany, its political institutions, and its people? Is it, as far as government policy and public mood are concerned, becoming a 'normal power' (Philip Gordon)?

In answering these questions, I will deal with:

1. the transformation of institutions in and through which Germany is acting;
2. multilateralism as the standard mode of German foreign policy action;
3. the evolving challenges and risks for German foreign policy.

1. THE TRANSFORMATION OF INSTITUTIONS

Even though the burdens of the post-war period have been overcome, neither Germany's integration into international organizations nor its economic involvement in the global market place have changed. Although I will deal less with its participation in economic affairs,[8] it should be kept in mind that Germany is heavily involved in the OECD, the GATT/WTO, the Group of Seven (G7), the World Bank and the International Monetary Fund (IMF).

The European Union as the Dominant European Institution

The motives for the foundation of the European Community (EC) were not entirely economic. The establishment of the European Coal and Steel Community (ECSC), the European Economic Community (EEC), the European Atomic Energy Community (EURATOM), and the European Monetary System (EMS) were eminently political undertakings with the goal of integrating Germany into the community of Western democracies, to control its still nascent economic power, and to overcome the historical French–German differences. A new German dominance in a reconstructed Europe due to its economic and political potential was to be prevented.

Integration within the EC implied that member states had to give up certain sovereign rights. The Federal Republic freely delegated these rights to the Community, because the EC also broadened its room to manoeuvre. Some partners, like France, accepted these constraints for *raison d'état,* whereas others, like Great Britain, only adopted them with reservations. Presently the European Union (EU) has the competence to make decisions on a broad spectrum of economic, monetary and social affairs.

At first the Community's policy was limited to trade issues. In the 1970s the Community tried to achieve a greater harmonization of foreign policy through the instrument of European policy coordination (EPC). However, this did not go beyond the coordination of policies in selected fields. The turning point came in the mid-1980s with the Single European Act (SEA), in which the cooperation of member states was extended to include foreign policy and security issues. The next step was the Maastricht Treaty, whose goal is the establishment of 'an ever closer union of the peoples of Europe'. This treaty is based upon three pillars: the Economic and Monetary Union (EMU), the Common Foreign and Security Policy (CFSP), and justice and home affairs (interior policy).[9] Thus, the Treaty of Maastricht has created a hybrid in which both supranational and intergovernmental forms of organization exist. Most precise are the prerequisites for the EMU. The transition into the next phase, nevertheless, requires a decision from the Council of Ministers, which will be prepared by an intergovernmental conference scheduled for 1996. It is at the discretion of the members states' governments to cooperate voluntarily in other sectors. The relinquishment of national sovereignty thereby remains limited.

At present, the future evolution of the European Union is not yet fully predictable. If it is successful and produces a dynamic community-building force, the pressure to cooperate in foreign policy and security, legal and domestic issues will increase. If the Union develops into a European Federation, it could become an important pillar of security in Europe. Considering the size of this task and the tendency of many countries to adhere to the *status quo,* it is also possible that the *tour de force* of Maastricht will lose its momentum, and that a reverse movement could again emphasize national identities and interests. A first test will come at the

1996 Inter-Governmental Conference. Its results will indicate whether the European Union is really proceeding towards 'an ever closer union of the peoples of Europe', or whether national concerns continue to dominate.

While being involved in a process of deepening, the Union has committed itself to an enlargement to include the economically most advanced nations in Central and Eastern Europe. A prerequisite is that political reform in the countries that wish to join the European Union is successful and that their economic level reaches that of the old member states. The European treaties with these states are a step in the right direction, but they do not yet go far enough in opening up European markets for their products. Further, the EU has to undergo institutional reform to accommodate a greatly increased membership. If the EU neglects these tasks, it cannot be a stabilizing factor.

The Janus face of the present Union meets the interests of both the French and the British. The Union constrains Germany's most important resource, its economic power, and it provides an opportunity to break the domination of the Deutschmark. At the same time, both France and Great Britain retain their political autonomy, especially with regard to security issues. Neither their status as nuclear powers nor as permanent members of the UN Security Council are encroached. Thus, it remains unclear whether the ambitious goal of a European Political Union will be realized within a reasonable time-frame. The reservations and opposition against it constitute a considerable factor of uncertainty.

In Germany, a combination of a nostalgia for the *status quo*, economic malaise and critique of the democratic deficit of the European Union has caused concerns over whether the route carved by the Maastricht Treaty really meets German interests. The appeal to the federal constitutional court and the decision of the German Parliament to reserve the right for a final vote before the Monetary Union becomes binding are symptoms of these concerns. In its decision of October 1993, the constitutional court partly acceded to these apprehensions. Its ruling emphasized that the goal of the Maastricht Treaty is to form a closer union of states, but not to establish a 'United States of Europe'. The national identity of the member states should not be encroached upon, but at its core should be an intergovernmental cooperation controlled by democratically elected national parliaments that could be revoked if necessary.[10] This provides for a process of Union-building that is not automatic, but remains dependent on the political will of its members.

The Future of the Atlantic Alliance

Like the European Community, the Atlantic Alliance securely anchored the Federal Republic to the West. Germany was protected against an imminent Soviet threat by a combination of NATO and US guarantees; it contributed to European defence while accepting limitations established by the Alliance as well as the Western European Union (WEU). Still today, NATO is, next to the EU, the most important international organization of which Germany is a member. During the time of the cold war, it not only guaranteed Germany's security, but established a common framework for Western policy and institutionalized a close link to the United States. In NATO, intergovernmental elements are combined with supranational structures. While the political organization of the Alliance is based upon the cooperation among sovereign states, the military apparatus functions supranationally. This especially affected the Federal Republic, which had relinquished a national decision-making power in military affairs. It had placed all its armed forces under the military authority of the Alliance, except those earmarked for territorial defence. Considerable military contingents of other NATO states (as well as large Soviet forces in the east) were based on German territory. As it had to renounce the possession of nuclear weapons, the Federal Republic was dependent upon a nuclear deterrent guaranteed by the USA. Germany had a limited voice in the deployment of nuclear weapons, but did participate in the decision-making process on their use.

In the course of the reunification process, Germany pledged to limit the size of the Bundeswehr to 370 000 men in place of the original ceiling of 500 000 troops. It also reaffirmed its renunciation of nuclear weapons. At the same time Germany attained the withdrawal of Soviet/Russian troops from the territory of the former GDR, and an agreement was reached on a special security status for that region. The Forces Convention of 1954,[11] which regulated the stationing of NATO troops on the territory of the Federal Republic, was revised: substantial numbers of NATO forces remain stationed on German soil. The major divisions of the Bundeswehr are integrated into multinational corps and, in a crisis, will not be under national command. Of late, the Bundeswehr has participated in international peacekeeping and peacemaking activities, such as in Bosnia, though under terms specified by a federal constitutional court decision. As the necessity for a strong military presence in Europe and a credible nuclear deterrent have dwindled with the decline of an imminent threat, Germany's remaining – and freely negotiated – military constraints have lost most of their significance.

With the end of the East–West conflict, one of the pillars upon which the 'Atlantic security net' was based has disappeared. During the cold war, this net had both confined and secured manoeuvring room for all partners, especially for West Germany. A change of alliances was not possible for anyone. Each of the partners did everything within its power to preserve the post-war system, until the conditions upon which it had been established changed. With the demise of the Warsaw Pact and the collapse of the Soviet Union, the Atlantic Alliance had to change too. Its function as a framework for the collective defence of Europe has lost significance.[12] As the future course of Russia remains uncertain, NATO needs a capability for reconstitution should a 'Russian threat' or some other distinct threat arise again. Instead of focussing on a single dominant threat, the Alliance has recently been re-examining its military missions by concentrating on more heterogeneous risks not limited to the NATO territory. The concept of Combined Joint Task Forces (CJTF) takes account of the need for a more differentiated response by a select number of countries, but it also raises the question of how the Alliance would in the future combine selectivity with commitment. Besides common defence, NATO has adopted three new tasks. One is proactive crisis management, and the second peacekeeping and peace-enforcement missions mandated by the United Nations or the OSCE. Accordingly, NATO has made forces available for surveillance as well as for military action under UN auspices in the Bosnian conflict. A third task is advocated under the name of coalition strategy by the United States. In return for a US commitment to participate fully, including if necessary the use of ground troops, in all conflicts in Europe in which there was a NATO consensus to act, the allies would pledge to share fully with the USA through NATO the military burdens and risks in meeting mutual security threats outside Europe.

The end of the cold war thus has a profound impact on the political character of the Alliance. New political constellations are possible that were inconceivable during the period of the East–West conflict. This especially applies to the United States, whereas Germany will maintain its commitment from the post-war period for reasons which mostly lie in its historical legacies. However, in Germany's view it is important that America remains politically and militarily coupled to Europe. During the East–West conflict Western Europe functioned as a military outpost for the USA to check the potential of the Soviet power. After that, Europe became an overseas depot and switching yard for the deployment of American European-based forces for global intervention. The USA now looks at NATO primarily in the framework of a coalition strategy, hoping to attain a higher level of burden-sharing.[13] These developments greatly change the character of the Alliance as a system of collective defence and involve risks to its coherence and credibility.

Germany is confronted with the dilemma that it wishes, on the one hand, to preserve NATO as an Atlantic security community – as a basis for common values and interests – and, on the other, to empower the European Political Union's authority in foreign and security policy. In order not to undermine NATO cohesion and effectiveness, it has been decided to establish the WEU both as an inner-European coordinator within NATO and as the defence arm of the EU. It will thus serve as a link and as a halfway house between both organizations. When this institutional reform is implemented, the Alliance will develop a more binary structure. Though there is the danger that it might produce some rifts between Europe and America, it would strengthen the decision-making process within the EU on common foreign and security policy as well as affording the USA a greater selectivity in its global strategic responses.

A highly debated issue is whether the Atlantic Alliance should admit as members some of the Central European countries. The Višegrád States – Poland, Hungary and the Czech and Slovak Republic – as well as Slovenia and the Baltic Republics, have expressed their wish to be admitted to both EU and NATO. The North Atlantic Cooperation Council (NACC), due to the non-binding nature of its consultations, cannot give these states the guarantees that they feel they need for their own security and a stable domestic development. At its January 1994 summit, NATO offered to conclude bilateral 'Partnership for Peace' agreements for all those countries that so desired. They provide for consultation under Article 4 of the Treaty of Washington as well as for joint exercises and other forms of cooperation. By 1995, some 20 European states which were not previously members of NATO had concluded PfP agreements. The status of the resulting relationship is below that of regular membership, but can, for some at least, though not Russia, be seen as a preliminary step towards full membership.[14] Enlarging NATO is, however, only one option for projecting stability into Central and Eastern Europe; and the balance of benefits and costs has to be well considered. Germany's prime interest is the establishment of a stable security space between its border and the Russian frontier.

Russia, however, has insisted that any enlargement of NATO and any deployment of NATO forces close to Russian borders would be a very unfriendly act. This does not prevent Poland, the Czech Republic and Hungary from continuing to lobby for full NATO membership. With a change in the Clinton administration's position, they have found a potent supporter within the Alliance. Other members are more reluctant to go ahead with NATO enlargement, partly out of concern about alienating Russia, and partly weary of extending Alliance commitments for which they feel their countries are not yet ready. NATO is faced with the dilemma that expansion and the resultant obligation to provide assistance as well as the refusal to do so might weaken the cohesion of the Alliance and its capability to maintain collective defence. In this situation, NATO decided to do an analysis of the problems associated with an enlargement and present its findings to the NATO Council in December 1995 for further decision. On 28 September 1995, aspirant countries were briefed on the conditions of membership – democratic stability, respect of human rights, unqualified acceptance of the Treaty of Washington (1949) – though the report did not specify which countries were considered eligible nor when enlargement could take place. At the same time Washington sought to reassure Moscow that NATO membership of former Pact members was not directed against Russia and that no nuclear weapons would be deployed nor large military manoeuvres conducted on new member states' territory. These assurances could become part of a bilateral agreement between the Alliance and Russia. Further, the USA has offered Russia a strategic partnership and has sought to establish multilateral frameworks in which Moscow could closely cooperate with the major Western powers. For this, the Contact Group created to search for a peace arrangement in Bosnia provides a good example. It is important that Russia will in some way be involved in the emerging new European security structures, as there will be neither peace nor security for Europe that is not also provided for Russia.

It is in German interests to keep NATO intact and well adjusted to the new international challenges. For the time being the situation in Russia and in South-eastern Europe is still completely unsettled. It is conceivable, on the one hand, that Russia will develop into a European–Asiatic power which is capable of stabilizing its region non-hegemonically and of cooperating with Western Europe on an equal basis. On the other hand, a situation could emerge in which Russia again threatens European security and could only be checked or balanced by a strong military alliance. It would therefore be premature to put NATO at stake, an institution that has guaranteed security and stability in Europe for the last 45 years.

The CSCE as a Collective European Security System?

In the past, the Federal Republic has strongly promoted the CSCE process. Under the conditions of the East–West conflict it played an important role in overcoming the confrontation. On one side, it stabilized the *status quo* in Europe, while on the other side it supplied flexible formulas by which its division could slowly be overcome. After the reunification of Europe and Germany, the latter had hoped that a new order of peace would take the place of the old system of confrontation. However, at present the CSCE/OSCE does not yet fulfil the prerequisites to function successfully as a collective security system. What are the prospects that it might do so in the future?

With the 'Charter of Paris' the CSCE took the first steps in this direction by establishing instruments and institutions to resolve conflicts and manage crises. These have been further developed by the decisions agreed upon at the 1994 Budapest follow-up conference. The former *conference* was transformed into an *organization,* the OSCE. Its failure to act in the Bosnian conflict, however, shows that it cannot yet be relied upon to guarantee stability and security in Europe. This is tragic considering that the OSCE is the only European institution to which all of the European states, along with the USA, Canada and Russia, belong. Presently there is no consensus among the member states binding them to joint action against a state that has violated the principle of the non-use of force. Indeed if an agreement were reached for a specific case, the member states lack the resolve to take action or, if necessary, to use military power to punish an aggressor. National interests still widely dominate and are reinforced by the size and political heterogeneity of its members. The awareness that conflicts in Europe affect all states in the region and therefore should concern them is not yet widespread enough. No carefully crafted institutional arrangement will remedy this fact. A stronger European resolve, however, does not seem to be within easy reach.

In spite of its inadequacies, the CSCE/OCSE remains an asset for Germany. Because of its emphasis on norms and standards, especially its strong human rights record, the OSCE responds nicely to the moral impetus in German politics. Another of its positive achievements have been the various agreements on confidence-building measures and on conventional arms control, such as the CFE Treaty. The 1996 Lisbon CSCE/OSCE follow-up conference, as well as the CFE review conference, will show whether its members are prepared to adjust to a Europe without blocs (the CFE Treaty called for proportionate military cuts in both West and East). If this can be achieved without major disturbances, the OSCE might still not qualify for a collective security system, but both institutions could provide the pillars on which an all-encompassing European security platform in the future could be built.

The Feasibility of Securing Peace within the United Nations

Although its activities have not yet reached the level prescribed by Secretary General Boutros Ghali's ambitious programme, the 'Agenda for Peace',[15] the United Nations is at present the only organization that has the capability to take effective action in resolving conflicts. Contrary to the situation during the cold war, the Security Council has been able to reach common agreements on peacekeeping operations in the second Gulf War, in Somalia and in Bosnia with the support of the three Western powers and Russia. However, the organization of a joint military force under UN command or the establishment of the Military Staff Committee as specified in the UN Charter have not yet occurred. The United Nations has also not effectively contributed to ending the war in Bosnia due to the clash of interests among the states concerned and among the members of the Security Council.

In the past, Germany's capability to participate in United Nations peacekeeping and peacemaking missions has been limited by a narrow interpretation of the Basic Law concerning an out-of-area deployment of the German Bundeswehr. This self-imposed limitation had constrained German interests in achieving a stable global environment and was not in accordance with the country's claim to a permanent seat in the Security Council. With the ruling of the federal constitutional court in July 1994, the participation of Germany's armed forces in peacekeeping operations is now considered constitutional, provided the German Bundestag approves their specific mission.

The work of the United Nations, however, is not limited

to peacekeeping activities. Germany's policy towards the UN has been as under-developed as its economic aid policy. Germany's claim to a seat in the UN Security Council is mainly a verbal declaration since it cannot support its claim with extraordinary assistance to countries of the Third World – German official development assistance is only 0.2 per cent of its gross national product (GNP) which lies in the lower third category of the OECD states. Furthermore, so far Germany has only marginally contributed to UN peacekeeping missions. The logical step, establishing a common permanent seat for the European Union, cannot be realized due to the reservations of France and Britain, both of which want to preserve their special status in the United Nations system and *vis-à-vis* Germany.

In the past, its membership in the world organization was not a burden. The Federal Republic paid its dues, but did not involve itself in critical political decisions and took a stance of caution with regard to military actions. The so-called 'Enemy State Clauses', Articles 53 and 107 of the UN Charter, did not inflict restrictions upon Germany because they were neutralized by the bloc structure of the post-war period as well as by assurances of its partners. Should the charter be revised and Germany receive permanent status in the Security Council in the future, then it will not only be expected to make a greater contribution to the budget, but also to assist at a higher level in international peacekeeping operations.

2. MULTILATERALISM AS A STANDARD MODE OF FOREIGN POLICY ACTION

The characteristic of Germany's post-war foreign policy has been its distinct multilateralism. Membership in international organizations offered the Federal Republic an opportunity to change external restrictions upon its sovereignty into voluntary commitments. Through its membership it was increasingly able to take part in the organizations' policy-making. The history of the Group of Four (representatives from Bonn and the three powers with special rights and responsibilities regarding Germany as a whole and Berlin) further shows that Germany could employ an institution which had been established as a guardian for Germany to gain political influence as a 'Fourth Ally' due to the cold war circumstances and the absence of the Soviet Union as a partner in allied cooperation.[16] It would therefore be incorrect to speak of German 'oblivion from power' as some observers (Hans-Peter Schwarz) have done.[17] Under the conditions of the cold war, Bonn viewed a multilateral approach to foreign affairs as a cost-effective policy variant in advocating their national interests and used it accordingly. Hence, the EU, NATO and the OSCE owe much of their present form and function to the contributions of the Federal Republic. In order to gain acceptance for and secure German unification at the international level, the Federal Republic not only worked to make united Germany a member of an unaffected Atlantic Alliance, but also to strengthen its integration into the EC. It wanted to tie itself more strongly than ever into Western Europe in order to acquire coherent and stable surroundings for the united Germany.[18]

Institutions offered tried methods to German politics and ensured that expectations were met and national behaviour could be assessed. They also created a time pressure and thereby fostered decision-making. In the past, institutions also brought military, political and economic power into alignment. This was particularly important considering Germany's weaknesses. The US predominance was mediated in NATO, and French pressure was counterbalanced in the EC. The Federal Republic could only indirectly utilize its economic weight and had to accept compromises in order to safeguard the processes into which it was integrated. Institutions themselves seldom act directly, but they offer a framework for international policy-making. As in the past, Germany in the future will need partners for cooperation with whom it can realize its political interests. This requires a willingness to adapt to its partners interests and an ability to reach compromises. Germany can thus be expected to continue playing a key role as initiator, inducer and participant in various institutional frameworks.

Germany and France as Leading European Powers

France is one of Germany's closest allies in Europe. The intimate cooperation between Bonn and Paris has become a structural landmark in European politics and will continue to be so in the future.[19] From the French perspective, Germany has always been a factor of insecurity as well as a political rival for historical, demographic and geographical reasons, a partner which France wanted to attach to itself and submit to a European orientation. It has always been a goal of French policy to prevent German dominance even if this meant renouncing its own dominance and to offer co-leadership. This was Charles de Gaulle's primary motive for the Franco-German Treaty of 1963 as well as for the initiatives of President François Mitterand and Chancellor Helmut Kohl to jointly build the European Union in December 1990. French policy of binding relations between the two countries has not changed since German reunification. In fact, it has become an even higher priority for Paris, as the German partition no longer functions as a system of checks and balances.

In the future, the German–French couple as an alliance of Europe's leading powers will not only be a central actor in (continental) Europe, but will also control both route and speed of a closer political union. This alliance will function as long as the German side takes the French global concerns into consideration and France tolerates the German interest in preserving its Atlantic ties. Great Britain has not yet politically overcome its geographic isolation to propose an alternative to this German–French duo or to further develop it into a European triumvirate. For Paris, only a Political Union offers a long-range guarantee to prevent a German hegemony in Europe – a 'German Europe'. At the same time, the establishment of the Political Union fulfils Germany's goal to permanently tie its destiny to those of the other Western democracies and thereby gain external security and domestic stability.

Close Relations with Poland and the Czech Republic

With reunification, Germany obtained new neighbours and took on greater responsibilities for its relations with Central and Eastern European countries. While the purpose of the policy of *détente* in the 1970s and 1980s was to lessen mistrust and to provide guarantees regarding the *status quo*, the present task is to develop close cooperative ties with these states that enable them to progress towards democracy and market economy. It is in Germany's fundamental interests to stabilize its eastern perimeter and prevent tremors in its own political and social systems that could be caused by new influxes of refugees, a further penetration of organized crime, or the spread of ethnic conflict and civil war.

Germany is especially interested in developing trusted relations with Poland and the Czech Republic which have suffered tremendously under German war-time occupation. But also millions of Germans have suffered when they were expelled in 1945 from areas that were their home for centuries. Today, most European borders have lost their separating character. This is especially true for the Oder-Neisse border between Poland and Germany that evolved from a bone of political contention into a starting point for transborder cooperation. The German refugees from what were once the German provinces of Silesia and Pommerania are now slowly becoming the spokespeople not for revanchism, but for reconciliation. But reconciliation is not enough: Warsaw – and on a smaller scale also Prague – expect Germany to act also as a spokesperson for their interests in the West.

For Bonn, the Central and Eastern European states' desire to be accepted in the near future as members into the European Union has taken top priority. Thereby the 'Wall of Prosperity' at the Oder-Neisse and Bohemian Forest should be levelled and these countries domestically and politically stabilized. A concern is, however, that this wall should not be re-erected eastward at the Carpathian Mountains and the Bug River. What should happen to the Baltic States and those of the Balkans, to the Ukraine and Belarus, not to mention Russia and the other former members of the Council on Mutual Economic Assistance (COMECON), is still an open question. Further, the European Union's desire to expand to the East has to be carefully weighed against the goal to strengthen and to develop the EU into a Political Union. There is, however, no alternative. Poland, the Czech Republic and Hungary are part of Europe and have a historical right to return to it. At present, a decision to start membership negotiations has been taken, but a precise date for their admission has not yet been set. It is likely that enlargement will increase the tendency of European integration to proceed with variable speeds and status levels.[20] The result could be the evolution of a European core group surrounded by a somewhat less tightly organized belt of states.

Germany's interests with regard to the states of Central and Eastern Europe is of a political, military, and economic nature. It would like the process of democratization and liberalization to continue and the countries to develop stable political structures. Military priorities dictate a reduction of the existing arms arsenals in the region and the prevention of military conflicts between and within these states. From an economic point of view, market-orientated economies in Central and Eastern Europe would offer export markets for German goods, investment possibilities for German capital, and resources for necessary raw materials. Support for democratic reforms is therefore of vital German (and European) interest. It can conceivably be best helped by offering the states undergoing reform economic and technical assistance as well as the necessary management know-how, and by supporting the opening of the Western markets to their products. Germany's past financial contributions are in the range of 90 billion Deutschmarks, but they do not suffice. Only a joint effort by the West – especially the members of the G7 – will enable the Central and Eastern European countries to catch up to their level of industrial development.

Close Cooperation with the United States

Outside Europe, the close cooperation with the United States is a fundamental axiom of German policy. In the post-war period the USA, through its presence in Europe, not only guaranteed the Federal Republic's security, but also protected its room to manoeuvre in foreign policy from the concerns of its neighbours. Friction occurred in the German–American relationship when both sides assessed the military threat differently, as in the first phase of the American *détente* policy in the 1960s or, with a complete reversal of perspectives, in the period of neo-containment during the Reagan administration. Furthermore, the economic and monetary ties between the two countries have always been very close. The American economic assistance in the form of the GARIOA Program and the Marshall Plan made the economic reconstruction of West Germany and its integration into the world market possible. However, the potential for conflict within this relationship increased with the Federal Republic's growing economic importance, as has been illustrated in the 'Chicken War', the 'Nixon-Shock', and the nuclear export and gas-pipeline conflicts. When the USA wanted to force its position by constructing linkages with vital West German security interests, Bonn tried to secure support from its partners in the European Community. Nevertheless, Bonn's and Washington's political interests were close enough that the benefits from the close rapport between the two countries were greater than their costs. This identity of interests culminated in George Bush's offer of a 'partnership in leadership' to Germany, made during his visit to Germany in May 1989.[21]

Germany also needs to cooperate closely with the United States. In Europe the USA continues to represent a factor of stability. It relieves the concerns of some of Germany's neighbours that Germany could strive to attain a hegemonial position in Europe. It also makes Germany's leading economic role politically acceptable for the other European states. However, this only operates under the condition that the United States' 'balancing function' is not directed against German policy.[22] This is one of the concerns of German politics in the future.

In the future Germany and the United States will continue to be interested in a close mutual relationship. This, however, has become more difficult for a number of reasons. In both countries the end of the East–West conflict caused a new orientation of foreign policy. The USA has retained its normative principles – democracy and free-market economics – as well as its claim to global leadership; its methods of implementation, however, have changed. On the one hand, the administration is following a strategy of 'Enlargement'[23] that aims at the further integration of states and regions into the democratic and free-market structures of the West. On the other hand, the USA has given up its primary focus on Europe which had been a result of the political and military conflict with the Soviet Union and had served its policy of 'Containment'. Alliances have become instruments for achieving certain political goals, and allies are seen as partners in burden-sharing. In this respect the USA has high expectations for Germany which the present administration views as the most powerful partner in Europe due to its demographic potential, stable political structure and economic power.

The United States remains the dominant economic power world-wide. It is a corner-stone in the global economic triangle – USA, (Western) Europe, Japan – whose institutional structure can be found in the G7, the OECD and the new WTO, and which is a deciding factor in Europe's future prosperity as well as that of Germany.[24] The latter participates both directly and indirectly through the European Union in decision-making within these institutions. At the same time, the USA, the EU and Japan are also competitors in world markets, whose rivalry is becoming more intense as each is fighting to secure its position and competitiveness. One of the greatest risks for the future of free world trade lies in its increasing regionalization through the creation of large economic blocs – the European Economic Area (EEA), the North-American Free Trade Zone (NAFTA) and the Asia–Pacific Economic Cooperation (APEC).

With unification, Germany's political and economic interests have become more 'Eastern' (in that they transcend Europe and the NATO area) though Germany has not given up its character as a Western country and its corresponding desire for close bonds to (Western) Europe and the USA. After the decline of the military threat, Germany might in the future wish to realize its interests concerning Eastern Europe and Asia in the future more directly and with less multilateral protection. Conflicts in foreign and economic policy are therefore pre-programmed. Additional problems lie ahead as Germany must consider, along with its own interests, those of its partners in the EU. Since trade-offs in other fields of policy are less likely than in the past, growing friction in the German–American relationship can be expected even though their political goals remain similar.

US policy is also influenced by its international environment. Germany's room to manoeuvre in foreign policy will therefore depend upon whether Russia remains America's most important strategic partner or competitor, like the Soviet Union was before, or if China takes on this role. In the former case, German politics with regard to Eastern Europe will have to take American interests into account while, in the latter case, German responsibility for the development of the region would grow, but it could be obliged to be more considerate of American concerns in its policies towards Asia.

Japan and Asia

Japan and South-East Asia are acquiring a special significance for Germany. Its new 'programme on Asia' (1993) testifies that it sees Japan not primarily as an economic competitor, but as a political partner.[25] As leading 'civilian powers'[26] of the post-war period (Hanns Maull), both find themselves in a state of transition in which they are expected to take on increasing responsibilities although their societies are not fully prepared for it. German interests in Asia (including China) result from the fact that this region presently has the highest prospect for growth and is particularly attractive for long-term investments by German business due to its relatively high level of political stability – especially in comparison to Eastern Europe. The strengthening of bilateral and multilateral relations with this region, for example between the EU and ASEAN, should further secure its political involvement.

3. CHALLENGES AND RISKS FOR GERMAN FOREIGN POLICY

Setting Priorities Between Conflicting Demands

The various demands upon German policy are not easily compatible with one another. They result from the different institutional patterns of involvement and the multilateral character of its diplomatic practices. In Western Europe the tendency to strengthen European integration will continue to dominate. Since Germany is not likely to revise its fundamental decisions of the 1950s to tie itself securely to the West and to cooperate closely with France, it must accept the resulting limitations on its political manoeuvring space. However, a situation might come when the country's leaders and people perceive its national interests at risk and could refuse to implement supranational decisions. Concerning European integration, a prognosis is not yet possible because EU common policy until now has been limited to economic questions. The yielding of national sovereign rights within the framework of the Maastricht Treaty so far has had little political impact. Many filters have been built into the process of reaching a common foreign and security policy that will slow down rather than accelerate the process of union-building. Early limitations have already revealed themselves with the harmonization of economic and monetary policy. They are most visible in those cases where beloved traditions and practices are at stake: for example, relinquishing the Deutschmark in favour of a European Currency Unit (ECU). In this case, voices warning against a surrender of national identity are increasing in numbers even in Germany.[27]

European integration policy, with its goal of creating a close Political Union, might also come into conflict with the objective to preserve and further develop the ties to the United States as well as its institutional hinge, the Atlantic Alliance. Despite its interest in empowering the Political Union with new and stronger authority in the areas of foreign and security policy, Germany has to ensure that the EU–WEU structure does not develop into an alternative to NATO, but enhances the 'two-pillar concept' on which European security rests. Such a policy implies a difficult balancing act between the interests of its partners. Further, it will not be easy to combine the strengthening of the Union with the task of expanding the European Union to the Central and Eastern European states and thereby contribute to the political and economic stabilization of this region.

In history, Germany has entertained both friendly and hostile relations with Russia. In the 19th century cooperation dominated, in the 20th century they were mostly marked by confrontation. But even during the cold war, periods of tension alternated with those of *détente*. The Federal Republic found it useful to provide for its security by, on the one hand, joining and contributing to NATO and, on the other, constructing, together with its partners, a policy of *détente* with the Soviet Union (the so-called 'Harmel formula'). Its future interests demand that it continues to assist Russia in its political and economic modernization as a higher degree of domestic stability should make it more accountable in international affairs. At the same time Russia should not again dominate Eastern Europe and constitute a security threat to the West. Germany has further to balance its assistance and support of Russia with that of the other states of Central and Eastern Europe with whom it has well-defined common interests.

I have mentioned earlier the problem of NATO enlargement. Such a step should not accelerate the process of reducing NATO from a defence alliance to a mere pact of military guarantees. In the German point of view, it is important that NATO both retains its capabilities for collective defence of its territory and develops further capacities for crisis-management and peacekeeping outside the NATO area. There might be no alternative to granting membership to Poland, Hungary and the Czech Republic both of the European Union and of NATO. One of the most important tasks facing German politics is therefore the development of strategies compatible with the preservation and further evolution of the EU and NATO. The other relates to the development of strategies for the defence of its interests outside the EU–NATO perimeters: for example, to secure access to raw materials and other critical resources.

To prevent divergent interests on both sides of the Atlantic, or trade conflicts in the economic triangle, from straining the relationship between Europe and the United States, the links between both sides need to be strengthened. In order to raise the awareness of their peoples, both might develop a joint declaration of principles, dwelling upon but also enlarging those of 1974 and 1990. It would be too cumbersome, however, to agree on a new Transatlantic Treaty as some have proposed[28] and have it ratified by the national parliaments. The existing organizations need minor adjustments but are otherwise fully equipped to safeguard a constructive transatlantic relationship. It would be further advisable if Germany and Japan deepen their relationship by intensifying their joint consultations and fostering a broader cultural exchange.

Acceptance of International Responsibility

With the cold war legacies left behind and the burden of national division overcome, Germany's allies and partners encourage it to assume larger international responsibilities and to accept a leadership role in international affairs. Fulfilling these expectations and combining this with its traditional multilateral style is indeed the biggest foreign policy challenge Germany has faced since unification. Though Germany not only was an important paymaster in the Gulf War, but has also given the lion's share of assistance to Eastern Europe, more is expected from it, especially that it becomes a reliable exporter of security – understood in a very broad context[29] – whereas the old Federal Republic had to import its security mainly from the USA. The demand for the shouldering of greater burdens is not focussed primarily on greater participation of the Bundeswehr in UN peacekeeping missions instead of remaining in the rear. Germany should participate more, on its own political initiative, in the formation of international politics. This also involves making well-thought-through choices instead of deferring them to her allies.

Germany will take pains to meet these expectations in the years to come. Prominent German politicians have pledged Germany's willingness to play a full international role along with its partners. I quote Chancellor Helmut Kohl, speaking at the final departure of allied troops from Berlin in September 1994:

> We will never forget what our American, British and French friends have done for us. Germany will not stand on the sidelines where peace and freedom in the world are at stake. We Germans are aware of our responsibility and will fulfil it alongside our partners.

President Roman Herzog concurs that Germany can no longer enjoy a 'free-rider' role:

> Germany belongs to the concert of the great democracies, whether she likes it or not; and if one of these democracies stands aside, it is inevitably not just doing harm to others but in the end to itself.

Even politicians from the political opposition, such as former SPD leader Rudolf Scharping, recognize (though not uncontested from some of its party rank and file) Germany's 'unquestionable obligations' to participate in UN peace-keeping and peacemaking operations along with its allies when he pointed out that 'NATO is an alliance committed to sharing burdens.'

A more self-confident international role, however, does not imply that Germany will adopt a unilateral strategy in foreign policy. German élites are aware that the increased political weight of their country not only elicits support, but also raises concerns based on unhappy historical experiences with a German bid for European domination. It is Germany's dilemma that many of its partners on the one hand want it to provide political leadership, and on the other to remain weak and constrained enough not to threaten them and their role. In their eyes, Germany should be an elephant and a mouse at the same time. To find the right balance between strength and restraint in its foreign policy will thus be one of the biggest challenges of the future.

It is this dilemma, as well as Germany's multilateral tradition, that will make it seek for partners to cooperate with. The EU members, especially France, the United States and Japan, will be its preferred allies. A primary interest is thus that the EU makes progress in the harmonization of its member states' foreign and security policy. It is a precondition if Germany and its partners should have an impact at the international level. Cooperating with the United States offers Germany the chance to influence the world's leading power and, within limits, to participate in its leadership role. This cooperation provides Germany with opportunities for exerting power that are not available on a national scale alone. Coordinating policies with Japan could have positive effects on the realization of German interests in the Asiatic region as well as in the economic triangle. An option of having alternative partners in cooperation offers a chance to decrease Germany's dependence on its partners, but is only feasible under certain circumstances. It carries with it the risk that Germany could fall between two stools or find itself in a situation in which it has to choose between Paris and Washington, and possibly Tokyo. To prevent this from occurring in the future is even more important than it was in the past.

Another new challenge is developing coherent policies for regions outside Europe and the Atlantic area. Events in other regions will in the future have larger repercussions on German policy than in the past when they were contained in a bi-polar grid. Contacts with other parts of the world primarily arose from the EU framework (for example with ASEAN), from traditional ties (such as with the countries of the Near and Middle East), or in regard to US interests (as has been the case in Ethiopia/Somalia). In the future, Germany will no longer be able to afford such disinvolvement, but will have to define its interests beyond the European perimeters.

Mediation between Domestic Politics and Foreign Policy

Germany will only do justice to these growing international demands when it strengthens its ability to lead. It is important that its political élites as well as its people are aware that the European and global interdependence of German politics is growing. However, it will only be able to overcome those elements of self-restraint which are clearly out of step with today's challenges if its government's ability to combine foreign policy demands with domestic needs is strengthened. Thus, the links between foreign and domestic policy should be increased in strength and number. One way is an expanded involvement of the German parliament in the foreign policies consultation and decision-making processes. As decisions within the EU affect the political system and the society of the Federal Republic, the German representatives in Brussels must also take the demands of domestic policy into account. The necessary interaction between foreign and domestic policies can best be illustrated with the image of 'two tables' (Putnam) at which international consultations take place.[30] Because of the federal structure of German government, seats at the domestic 'table' have to be reserved for representatives from the federal government, from those of the Laender, and from the two chambers of parliament. As long as the European Parliament lacks full parliamentary powers, democratic legitimacy is attained by the endorsement of actions taken by European organs through national parliaments. Further, the direct and indirect possibilities for the individual citizen to voice his or her opinion have to be strengthened by means of a better flow of information and a higher transparency of the Union's political activities. Only through these means can political indifference on a national scale be prevented from being matched at the international level by a foreign policy fatigue in general or by a European fatigue in particular.

In order to be capable of mediating between foreign and domestic policies as well as coping with the demands resulting from Germany's integration into a complex international environment, its government further needs to enhance its institutionalized problem-solving capacity. Germany can only solve the conflict of priorities resulting from contradicting international and domestic demands with an efficient political structure that has the necessary operative and analytical capabilities. The fact that Bonn was poorly prepared for the events leading up to the 'Wende' (turn) of 1989 indicates the deficiencies in this capacity. New approaches should be considered for its improvement. The classical reporting of the German embassies does not suffice any more for adequately informing the government about developments and trends abroad. A network of observers should be established from policy research institutes and complemented by analyses from foreign experts on the spot.[31] The government needs seismographs to predict future foreign policy challenges as well as indicators of what is feasible. Thus, the transfer between the analytical centres and the operative institutions must be improved.

German policy, to be credible and accountable, has to be based on broad domestic support. Until now it seems as if many Germans have perceived neither the high level of international involvement of their country nor the resulting opportunities and constraints for its politics. The major problem is thus not to achieve a domestic consensus above the lines of party politics and regional divisions (such as between the old and the new Laender), but to transform the existing consensus on not getting very involved in international affairs (for many Germans, Switzerland is their international role model!) into a greater preparedness to enter into international commitments and bear their costs. The German people need to develop a higher degree of concern, so that they do not regard civil wars in the European perimeter as natural catastrophes which cannot be prevented and whose damage and resulting suffering can only be alleviated. This also means overcoming a deep-seated popular pacifism that resulted from the experience of the Second World War, American re-education, and the after-effects of the missile debate of the 1980s. Germany needs to formulate its own interests and make choices if necessary. This is by no means an advocacy for a nationalistic foreign policy, but the traditional multilateral approach has to be filled with new concepts and has to reach beyond the European borders if it is to be politically effective. This is the only way that Germany will be capable of co-leadership in international affairs and be respected by its partners as a leading power.

It is not the dwarves that tie Gulliver down, but he himself does not yet know which bindings he has to cast away, and which institutional or multilateral bonds he has to accept and even strengthen for his own good.

NOTES

1. An earlier version has been published as 'Gulliver in der Mitte Europas. Internationale Verflechtung und nationale Handlungsmöglichkeiten' in *Deutschlands neue Außenpolitik*, Vol. 1, Grundlagen, Ed. Karl Kaiser and Hanns W. Maull (Munich: Oldenbourg Verlag, 1994) pp. 129–152. The author thanks Genevieve Libonati and Benjamin Kiersch for their expert translation into English.
2. See Treaty on the Final Settlement with Regard to Germany, 12 September 1990, *NATO Review*, Vol. 38, No. 5 (October 1990) pp. 30–32.
3. See London Declaration on a Transformed North Atlantic Alliance,

6 July 1990, *NATO Review*, Vol. 38, No. 4 (August 1990) pp. 32–33.

4. See Alfred Grosser, *Die Bundesrepublik Deutschland – Bilanz einer Entwicklung* (Tübingen: Wunderlich, 1967) p. 12.

5. See Andrei S. Markovits and Simon Reich, 'Deutschlands neues Gesicht: Über deutsche Hegemonie in Europa' *Leviathan* 1 (1992) pp. 15–63.

6. See Werner Link, 'Perspektiven der europäischen Integration', in Karl Kaiser and Hanns W. Maull (Eds), *Die Zukunft der europäischen Integration: Folgerungen für die deutsche Politik* (Bonn: Forschungsinstitut der Deutschen Gesellschaft für Auswärtige Politik, 1993) pp. 7–26 (Arbeitspapiere zur Internationalen Politik, No. 78).

7. See Helga Haftendorn, 'Außenpolitische Prioritäten und Handlungsspielraum. Ein Paradigma zur Analyse der Außenpolitik der Bundesrepublik Deutschland' *Politische Vierteljahresschrift* 1 (1989) pp. 31–49.

8. For this aspect see Norbert Kloten, 'Die Bundesrepublik als Weltwirtschaftsmacht' *Deutschlands neue Außenpolitik*, op. cit., pp. 63–80.

9. Cf. The Treaty on European Union, Articles A and B, *European Union: Selected Instruments Taken from the Treaties*, Book 1, Vol. 1 (Luxembourg: Office for Official Publications of the European Communities, 1993) pp. 15–68.

10. See 'Der Vertrag von Maastricht ist keine Preisgabe des Staates Bundesrepublik', *Frankfurter Allgemeine Zeitung* (13 Oct. 1993).

11. See Convention on the Presence of Foreign Forces in the Federal Republic of Germany of October 23, 1954 *Documents on Germany, 1944–1985* (Washington, DC: Department of State Publication) No. 9446, pp. 610–612.

12. See also Uwe Nerlich, 'Neue Sicherheitsfunktionen der NATO' *Europa Archiv*, 23 (1993) pp. 663–672.

13. See Les Aspin, 'Forces and Alliances for a New Era', speech delivered by the US Secretary of Defense on 12 September 1993 at the IISS Conference in Brussels, manuscript. Also see Les Aspin, 'A Bottom-Up Review: Forces for a New Era' (Department of Defense, 1 September 1993).

14. See Declaration of the Heads of States and Government participating in the meeting of the North Atlantic Council held at NATO headquarters, Brussels on 10–11 January 1994 and the Invitation and Framework Document to the 'Partnership for Peace', *NATO Review*, Vol. 42, No. 1 (February 1994) pp. 28–33.

15. Cf. *Agenda for Peace. Preventive Diplomacy, Peacemaking and Peace-keeping*, report of the Secretary General Boutros Boutros-Ghali pursuant to the statement adopted by the Summit Meeting of the Security Council on 31 January 1992, United Nations Document DPI/1247 (New York: United Nations Publications, 1992).

16. See Helga Haftendorn, 'Am Anfang waren die Alliierten. Die alliierten Vorgehaltsrechte als Rahmenbedingung des außenpolitischen Handelns der Bundesrepublik Deutschland', in Hans-Hermann Hartwich and Göttrik Wewer (Eds), *Regieren in der Bundesrepublik V: Souveränität, Integration, Interdependenz – Staatliches Handeln in der Außen- und Europapolitik* (Opladen: Leske und Budrich, 1993) pp. 41–92 (p. 68).

17. This term originates from Hans-Peter Schwarz, *Die gezähmten Deutschen*.

Von der Machtbessenheit zur Machtvergessenheit (Stuttgart: Deutsche Verlag-Anstalt, 1985).

18. Peter Schmidt, 'Der politische Umbruch in Mittel- und Osteuropa – Folgen für die Sicherheitspolitik in Westeuropa', *Strategisch-Sicherheitspolitische Studien* 2 (1993) pp. 16–23 (Forschungsbericht des Ludwig Boltzmann-Institutes für International Kultur- und Wirtschaftsbeziehungen).

19. Here, I am contradicting the opinion of Renata Fritsch-Bournazel who states that the character of French–German relations has changed fundamentally since German reunification. Cf. Renata Fritsch-Bournazel, *Europe and German Unification* (New York/Oxford: Berg Publishers, Inc., 1992) p. 171.

20. See also Reimut Jochimsen, 'Die Europäische Wirtschafts- und Währungsunion. Chancen und Risken', *Europa Archiv* 13–14 (1993) pp. 377–388.

21. Cf. President George Bush's Speech on 31 May 1989 in Mainz, Germany, *U.S. Policy Information and Texts* (USIS, Bonn), No. 70 (1 June 1989) pp. 1–7.

22. Link brought this to our attention in 'Perspektiven der europäischen Integration', op. cit. (see note 8).

23. See Speech of Anthony Lake, National Security Adviser to the American President on 21 September 1993 at the Johns Hopkins University School of Advanced International Studies, Washington, DC, *U.S. Policy Information and Texts* (USIS Bonn), No. 97 (23 Sept. 1993) pp. 6–12.

24. See Werner Link, 'Handlungsmaximen deutscher Außenpolitik im neuen Internationalen System', in Werner Link, Eberhard Schütt-Wetschky and Gesine Schwan (Eds), *Jahrbuch für Politik*, Vol. 1 (Baden-Baden: Nomos, 1991) pp. 77–102. Link postulates a pentagonal structure of overlapping triangles as a new global political structure.

25. See Foreign Minister Hans-Dietrich Genscher's speech at the German–Japanese Society in Bremen on 13 September 1991, *Bulletin* (Presse- und Informationsamt der Bundesregierung), No. 101 (19 Sept. 1991) pp. 801–804; also see Chancellor Helmut Kohl's speech at the visit of Japanese President Kiichi Miyazawa on 30 April 1992 in Bonn, *Bulletin* (Presse- und Informationsamt der Bundesregierung), No. 46 (5 May 1992) pp. 417–419.

26. Cf. Hanns W. Maull, 'Germany and Japan: The New Civilian Powers', *Foreign Affairs* (Winter 1990/91), pp. 91–106.

27. See also the series of speeches given at the Christian Social Union (CSU) Convention in Munich, 8–9 October 1993, as well as the platform of the CSU that was passed at the convention, in which it is stated that the party would be against a European Federal Republic but supports the concept of a Europe of Nations.

28. See Gunther Hellmann, 'EU und USA brauchen ein breiteres Fundament: Plädoyer für einen "transatlantischen Vertrag"', *Außenpolitik* 2 (1994) pp. 236–245.

29. Thus spoke Wolfgang Ischinger in his lecture at the Center for Transatlantic Foreign and Security Policy in Berlin, Germany, on 19 January 1994.

30. Cf. Robert Putnam, 'Diplomacy and Domestic Politics: The Logic of Two-level Games', *International Organization* 3 (1988) pp. 427–460.
31. Due to its close contact to the government of the host country, embassy reports tend to over-interpret the thoughts and intentions of the government offices. The opinions of the opposition and private organizations are often neglected in spite of their possible relevance to future political developments.

BIBLIOGRAPHY

Aspin, Les, 'A Bottom-Up Review: Forces for a New Era', Department of Defense, 1 September 1 1993.
Aspin, Les, 'Forces and Alliances for a New Era'. Speech delivered by the US Secretary of Defense on 12 September 1993 at the IISS Conference in Brussels, manuscript.
Bulletin (Presse- und Informationsamt der Bundesregierung), No. 79, 17 July 1992, pp. 753–758. (Available in English as an OSCE document.)
Charter of Paris for a New Europe, 19 November 1990. *NATO Review*, Vol. 38, No. 6, December 1990, pp. 27–29.
Christian Social Union (CSU) Convention in Munich, 8–9 October 1993.
Convention on the Presence of Foreign Forces in the Federal Republic of Germany of October 23, 1954. *Documents on Germany, 1944–1985.* (Washington, DC: Department of State Publication), No. 9446, pp. 610–612.
Declaration of the Heads of States and Government participating in the meeting of the North Atlantic Council held at NATO headquarters, Brussels, on 10–11 January 1994, and the Invitation and Framework Document to the 'Partnership for Peace'. *NATO Review*, Vol. 42, No. 1, February 1994, pp. 28–33.
'Der Vertrag von Maastricht ist keine Preisgabe des Staates Bundesrepublik'. *Frankfurter Allgemeine Zeitung*, 13 Oct. 1993.
Fritsch-Bournazel, Renata, *Europe and German Unification.* (New York/Oxford: Berg Publishers, Inc., 1992).
Grosser, Alfred, *Die Bundesrepublik Deutschland – Bilanz einer Entwicklung.* (Tübingen: Wunderlich, 1967).
Hacke, Christian, 'Die Außenpolitik Deutschlands: Weltmacht wider Willen', in Hartwich, Hans-Hermann and Göttrik Wewer (Eds), *Regieren in der Bundesrepublik V: Souveränität, Integration, Interdependenz – Staatliches Handeln in der Außen- und Europapolitik.* (Opladen: Leske und Budrich, 1993) pp. 93–118.
Haftendorn, Helga, 'Am Anfang waren die Alliierten. Die alliierten Vorgehaltsrechte als Rahmenbedingung des außenpolitischen Handelns der Bundesrepublik Deutschland', in Hans-Hermann Hartwich and Göttrik Wewer (Eds.), *Regieren in der Bundesrepublik V: Souveränität, Integration, Interdependenz – Staatliches Handeln in der Außen- und Europapolitik.* (Opladen: Leske und Budrich, 1993) pp. 41–92.

Haftendorn, Helga, 'Außenpolitische Prioritäten und Handlungsspielraum. Ein Paradigma zur Analyse der Außenpolitik der Bundesrepublik Deutschland'. *Politische Vierteljahresschrift*, No. 1 (1989) pp. 31–49.

Haftendorn, Helga, 'Gulliver in der Mittel Europas. Internationale Verflechtung und nationale Handlungsmöglichkeiten'. *Deutschlands neue Außenpolitik*, Vol. 1, Grundlagen, Ed. Karl Kaiser and Hanns W. Maull. (Munich: Oldenbourg Verlag 1994) pp. 129–152.

Hellmann, Gunther, 'EU und USA brauchen ein breiteres Fundament: Plädoyer für einen "transatlantischen Vertrag"'. *Außenpolitik* 2 (1994) pp. 236–245.

Jochimsen, Reimut, 'Die Europäische Wirtschafts- und Währungsunion. Chancen und Risiken'. *Europa Archiv* 13–14 (1993) pp. 377–388.

Kloten, Norbert, 'Die Bundesrepublik als Weltwirtschaftsmacht'. *Deutschlands neue Außenpolitik*, Vol. 1, Grundlagen, Ed. Karl Kaiser and Hanns W. Maull. (Munich: Oldenbourg Verlag 1994) pp. 63–80.

Link, Werner, 'Handlungsmaximen deutscher Außenpolitik im neuen Internationalen System', in Werner Link, Eberhard Schütt-Wetschky and Gesine Schwan (Eds), *Jahrbuch für Politik*, Vol. 1 (Baden-Baden: Nomos, 1991) pp. 77–102.

Link, Werner, 'Perspektiven der europäischen Integration', in Karl Kaiser and Hanns W. Maull (Eds), *Die Zukunft der europäischen Integration: Folgerungen für die deutsche Politik 5*, Arbeitspapiere zur Internationalen Politik, No. 78 (Bonn: Forschungsinstitut der Deutschen Gesellschaft für Auswärtige Politik, 1993) pp. 7–26.

London Declaration on a Transformed North Atlantic Alliance, 6 July 1990. *NATO Review*, Vol. 38, No. 4, August 1990, pp. 32–33.

Markovits, Andrei S. and Simon Reich, 'Deutschlands neues Gesicht: Über deutsche Hegemonie in Europa'. *Leviathan* 1 (1992) pp. 15–63.

Maull, Hanns W., 'Germany and Japan: The New Civilian Powers'. *Foreign Affairs*, Winter 1990/91, pp. 91–106.

Nerlich, Uwe, 'Neue Sicherheitsfunktionen der NATO'. *Europa Archiv* 23 (1993) pp. 663–672.

Putnam, Robert, 'Diplomacy and Domestic Politics: The Logic of Two-level Games'. *International Organization* 3 (1988) pp. 427–460.

Rittberger, Volker, 'Nach der Vereinigung – Deutschlands Stellung in der Welt', in Hartwich, Hans-Hermann and Göttrik Wewer (Eds), *Regieren in der Bundesrepublik V: Souveränität, Integration, Interdependenz – Staatliches Handeln in der Außen- und Europapolitik*. (Opladen: Leske und Budrich, 1993) pp. 119–144.

Rome Declaration on Peace and Cooperation, 7 November 1991 (including the Alliance's New Strategic Concept and other documents). *NATO Review*, Vol. 39, No. 6, December 1991, pp. 19–32.

Rosecrance, Richard, *The Rise of the Trading State. Commerce and Conquest in the Modern World*. (New York: Basic Books, 1986).

Schmidt, Peter, 'Der politische Umbruch in Mittel- und Osteuropa – Folgen für die Sicherheitspolitik in Westeuropa'. *Strategisch-Sicherheitspolitische Studien* 2 (1993) pp. 16–23.

Schwarz, Hans-Peter, *Die gezähmten Deutschen. Von der Machtbessenheit zur Machtvergessenheit*. (Stuttgart: Deutsche Verlag-Anstalt, 1985).

Speech of Anthony Lake, National Security Adviser to the American President on 21 September 1993 at the Johns Hopkins University School of Advanced International Studies, Washington, DC. *U.S. Policy Information and Texts* (USIS Bonn), No. 97, 23 September 1993, pp. 6–12.

Speech of Chancellor Helmut Kohl at the visit of Japanese President Kiichi Miyazawa on 30 April 1992 in Bonn. *Bulletin* (Presse- und Informationsamt der Bundesregierung), No. 46, 5 May 1992, pp. 417–419.

Speech of the Foreign Minister Hans-Dietrich Genscher at the German–Japanese Society in Bremen on 13 September 1991. *Bulletin* (Presse-und Informationsamt der Bundesregierung), No. 101, 19 September 1991, pp. 801–804.

Speech of President George Bush on 31 May 1989 in Mainz, Germany. *U.S. Policy Information and Texts* (USIS, Bonn), No. 70, 1 June 1989, pp. 1–7.

Treaty on European Union, Articles A and B. *European Union: Selected Instruments Taken from the Treaties*, Book 1, Vol. 1 (Luxembourg: Office for Official Publications of the European Communities, 1993), pp. 15–68.

Treaty on the Final Settlement with Regard to Germany, 12 September 1990. *NATO Review*, Vol. 38, No. 5, October 1990, pp. 30–32.

United Nations, *Agenda for Peace. Preventive Diplomacy, Peacemaking and Peace-keeping.* UN Document DPI/1247. (New York: United Nations Publications, 1992).

5 Will Germany Assume a Leadership Role in the European Union?[1]

Michael Kreile

The primary question of this chapter can be interpreted in two ways. First, it could mean investigating an empirically observable tendency which would manifest itself in the changed behaviour of the Federal Republic of Germany in the institutions and decision-making processes of the European Community. In other words, is united Germany about to gain greater support within the EU for its political concepts and goals or even to determine the course of European integration? Critical observers could pose the question: Is Germany perhaps now in a position to reach and develop the hegemonic position previously unattainable due to the unresolved national question, the status differences from the Allied powers and doubts as to the permanence of its commitment to the Western alliance? The second way of interpreting the question would be normative: i.e., should Germany assume a leadership role in the European Union? Providing an answer to this question presupposes a clear determination of the goals that role should serve, and which factors could favour or hinder the exercising of this leadership role.

An analytic interpretation of the problem requires clarification of the concept of political leadership with regard to international politics and especially the regional context of the European Union. The widely accepted idea that a political leadership role facilitates the successful realization of national interests in competition with the claims of other states should be critically compared to the central thesis of the 'theory of hegemonic stability'. According to this theory, the primary accomplishment of the hegemonic power is providing public goods and fulfilling an ordering function in the world economy in the interest of the community of nations. To achieve this order, the hegemon is even willing to forego short-term advantages if required. In the words of Robert Gilpin:

> Hegemony or leadership is based on a general belief in its legitimacy at the same time that it is constrained by the need to maintain it; other states accept the rule of the hegemon because of its prestige and status in the international political system . . . A considerable degree of ideological consensus . . . is required if the hegemon is to have the necessary support of other powerful states. . . . If other states begin to regard the actions of the hegemon as self-serving and contrary to their own political and economic interests, the hegemonic system will be greatly weakened.[2]

Certainly, this thesis must be differentiated to take into account the different types of hegemony. One could also object to the equating of 'hegemony' with 'leadership'. Of course, this simultaneously raises the question of whether and how political leadership can be exercised over a longer period of time without hegemony. Neither the conceptual creativity of those governing, nor the professionalism of the diplomatic apparatus, as far as they exist, can suffice for this purpose. In addition, leadership requires both the ability to integrate the interests of the partner countries in a strategic concept and to mobilize resources for its realization, as well as the partners' willingness to follow the leader. This willingness to follow can be based on conviction, expectations of profit or weakness of resolve in acting. Economic dominance, defined as asymmetric relations of influence between economic units,[3] might create a basis for it but should not be confused with either hegemony or leadership ability.

This chapter will approach the question of Germany's future role in the European Union in the following manner: first, one must determine how the position of the Federal Republic in the EC has changed as a result of reunification. In particular, we will have to examine how unification has affected the strength of the German economy as well as its international performance. Second, one must clarify to what degree the changes influence the leadership ability of the Federal Republic and the willingness of the other EU nations to follow German initiatives. And finally, one must discuss to what extent the structures of the common decision-making process open up leadership options or require a stronger institutionalization of political leadership. The investigation of these questions will substantiate the thesis that the need for leadership in the EU cannot be met by a hegemonic power, however restrained or controlled, but only by the strengthening of supranational Community organs.

UNIFIED GERMANY: INTERNATIONAL STATUS AND EXTERNAL ROLE ASSIGNMENT

The regaining of national unity, the end of the East–West conflict, and the break-up of the Soviet empire have enhanced both Germany's international status and its international political responsibility, and are the basis of Germany's predominant position in Europe. This view, which is primarily to be found in the Anglo-Saxon countries and among German policy-makers and academics (here with an emphasis on responsibility), is based, to a large degree, on factors like the size of the population or Germany's anticipated economic strength after the successful transformation of the East German economy. Moreover, the role reversal German foreign policy is supposed to achieve has been traced back to the changed constellations in the international arena.[4] A French expert on Germany, Anne-Marie Le Gloannec, has characterized the change as follows:

> The rediscovery of European unity and German unification has pushed France, until now the geopolitical heart of the European Community, back to the edge of the Atlantic. By contrast, Germany has not only regained power, but also its central position. As a member of the European Community bound by a thick network of obligations to the less powerful and yet equal partners, Germany will nevertheless become the master of the Pan-European and international game.[5]

Undoubtedly, the Treaty on the Final Settlement with respect to Germany ('Two plus Four Treaty'), which recognized Germany's 'full sovereignty over its internal and external affairs' (Art. 7), levelled out differences in status from the victorious powers of the Second World War. The resulting gain in specific freedom of manoeuvre appears for the Federal Republic, however, to be smaller than the loss of status which the governing political élites of the smaller major powers apparently feel. The confirmation of the renunciation of ABC weapons, the reduction of the armed forces to less than 370 000 men and, above all, the NATO membership of reunited Germany demonstrate that the Federal Republic does not emulate the traditional great powers nor consider playing an open game on the East–West axis with changing alliances or partners. Without wanting to replace geopolitical modes of thought with economic determinism, one can once again call attention to the fact that the gravity of its foreign economic interests firmly anchors the Federal Republic in Western Europe and the Atlantic Alliance. This is just as true for the continuity of Germany's need to guarantee its security by being included in the Alliance structures, for the institutions of its polity,[6] and for the political and professional socialization of the élite in the middle and younger generations as well as the expectations of its citizens.

The premise that Germany's international weight has increased leads to the conclusion that Germany must be assigned a new role. This was clothed in the phrase 'partners in leadership' and includes the request that Germany make its contribution to UN peacekeeping operations and 'out-of-area' NATO expeditions. Among German government officials and academics, talk about Germany's new 'international responsibility' has become fashionable.[7] Sometimes this term is simply used as a code-word for 'power' and expresses ambitions that befit a now more powerful country. The demand for a permanent seat on the UN Security Council has thus been presented as an almost selfless endeavour to cope with Germany's new responsibility. The second meaning of the term refers to the expectations and role assignments formulated by Germany's allies in NATO and the European Union. According to Helga Haftendorn, the partner countries are no longer satisfied with Germany playing the role of paymaster as in the Gulf War and in the aid programmes for Eastern Europe; they rather expect Germany to become a reliable exporter of security and a source of initiatives designed to shape international politics beyond the European region.[8] However, the 'continental power with global weight'[9] may well be a self-fulfilling prophecy to the extent that the self-image derived from external role assignments encourages assertive behaviour by German actors, which in turn is read as proof abroad that Germany has returned to the world stage as a great power. Of course, this game of mirrors takes no account of the domestic and international restrictions that limit the range of German foreign policy as well as the exercise of German power.

The third usage of 'international responsibility' is meant to stress the value orientation of German foreign policy. Politicians of all parties invariably proclaim their commitment to the world-wide defence of human rights. Germany, defence minister Rühe (CDU) holds, must be prepared to assume co-responsibility for peace, freedom and justice in the world, while the SPD emphasizes the preservation of the environment and sustainable development in the South.[10] Occupying the high moral ground is also the passion of TV commentators and newspaper columnists. The foreign policy discourse in united Germany not so much reveals a Wilhelminian quest for 'a place in the sun', but is rather imbued with a strong dose of Wilsonianism. Unfortunately, the Federal Republic still faces difficulties in combining credibly the role of international social worker and moral referee with its role as mercantilist or weapons trader. Moreover, the consensus on values breaks down when it comes to the question of whether military force is a legitimate instrument of foreign policy to be used in order to protect human rights and to enforce international law.

External role assignments and domestic soul-searching have therefore fuelled the debate on the future mission of the Bundeswehr. Since the threat to the integrity of the Federal Republic from the Warsaw Pact has vanished, the Kohl government has embarked on a restructuring of the Bundeswehr. The building of highly mobile 'crisis reaction forces' is to enable the Bundeswehr to participate effectively in UN peacekeeping and peace-enforcement missions as well as in operations of multilateral crisis-management in the framework of NATO and WEU. This redefinition of the Bundeswehr missions was challenged by the SPD and the Greens in the constitutional court. However, the court ruled that Article 24 of the Basic Law (the constitution) authorizes the employment of the Bundeswehr for purposes that stem from membership in a system of collective security. In a generous interpretation (though at variance with international relations theory) the court declared NATO and WEU to be systems of mutual collective security.[11] The court also ruled that any deployment of German troops abroad requires the prior approval of the Bundestag. After having received the go-ahead for its broadened security policy, the government took care to emphasize that it felt committed to a 'culture of restraint'. The Bundestag election of October 1994 provided the CDU/CSU-FDP coalition with a narrow majority of ten seats. This outcome is unlikely to encourage an activist policy of international crisis-management. After all, there is a strong current of pragmatic welfare state pacifism among the public, which is reluctant to pay for international responsibility with the blood of German soldiers.

THE ECONOMIC CONSEQUENCES OF GERMAN UNITY

> After the pullback of the superpowers, Europe will require a generous hegemon which is willing to distribute its riches to the poor countries on the periphery of Europe and to be concerned about the interests of the entire region instead of just its own interests.[12]

This appeal from William Wallace continues to reflect the expectations of a number of countries towards united Germany. There can be no doubt that many governments prefer to be recipients of 'cheque-book diplomacy' rather than seeing Germany promoted to international policeman. Yet, it is necessary to point out that the ability to conduct foreign policy with economic means has not grown as a result of unification – quite the contrary. For as far as economic performance is concerned, Germany has become a more ordinary European country and less of a model to be envied or imitated. It now has to face the tensions arising from economic dualism and to support a less developed region through large-scale income transfers. This has led to a record increase in public sector borrowing and a drastic deterioration in the current account of the balance of payments. Consequently, as long as this situation prevails, international commitments with budgetary implications will have to be scaled down rather than extended.

Of course, it can be argued that the reconstruction of the East German economy will usher in a new economic miracle and that Germany will be the main beneficiary of the emerging new intra-European division of labour.[13] But these are long-term prospects fraught with uncertainties while, in the medium term, German policy-makers will have to cope with the legacy of socialism and the errors committed in the conduct of post-unification economic policies.

The integration of two societies divided by 45 years of separate histories, by disparate levels of economic development, and by widely different collective experiences has turned out to be a much more difficult and painful process than the political architects of German unity had originally expected. In terms of economic geography, unification has added a large but structurally weak region with 16 million inhabitants to the Federal Republic. The relative backwardness of the East German economy is at the root of a protracted crisis of adjustment with far-reaching social and political ramifications. The merger of the two economies in July 1990 immediately revealed the lack of competitiveness of East German firms in an open market. By mid-1991, gross domestic product in East Germany had declined to one half of its 1989 level, while industrial output had decreased by two thirds. As the Council of Mutual Economic Assistance disintegrated, East German industry lost traditional outlets in Eastern Europe and the Soviet Union. The magnitude of the decline in employment which resulted from the contraction of the East German economy is staggering, even when one takes into account the artifical nature of full employment in the GDR. At the end of 1992, six million people were employed – 3.5 million less than three years before. The social 'safety net' provided by the welfare state and, in particular, the massive use of labour market policy instruments have prevented large-scale social unrest. The development of incomes and demand has been largely uncoupled from the decline in production and employment. In 1993, for instance, aggregate demand was almost twice as high as East German output, and 'total compensation of employees exceeded national income implying negative profits'.[14]

Looking at the bright side, one finds that the East German economy is in the process of catching up with West Germany. Massive investment in industrial equipment and the modernization of the infrastructure are showing their effects. Rising from a very low level, East German output grew by 7.8 per cent in 1992, by 5.8 per cent in 1993 and by 9 per cent in 1994, with another 9 per cent being forecast for 1995. 'Between 1991 and 1993 eastern Germany's contribution to all-German GDP rose from around 7 per cent to almost 10 per cent.'[15] In 1994, productivity (GDP per employee) reached 51.8 per cent of the West German level as compared to 42.5 per cent in 1992. Yet wages and salaries stood at 70 per cent of West German levels. Although total employment increased to 6.3 million people in 1994, open and disguised unemployment still added up to 2.4 million people.[16]

Conduct of Economic Policies

The impact of unification on the German economy has partly been a function of the errors committed in the conduct of economic policies. The strategies of key actors resulted in a mismatch between wage policy and fiscal and monetary policy, until the recession of 1992/93 imposed a reassessment of priorities. From the very beginning, the rapid equalization of living conditions between the two parts of the country has been the declared objective of the wage policy carried out by the unions in East Germany. The competitiveness of many East German firms suffers from the fact that wages have been treated as an independent variable unrelated to productivity trends.[17] The high-wage strategy was predicated on the expectation that employment would be subsidized by the Treuhandanstalt or the federal government in order to prevent plant closures. In the West, the unions acted on the assumption that the unification boom (brought about by the spending spree of East German consumers) entitled them to real wage increases above the rise in productivity. Wages, they felt, had not kept pace with profits, and wage earners deserved compensation for higher taxes and social security contributions raised by the state in order to finance a fraction of the costs of unity.

The Kohl government offered convenient arguments for an aggressive wage policy as its fiscal policy lacked credibility and favoured higher-income groups. Fiscal policy was guided by a muddling-through approach relying heavily on public sector borrowing. Distributional conflict assumed an East–West dimension, and the government tried to defuse it by extending the bill for German unity into the future. Its initial refusal to impose higher taxes was determined by the basically accurate perception that the West Germans were not prepared to make substantial sacrifices for national unity, but also by the attempt to save the supply-side fiscal policy practised since 1982. The corrective measures taken in 1991 and 1992 were not sufficient to reduce public sector borrowing requirements. This was also due to the spending behaviour of the Western Länder and municipalities which failed to adjust their budget policies to the requirements of fiscal redistribution in favour of the Eastern states. With the transfers to East Germany amounting to between 4 and 5 per cent of West German GDP per year, 'the rise in public spending virtually wiped out the fiscal consolidation gains achieved between 1982 and 1989, a period over which the general government budget was brought back into financial balance'.[18] In 1993, the deficit reached 3.3 per cent of GDP, while the borrowing requirement of the enlarged public sector (including the Treuhandanstalt and the public enterprises) came to 5.2 per cent of GDP, 'equivalent to about half of domestic savings'.[19]

True to its mandate of safeguarding currency stability, the Bundesbank reacted to the inflationary effects of fiscal laxity and of an aggressive wage policy by tightening monetary policy. By the summer of 1992, the discount rate had been raised to an unprecedented 8.75 per cent. High interest rates were also intended to prevent a weakening of the D-mark in foreign exchange markets.[20] This policy met with strong criticism from the Bush administration and from governments throughout Western Europe. Germany, they complained, had embarked on a beggar-thy-neighbour policy, shifting the costs of national unity to partner countries.

The recession which hit the German economy in late 1992 (causing an unexpectedly steep decline in GDP of 1.7 per cent in West Germany and 1.1 per cent in Germany as a whole in 1993) had a sobering effect on the main institutional actors and created the risk-awareness required for political compromises. In March 1993, the federal government reached a package agreement with the Länder, the SPD, the unions and the business associations. The 'Solidarity Pact' provided for a concerted effort in favour of economic reconstruction in the East, a reform of intergovernmental revenue-sharing, and a medium-term strategy designed to rein in the deficit ('Federal Consolidation Programme').[21] The unions accepted low pay deals which entailed real income losses. The Bundesbank cautiously eased its monetary policy. And the government's fiscal policy set out 'to halt by 1995 and then to reverse the trend towards an ever-expanding public sector'.[22] In 1994 modest progress towards fiscal consolidation was facilitated by the economic recovery which yielded real GDP growth of 2.8 per cent. Nevertheless, a determined effort is still required so that one of the Maastricht criteria for fiscal discipline, the debt-to-GDP ratio of 60 per cent, will be met in the medium term.[23]

International Economic Performance

As far as Germany's international economic performance is concerned, unification has transformed the high current account surplus which characterized the balance of payments in the late 1980s into a sizeable deficit. Between 1989 and 1992, the swing in the current account amounted to DM 142 billion, as the surplus of DM 108 billion turned into a deficit of DM 34 billion. The deterioration of the current account mainly reflected the surge in imports (and decline in exports) caused by the boost to domestic demand which the budget transfers to the East had generated. About one third of the swing was due to higher expenditure on tourism, a decline in net investment income, the fall in military receipts following the withdrawal of Allied troops, and rising transfers to the European Community.[24] By 1994 the current account deficit widened to DM 56 billion in spite of a rising trade surplus, as the deficit on services and transfers soared. Since German savings are not sufficient to finance both investment and the budget deficit, Germany has become a net capital importer. Huge capital inflows attracted by high interest rates were more than enough to finance the current account deficit. Critics have argued that Germany has thereby become more vulnerable as it exposes itself to the risk of a crisis of confidence in international financial markets.[25]

The Bundesbank, however, takes comfort from the fact that the German economy is in better shape in 1995 than anybody would have predicted in early 1993 and points to the improvement in the current account balance expected for the coming years.[26]

As long as the twin deficit (budget and current account) persists, there will be strong domestic pressure to limit rather than expand costly international commitments. Without a limitation of the expectations directed at the Federal Republic and the obligations to be assumed, Germany runs the risk of a domestic acceptance crisis which could undermine the cooperative internationalism which is the hallmark of German foreign policy. A stabilization policy for current and potential crisis regions, whether the CIS, North Africa or the Middle East, the success of which would help all the Western industrial countries, requires collective sponsorship, sober means-and-ends analysis and a distribution of the burden according to the ability to pay.

With regard to Eastern Europe, burden-sharing among Western countries has been less than equitable. In fact, Germany has been the principal source of financial assistance to this region accounting for about 50 per cent of total transfers by OECD countries.[27] By the end of 1994, Germany's total commitments added up to DM 145 billion, of which DM 100 billion were earmarked for the Soviet Union and its successor states. However, these figures are somewhat inflated, at least when they are classified as aid, since the DM 100 billion for the Soviet Union include such items as the payments related to the withdrawal of Russian troops (DM 14 billion), export credit guarantees (DM 33 billion) extended partly to support employment in the East German engineering industry, and Soviet debt in transferable rubles (DM 20 billion) to the former GDR.[28]

On the other hand there is no doubt that Germany is the country that is likely to benefit most from a successful economic transformation in Eastern Europe. It is the most important trade partner for Poland, the Czech Republic and Hungary, as well as a major source of direct foreign investment. The share of Eastern Europe (including the former Soviet Union) in West German exports increased from 3.6 per cent in 1990 to 5.9 per cent in 1993, or – in absolute figures – from DM 23.5 billion to DM 36.4 billion, while exports from East Germany fell from DM 29.8 billion to DM 6.3 billion (of which DM 4.9 billion went to the former Soviet Union). This, incidentally, demonstrates that East German industry needs to develop a competitive export base in order to recover 'traditional' markets in Eastern Europe. It should also be pointed out that the Central European reform countries are becoming highly competitive investment locations for manufacturing industry, a challenge which German industry will have to reckon with.

Expanding exports to Eastern Europe notwithstanding, the EU-12 remain Germany's most important export market with 50.5 per cent of total exports in 1993 (down from 54.5 per cent in 1990).[29] Over the same period, the US share was relatively stable (7.3 per cent, down from 7.5 per cent in 1990), while developing countries (excluding OPEC) increased their share from 7.3 per cent to 9.5 per cent. The federal government, in concert with business associations, has launched a new Asia policy in order to strengthen Germany's presence in this particularly dynamic growth region. But it remains to be seen whether this will change the situation as aptly described by W.R. Smyser: 'Germany has a global currency but it does not yet have a global economy.'[30]

ECONOMIC DOMINANCE AND POLITICAL PSYCHOLOGY

The size of the West German economy and the dimensions of its foreign trade have linked the Federal Republic to other West European countries in a pattern of asymmetrical interdependence. In 1986, the FRG accounted for 26 per cent of the European Community's GDP, its share of the population being 19 per cent. Its high trade and current account surpluses exposed it to the criticism that German economic policy neglected the adjustment obligation of a surplus country by sticking to a deflationary strategy which affected the growth prospects of other European countries negatively.[31] Through the key currency role played by the D-mark, the Bundesbank imposed both the constraints and the benefits of a stability-orientated monetary policy on partner countries.

How has the position of the Federal Republic in the EC been changed by reunification? The increase in population and a modest increase in GDP have added to Germany's weight but every enlargement of the community modifies this purely arithmetic effect. In 1993, Germany accounted for 29.5 per cent of the GDP and 23.3 per cent of the population of EU-12; with the enlargement to EU-15 these shares declined to 27.6 per cent and 21.9 per cent respectively. It may also be recalled that West Germany's share in the GDP of EC-9 came to 31.5 per cent in 1975.[32] The reduction of German trade surpluses and the economic growth impulses provided by reunification were well received in partner countries. However, the Bundesbank's high interest rates, which were to demonstrate domestically and internationally the credibility of the stability-orientated monetary policy, were criticized as an expression of German efforts at dominance.[33] In any case, they contributed to the disintegration of the European Monetary System which has jeopardized the timetable, if not the substance, of Economic and Monetary Union (EMU).[34]

The asymmetry of interdependence resulting from the different sizes of the national economies and their different capacities to adapt to change is necessarily a source of political conflict as long as there is no coordination of national economic policies which could distribute the burden of adjustments justly. Yet governments which orientate their economic policy primarily towards domestic economic requirements have little reason to complain that other countries are trying to do the same. 'Sacro egoismo' is not a specifically German vice.

When, in Maastricht, Germany's partner countries accepted the Bundesbank as a model for the creation of the European

Central Bank this was not a result of newly won German leadership strength, but rather a ratification of the consensus already reached in the Delors Report of 1989.[35] In Germany, there exists a current of opinion that considers the Maastricht Treaty – and EMU in particular – as the price to be paid to France in exchange for French acquiescence in German unification. Yet this point of view fails to recognize the continuity of the Federal Republic's European integration policy. In fact, the course for EMU was set long before anybody seriously expected German unity to materialize.[36] On the other hand, there is no doubt that the Kohl government used the interest of its European partners in controlling German power as a lever to promote political integration. However, as the imbalance of the Maastricht Treaty shows, it was not very successful in this respect and had to set its hopes on the 1996 review conference. Manifestations of new German assertiveness, such as the conquest of 18 additional seats on the European Parliament or the unilateral recognition of Croatia and Slovenia ahead of the EC schedule, do not really add up to a hegemonial strategy.

Perceptions of German Dominance

One of the most important developments resulting from the German unification process is a change in the perceptions of the partner nations which exaggerates the real increase in status and also the changes in the foreign policy behaviour of German actors. The reactions of West European political élites and the media often mix traumatic memories of German power politics and occupation with instinctively activated historical clichés, frustrated great power ambitions or the small neighbours' fear of becoming satellites of their 'big brother'. In Stanley Hoffmann's words:

> For many years, the French, who dominate the Brussels bureaucracy, saw in the EC a vehicle for French influence and for imposing restraints on the power of West Germany. Today, and for good reasons, the fear of Germany dominating the Community has replaced (as also in Denmark) the old fear of an unshackled Germany outside the Community. For France it is worth staying in the EC

as long as Germany is in it, but the French have increasing doubts about who is the guard and who is the captive.[37]

One could just as well argue that progress in the economic and political integration of Europe must be justified by other goals than the containment of German power.

The preoccupation of the Western countries with the *incertitudes allemandes* and the unease caused by German dominance, but also by the impression of German weakness, are phenomena which most often appear when Germany seems to deviate from the path of Atlantic or European virtue or when economic crisis symptoms in partner countries make Germany appear an either admirable or irritating example. A brief review of the last decades makes clear how constant the obsessions and how variable the diagnoses are.

As, at the beginning of the seventies, the social–liberal coalition achieved a certain degree of foreign policy emancipation with its active Ostpolitik, it was the newly won manoeuvring space which reawakened memories of Rapallo abroad and, in France, intensified a sense of rivalry since West Germany threatened to replace France in its role as the Soviet Union's privileged partner in Western Europe. Under Helmut Schmidt's leadership it was the economic success of the 'German Model' which led to the horror vision in France and Italy of a Germanization of Europe. In 1978, the allegedly European hegemonic power gave in to the concerted pressure of the United States and the EC partners and initiated a programme of fiscal expansion in order to fulfil its role as a 'locomotive' of the world economy. In the autumn of 1980, the *New York Times* celebrated Helmut Schmidt in its magazine under the title 'Asserting Germany's New Leadership', only a few months after Zbigniew Brzezinski, President Carter's security adviser, had accused Germany of 'self-finlandization'. The INF debate revived suspicions of neutralism and the victory of 'Reaganomics' and 'Thatcherism' led to a re-evaluation of Germany's economic vigour. In 1987, the *Financial Times* complained about 'a debilitating lack of economic flexibility' and the loss of the 'risk-taking postwar spirit'. *Fortune* magazine wrote in July 1988 that 'Germany's persistent decline is deeply disturbing' for the West.[38] Higher growth rates and the German reunification process then led to renewed appreciation of Germany's leadership and hegemonic roles.

The mood and perceptions in the partner countries are realities that German foreign policy cannot ignore, least of all when they have an effect on political behaviour. However, they do not offer solid points of orientation because they often vary from country to country (and within the individual countries according to political convictions), reflect economic and political trends or are based on situations (differences in size, asymmetrical interlinkage) which cannot be changed politically without major disruption.

ABILITY TO LEAD AND WILLINGNESS TO FOLLOW

The question of whether Germany has the 'right stuff' to be a European leader should be separated from the question of whether this is desirable. If the preconditions for a leadership role do not exist, then, of course, the question as to its desirability becomes academic. The necessary attributes of a leading power could include: continuity and coherence of political strategy with regard to Europe; predictability of foreign and security policy which requires a domestic political consensus on fundamental questions; the capacity of the government apparatus to develop concepts and to coordinate action; the availability of financial resources and the willingness to use these as an incentive for partners and as a means of compensating and offsetting competing interests.

The predictability of foreign policy and the continuity of the European strategy have been embodied by Chancellor Kohl since 1982. However, Foreign Minister Kinkel and Defense Minister Rühe do not see eye to eye on issues like the Eastern enlargement of NATO, and the CSU sometimes likes to engage in anti-Maastricht populism. As was demonstrated in the Bundestag vote on the Maastricht Treaty, the SPD shares a basic consensus with the governing parties on European integration policy. With regard to a European security policy one cannot, of course, overlook the fact that, since the end of Helmut Schmidt's chancellorship, the SPD has been unable to develop a security policy concept which would be acceptable to both the Western partners and to the party's rank-and-file.

According to Bulmer and Paterson, German European policy lacks coherence because it is strongly splintered between different policy fields ('sectorization'), because changes are only performed in small steps ('incrementalism'), and because it is based to a large degree on consensual relations within 'policy communities'. 'In fact, effective co-ordination comes mainly from crisis-management in the Cabinet, the increasing awareness of the interlinkage of policies through the EC budget and from the Finance Ministry's caution about Community expenditure.'[39] The 'institutional pluralism' which characterizes the system of government of the Federal Republic is, according to the two authors, a serious obstacle to assuming a leadership role in the EC. The federal government has sometimes had difficulties indeed in finding a common denominator for its own European policy positions. Support for higher environmental standards, for instance, is not made more convincing when there is no speed limit on German motorways. The Bundesbank's criticism of the Maastricht Treaty provided a superfluous illustration of institutional pluralism, especially since decisions regarding integration policy do not belong to the Bundesbank's sphere of competence. However, it will hardly be possible in practice to achieve coherence over all the relevant policy areas in the EC, because it is, after all, the Community's decision-making process itself which is characterized by a high degree of sectoral differentiation. Package deals between the member states are not orientated primarily towards policy coherence. If the organization of the decision-making process at the national level could guarantee the 'unité de doctrine' in the central questions of integration policy, then this would probably be sufficient for Germany to exercise a leadership role.

Rule of EU Partners

It is consequently not institutional factors of the political system which prevent Germany from taking over a leadership role in the EU. There is also no lack of ability to formulate strategic concepts for European policy. The real obstacles to a German leadership role are to be found, firstly, in the Union's institutional system and in the conditions for success of European integration, as will be explained in more detail in the next section. Second, the most important factor blocking the path to a leadership role is the lack of willingness of the other EU members to follow Germany's lead. Neither France nor Great Britain nor Italy are willing to abandon the claim to political parity with Germany within the EU and to forego co-determination in the leadership of the Community, in so far as this is performed by the member states. The two nuclear powers defend the symbolism of their great power status all the more strongly, as its correspondence to real freedom of action and resources diminishes. Pierre Hassner's formulation is still valid for France:

> It is a tradition for France to be aware of the gap between its situation and its ambitions or between its physical power and the requirements of its security. And so in order to bridge this gap France has no other choice but to replace its lack of power with superior diplomatic skill, which consists primarily in utilizing the strengths of others.[40]

The traditional self-conception of the political élite is rooted in a patriotic consciousness of history and includes the global importance of France as well as the idea that it deserves a political leadership position in Western Europe.[41] If France cannot perform this task on its own and is thus dependent on alliances this does not mean that the claim has been given up or ceded to others. However, in the practice of the EU decision-making process, the French claim to a leadership role cannot be realized and is instead reduced to an aggressive and consistent pursuit of its national interests.

The Conservative government in London holds on to the remnants of Britain's great power status but has never formulated a claim to a leadership role in European integration. The straggler role of Great Britain excluded this possibility just as much as the realism predominating in Whitehall and the preference for mere market integration. The peculiar combination of economic liberalism and nationalism which has a great deal of support among Conservatives explains the disinclination towards further political integration as well as the interest in possibilities for 'opting out'. Great Britain's dislike of the federalist integration policy of the Federal Republic, which in the view of the British would increase the centralizing tendencies in Brussels, is enough in itself to lead it to reject a German leadership role. If one considers the intact national pride of wide sectors of the population and the memory of imperial greatness as well as the victorious role in the Second World War, one can hardly see what could justify the support of a German leadership role by Great Britain, even if there were a change in government.

The new political élite in Italy do not need to live on great power nostalgia because the economic dynamism of the country has increased their self-confidence *vis-à-vis* the partner countries and has also increased the interest in an active and independent foreign policy. Italy is seen as a middle power which simultaneously belongs to three geopolitical spheres – the Atlantic, the European and the Mediterranean – and benefits from the profound changes in the international scene.[42] Signs of German leadership ambitions are observed suspiciously and one cannot overlook the fact that for Italy, as well as for France, a significant motive behind monetary integration is to replace the anchor function of the 'hegemonic currency' with a Community system of monetary control based on the 'principle of equality'.[43] The demand for German leadership is also not very great in the smaller EU states like Denmark or the Netherlands.

If in some of Germany's partner countries the world view of the political élite is more strongly determined by concepts like power, hegemony and balance, and if the configurations of cabinet diplomacy still characterize European policy thought, these points of view cannot simply be dismissed as an anachronism. Yet the limits of the utility of these ideas should become clear to the political actors when they realize that these ideas are relativized by the success of those states whose élite have adapted their perceptions to the realities of interdependence between highly developed industrial countries. The mode of expansion of these countries is no longer the annexation of territories or the creation of spheres of influence, but instead, under the conditions of an open world economy, the capturing of markets and presence in communication networks. Thus, the idea that Germany attempted with its Yugoslavia policy to establish a sphere of influence in the Balkans, a region divided by internal conflicts and suffering from economic instability, definitely reflects a static understanding of history. In addition, the conflicts of interest and cooperation problems in the West European alliance of welfare states can neither be reduced to the mechanics of power competition nor be described with the metaphors of war.

PROBLEMS OF POLITICAL LEADERSHIP IN THE EU SYSTEM

The European Union is a joint venture of nation states utilizing supranational organs and common policies for collective problem-solving, yet whose members nevertheless want to maintain the primacy of the nation state. The institutional system and the decision-making process of the Union are arranged to prevent hegemony. The principle of unanimity maximizes the veto power of each individual member and decisions according to the principle of qualified majorities require the formation of broad coalitions. Coalitions, in turn, often function on the basis of package deals extending beyond the individual policy fields. So far, the EU appears as an environment in which non-hegemonic leadership can thrive. Large member states, however, find it easier to form coalitions and provide resources for financing compromises. They also have a better chance of creating strategic links between the important objects of negotiation.

If one assumes that the EU system requires political leadership in order to appear as a potent actor to the outside world and in order to advance the integration process, then one must first ask whether the leadership role can be taken over by one country. Here one must clarify which fields of activity should be included in the leadership role. No single member state will pretend to exercise political leadership over the entire spectrum of the policy areas in the EU, from the common agricultural policy to the internal market to association policy. Also, specific initiatives or a temporary trail-blazer role should not be confused with political leadership. Integration policy as constitutional policy could be a central area of political leadership: i.e., the institutional 'deepening' of the Union. There is also a growing need for leadership in the area of foreign policy, if the Common Foreign and Security Policy is to become more than a paper tiger.

In the area of constitutional policy, Germany appears predestined to play a locomotive function, since the federalism which has proven itself on a national level can also function as a model for a political union. However, the Maastricht Treaty demonstrated that the willingness of the larger partner countries to accelerate the process towards political union lags far behind German ideas and goals. In the area of foreign policy it is still true that 'a heterogeneous actor faces the difficult task of having to conduct a foreign policy consisting of supranational, international and individual national components without a coherent overall strategy'.[44] The importance of the unanimity principle in the formulation and realization of the Common Foreign and Security Policy makes political leadership an extremely difficult task – a task that has the greatest chance of success when two or more states take the initiative together. A leadership role in the security area is not possible for Germany because neither of the nuclear powers France and Great Britain would accept this. France will not be able to take over this role because it keeps itself at too much of a distance from the USA. Neither will Britain because it has too little interest in European autonomy.

When, due to structural reasons, no single country can satisfy the need for leadership in the EY system, then one is faced with the question of whether the German–French tandem is up to this challenge. Since the founding of the EC, the German–French partnership has proven to be a dependable motor of integration. However, with successive rounds of enlargement, the greater number of member states and the new lines of conflict have led to more complex and diverse coalitions and even the triangle of London–Bonn–Paris would be greeted with mistrust and resistance by the other member states.[45] One can therefore assume that two- and three-nation directorates will hardly be more acceptable to the other member states than a German leadership role.

The conclusion that the possibilities of political leadership by individual states, or by several member states together, are rather limited does not mean that the EU system suffers from a general leadership deficit. The European Commission, under the presidency of Jacques Delors, certainly acted as a leadership organ by once again taking advantage of its right to initiate policy proposals. With the internal market project, the Commission launched a programme which opened up new perspectives for the Community. The strategic interlinking of market integration and policy integration cleared the way for a strengthening of Union policies and the development of Economic and Monetary Union. The Commission also demonstrated its ability to act in foreign relations. Its achievements included the integration of the EFTA countries into the internal market within the framework of the European Economic Area, the nearly perfect handling of German reunification, and the association policy for Eastern Europe.

No doubt, the vision, energy and political skill of Jacques Delors made a crucial contribution to this success. His successor is likely to cut a weaker figure, if only because the post-Maastricht backlash clips the Commission's wings. But the prerequisite for the Commission's potential success is its key position in the tangle of Community institutions. As a supranational authority it can and must define its own institutional interests via the ability to find a majority for its initiatives and it is less subject than the member states to zero-sum games for resources. While the leadership role of the Commission has, for the most part, proven itself in some central and less central policy areas, this does not apply to constitutional policy and the Common Foreign and Security Policy. CFSP remains primarily a reserve of the member countries. In constitutional policy one can hardly expect path-breaking initiatives from an organ that belongs to the beneficiaries of the institutional *status quo*. The goals of a constitutional policy project should be to strengthen the institutionalization of political leadership at the Union level, to make the governance structures more transparent and to enhance their democratic legitimation.

Widening and Deepening

The accession of Austria, Finland and Sweden definitely underlines the need for structures of governance which will be suited to a system including 20 or more member states. Although the three EFTA countries can still be handled by the existing institutional framework, it is unlikely that the accession of Malta, Cyprus, Poland, Hungary, the Czech Republic and Slovakia will take place without changes in the voting arrangements of the Council of Ministers, the number of commissioners, or the rotating presidency of the council. In order to prevent obstructionism, majority voting will have to become the rule. Radical reforms like the transition to a federal system might satisfy the requirements of both legitimacy and efficiency, but are unlikely to be accepted at the 1996 review conference.

In view of this conference, the German government's negotiating hand has been strengthened by the ruling of the constitutional court of 12 October 1993. The court rejected several constitutional complaints against the Maastricht Treaty but seized the opportunity to expound its position on the scope and limits of European integration. The court's message is that the main source of democratic legitimation consists of the parliaments of the member states which will increasingly have to be complemented by the European Parliament. This requires that the Bundestag must retain substantial functions and competences. The Community institutions are being reminded that substantial changes in the integration programme embodied in the Union Treaty require formal amendments and that amendments must not be circumvented by an extensive interpretation of the treaty.[46]

Both deepening and widening will thus be subjects of contention in the 1996 review conference. When Germany forcefully advocates the Eastern enlargement of the European Union, it is not guided by the ambition to establish itself as the pivotal power of Europe, but rather by an acute awareness of the risks which instability and crises in Eastern Europe involve, not only for Germany, but for Western Europe as a whole. The Central European countries are eager to diversify their trade and investment relations and will not line up to promote German hegemony. A more heterogeneous Union will be characterized by new coalition patterns and the emergence of new cleavages. However, the road to Eastern enlargement is littered with political dynamite since key policies of the EU – the CAP, the budget and the structural funds – will have to be reformed before new members can be admitted. The task is all the more difficult as the legacy of the Maastricht debate is risk-aversion and the defence of vested interests.

CONCLUSION

The demand that the Federal Republic of Germany assume a political leadership role in Europe is based on problematic assumptions, assigns roles which Germany cannot perform and misunderstands the rules of the game which the European Union follows. One does not have to reject completely the theory of hegemonic stability to argue that the European Community has done well without a hegemonic power until now and does not need one due to its institutional system. A sober observer can see no convincing evidence for the thesis that Germany is about to assume a leadership role in the EU system. The monetary hegemony of the Bundesbank (in so far as one can apply the hegemony concept to a policy field) can hardly be used as proof because it has mobilized opposition forces which have successfully worked for the project of a European monetary policy.

> It may seem excessive to say that, in the EC, what Germany wants, it gets, especially since the German government remains determined not to want anything that would cost it the external support it deems indispensable. Basically, however, Germany does get much of what it wants, and what it doesn't want doesn't get done.[47]

This last observation certainly applies no less to France, with the difference, however, that nobody cares to notice it.

The normative question of whether Germany should assume a leadership role must also be answered negatively. Far more important than the lack of necessary financial means is the lack of willingness, even the decisive opposition of smaller and larger partner countries, to follow the German lead. Political leadership in the EU system is provided by supranational organs which can be further developed and cannot simply be replaced by a leading power. After all, supranationality 'is the only remedy for the risk that the integration process degenerates into some sort of balance-of-power politics between the main member states'.[48] Yet, if the European Union does not develop stronger institutions of collective governance, Franco-German leadership by default may turn out to be a second-best solution and an alternative to political stagnation.

NOTES

1. This chapter is a thoroughly revised and enlarged version of my contribution 'Übernimmt Deutschland eine Führungsrolle in der Europäischen Gemeinschaft?', in Werner Weidenfeld (Ed.), *Was ändert die Einheit?* (Gütersloh: Verlag Bertelsmann Stiftung, 1993).
2. Robert Gilpin, *The Political Economy of International Relations* (Princeton, N.J.: Princeton University Press, 1987), p. 73.
3. See François Perroux, *L'économie du XXe siècle* (Paris: Presses Universitaires de France, 3rd ed. 1969), p. 71, p. 80.
4. See e.g. Beate Kohler-Koch, 'Deutsche Einigung im Spannungsfeld internationaler Umbrüche', *Politische Vierteljahresschrift* 32 (December 1991), pp. 605–620 (p. 616).
5. Anne-Marie Le Gloannec, *Die deutsch-deutsche Nation* (Munich: Hanser, 1991), p. 192 (translation M.K.).
6. See Werner Link, 'Handlungsmaximen deutscher Außenpolitik im neuen Internationalen System', *Jahrbuch für Politik* 1 (1991), pp. 77–102 (pp. 80–84).
7. See e.g. Volker Rühe, *Deutschlands Verantwortung* (Frankfurt/M.-Berlin: Ullstein, 1994); Karl Kaiser and Hanns W. Maull (Eds), *Deutschlands neue Außenpolitik*, Band 1: Grundlagen (Munich: R. Oldenbourg Verlag, 1994); for a stimulating reappraisal of Germany's international position see Hans-Peter Schwarz, *Die Zentralmacht Europas. Deutschlands Rückkehr auf die Weltbühne* (Berlin: Siedler, 1994).
8. Helga Haftendorn, 'Gulliver in der Mitte Europas. Internationale Verflechtung und nationale Handlungsmöglichkeiten', in Kaiser and Maull, *Deutschlands neue Außenpolitik*, pp. 129–152 (p. 149).
9. See Gregor Schöllgen, *Angst vor der Macht. Die Deutschen und ihre Außenpolitik* (Frankfurt/M.-Berlin: Ullstein, 1993), p. 25.
10. Volker Rühe, *Betr: Bundeswehr. Sicherheitspolitik und Streitkräfte im Wandel* (Berlin: Verlag E.S. Mittler & Sohn, 1993), p. 165; 'Das Regierungsprogramm 1994 der SPD', in Klaus-Jürgen Scherer and Heinrich Tiemann (Eds), *Wechsel '94* (Marburg: Schüren 1994), pp. 23–68 (p. 64).
11. Bundesverfassungsgericht, Urteil des Zweiten Senats vom 12 Juli 1994, Karlsruhe (mimeo), Leitsätze 5.b and p. 88.
12. William Wallace, 'Deutschlands zentrale Rolle: Ein Versuch, die europäische Frage neu zu definieren', *Integration* 13 (1990), pp. 13–20 (p. 20) (translation M.K.).
13. See e.g. Herbert Giersch, Karl Heinz Paqué, Holger Schmieding (Eds),

The Fading Miracle. Four decades of market economy in Germany (Cambridge: Cambridge University Press, 1992), pp. 271–276.

14. OECD Economic Surveys, Germany (Paris: OECD, 1994), p. 26.
15. Ibid., pp. 23–24.
16. *Frankfurter Allgemeine Zeitung*, 13 January 1995, p. 13; Jahresgutachten des Sachverständigenrates 1994/95 zur Begutachtung der gesamtwirtschaftlichen Entwicklung, Deutscher Bundestag, Drucksache 13/26, pp. 93, 100.
17. See also Michael Kreile, 'The Political Economy of the New Germany', in Paul B. Stares (Ed.), *The New Germany and the New Europe* (Washington, D.C.: The Brookings Institution, 1992), pp. 55–92 (pp. 74–76); Michael Kreile, 'Gli errori dell'unificazione', *Relazioni Internazionali* (March 1993), pp. 46–53.
18. OECD Economic Surveys, Germany (1994), p. 54.
19. Ibid.
20. See C. Randall Henning, *Currencies and Politics in the United States, Germany, and Japan* (Washington, D.C.: Institute for International Economics, 1994), p. 226.
21. See the excellent analysis by Razeen Sally and Douglas Webber 'The German Solidarity Pact', *German Politics* 3, 1 (April 1994), pp. 18–46.
22. OECD Economic Surveys, Germany (Paris: OECD, 1993), p. 85.
23. See the scenarios developed in OECD Economic Surveys, Germany (1994), pp. 65–67.
24. OECD Economic Surveys, Germany (1993), pp. 43–45.
25. See e.g. Manfred Lahnstein, 'Leben auf Pump', *Die Zeit*, 20 January 1995, p. 33.
26. *Frankfurter Allgemeine Zeitung*, 7 February 1995, p. 15.
27. *Frankfurter Allgemeine Zeitung*, 1 October 1994, p. 15.
28. Data provided by the Federal Ministry of Finance.
29. Figures from Sachverständigenrat 1994/95, pp. 43, 66, 417, 419.
30. W.R. Smyser, *The Economy of United Germany. Colossus at the Crossroads* (New York: St Martin's Press, 1992), p. 176.
31. See e.g. Elvio Dal Bosco, *Germania economica* (Rome: Ediesse, 1987), p. 87.
32. EU-Informationen, January 1995, p. 8; *OECD Observer*, May 1977.
33. See e.g. Daniel Vernet, 'L'année des rois nus', *Le Monde*, 31 December 1991, p. 2.
34. See Henning, *Currencies and Politics*, pp. 237–244; Wayne Sandholtz, 'Monetary Union: Tough Road Ahead, But No Road Behind', paper prepared for presentation at the Centre d'Etudes et de Recherches Internationales, Paris, 29–30 September 1994.
35. See Werner Weidenfeld, 'Back on the European Agenda: Economic and Monetary Union', in Rolf H. Hasse, *The European Central Bank: Perspectives for a Further Development of the European Monetary System* (Gütersloh: Verlag Bertelsmann Stiftung, 1990), pp. 9–18 (pp. 10–13).
36. See Elke Thiel, 'Europäische Wirtschafts- und Währungsunion', *Aus Politik und Zeitgeschichte*, B 7–8/1992, pp. 3–11 (p. 8).
37. Stanley Hoffmann, 'Goodbye to a United Europe?', *New York Review of Books*, 27 May 1993, pp. 27–31 (p. 30).

38. *Fortune*, 4 July 1988, pp. 108–110; *Financial Times*, 20 July 1987, p. 16, and 4 November 1987, p. 26.
39. Simon Bulmer and William Paterson, *The Federal Republic of Germany and the European Community* (London: Allen & Unwin, 1987), p. 41.
40. Pierre Hassner, 'Frankreich', in Eberhard Schulz (Ed.), *Die Ostbeziehungen der Europäischen Gemeinschaft* (Munich: R. Oldenbourg Verlag, 1977), pp. 171–188 (p. 172) (translation M.K.).
41. See Roland Höhne, 'Frankreichs Stellung in der Welt. Weltmacht oder Mittelmacht?', *Aus Politik und Zeitgeschichte*, B 47–48/1991, pp. 37–46.
42. See e.g. Carlo M. Santoro, *La politica estera di una media potenza* (Bologna: Il Mulino, 1991), pp. 29, 273.
43. See Carlo Azeglio Ciampi, 'Für einen Vertrag zur europäischen Währungsunion: Hegemonialwährung keine Lösung', *Integration*, 13, 1 (January 1990), pp. 3–8 (p. 5).
44. Werner Weidenfeld, 'Zur Handlungsfähigkeit Westeuropas in der internationalen Politik', in Peter Haungs (Ed.), *Europäisierung Europas?* (Baden-Baden: Nomos, 1989), pp. 109–121 (p. 116) (translation M.K.).
45. See Helen Wallace, 'Institutionalized Bilateralism and Multilateral Relations: Axis, Motor or Detonator?', in Robert Picht and Wolfgang Wessels (Eds.), *Motor für Europa? Deutsch-französischer Bilateralismus und europäische Integration* (Bonn: Europa Union Verlag, 1990), pp. 145–157 (p. 157).
46. Bundesverfassungsgericht, Urteil des Zweiten Senats vom 12 Oktober 1993, Karlsruhe (mimeo), pp. 44–46, 80–82.
47. Hoffmann, 'Goodbye to a United Europe?', p. 30.
48. Jan Q. Th. Rood, 'The EC and Eastern Europe over the longer term', in Gianni Bonvicini et al., *The Community and the Emerging European Democracies. A Joint Policy Report* (1991), pp. 13–16, 23.

BIBLIOGRAPHY

Bulmer, Simon and William Paterson, *The Federal Republic of Germany and the European Community* (London: Allen & Unwin, 1987).
Bundesverfassungsgericht, Urteil des Zweiten Senats vom 12 Oktober 1993, Karlsruhe.
Bundesverfassungsgericht, Urteil des Zweiten Senats vom 12 Juli 1994, Karlsruhe.
Ciampi, Carlo Azeglio, 'Für einen Vertrag zur europäischen Währung-sunion: Hegemonialwährung keine Lösung', *Integration* 13, 1, January 1990, pp. 3–8.
Dal Bosco, Elvio, *Germania economica* (Rome: Ediesse, 1987).
'Das Regierungsprogramm 1994 der SPD', in Klaus-Jürgen Scherer and Heinrich Tiemann (Eds), *Wechsel '94* (Marburg: Schüren 1994).
EU-Informationen, January 1995 p. 8.
Financial Times, 20 July 1987 p. 16; 4 November 1987.
Fortune, 4 July 1988 pp. 108–110.

Frankfurter Allgemeine Zeitung, 1 October 1994, p. 15.

Frankfurter Allgemeine Zeitung, 13 January 1995, p. 13.

Frankfurter Allgemeine Zeitung, 7 February 1995, p. 15.

Giersch, Herbert, Karl Heinz Paqué, Holger Schmieding (Eds), *The Fading Miracle. Four decades of market economy in Germany* (Cambridge: Cambridge University Press, 1992).

Gilpin, Robert, *The Political Economy of International Relations* (Princeton, N.J.: Princeton University Press, 1987).

Haftendorn, Helga, 'Gulliver in der Mitte Europas. Internationale Verflechtung und nationale Handlungsmöglichkeiten', in Kaiser, Karl and Hanns W. Maull (Eds), *Deutschlands neue Außenpolitik* Band 1: Grundlagen (Munich: R. Oldenbourg Verlag, 1994).

Hassner, Pierre, 'Frankreich', in Eberhard Schulz (Ed.), *Die Ostbeziehungen der Europäischen Gemeinschaft* (Munich: R. Oldenbourg Verlag, 1977), pp. 171–188.

Henning, C. Randall, *Currencies and Politics in the United States, Germany, and Japan* (Washington, D.C.: Institute for International Economics, 1994).

Hoffmann, Stanley, 'Goodbye to a United Europe?', *New York Review of Books*, 27 May 1993.

Höhne, Roland, 'Frankreichs Stellung in der Welt. Weltmacht oder Mittelmacht?', *Aus Politik und Zeitgeschichte*, B 47–48/1991, pp. 37–46.

Jahresgutachten des Sachverständigenrates 1994/95 zur Begutachtung der gesamtwirtschaftlichen Entwicklung, Deutscher Bundestag, Drucksache 13/26.

Kaiser, Karl and Hanns W. Maull (Eds), *Deutschlands neue Außenpolitik*, Band 1: Grundlagen (Munich: R. Oldenbourg Verlag, 1994).

Kohler-Koch, Beate, 'Deutsche Einigung im Spannungsfeld internationaler Umbrüche', *Politische Vierteljahresschrift* 32 (December 1991).

Kreile, Michael 'The Political Economy of the New Germany', in Paul B. Stares (Ed.), *The New Germany and the New Europe* (Washington, D.C.: The Brookings Institution, 1992), pp. 55–92 (pp. 74–76).

Kreile, Michael, 'Gli errori dell'unificazione', *Relazioni Internazionali* (March 1993), pp. 46–53.

Kreile, Michael, 'Übernimmt Deutschland eine Führungsrolle in der Europäischen Gemeinschaft?', in Werner Weidenfeld (Ed.), *Was ändert die Einheit?* (Gütersloh: Verlag Bertelsmann Stiftung, 1993).

Lahnstein, Manfred, 'Leben auf Pump', *Die Zeit*, 20 January 1995.

Le Gloannec, Anne-Marie, *Die deutsch-deutsche Nation* (Munich: Hanser, 1991).

Link, Werner, 'Handlungsmaximen deutscher Außenpolitik im neuen Internationalen System', *Jahrbuch für Politik*, 1 (1991).

OECD Economic Surveys, Germany (Paris: OECD, 1993).

OECD Economic Surveys, Germany (Paris: OECD, 1994).

OECD Observer, May (1977).

Perroux, François, *L'économie du XXe siècle* (Paris: Presses Universitaires de France, 3rd ed. 1969).

Rood, Jan Q. Th., 'The EC and Eastern Europe over the longer term', in Gianni Bonvicini et al., *The Community and the Emerging European Democracies. A Joint Policy Report* (1991).

Rühe, Volker, *Betr.: Bundeswehr. Sicherheitspolitik und Streitkräfte im Wandel* (Berlin: Verlag E.S. Mittler & Sohn, 1993).

Rühe, Volker, *Deutschlands Verantwortung* (Frankfurt/M.-Berlin: Ullstein, 1994).

Sally, Razeen and Douglas Webber, 'The German Solidarity Pact', *German Politics*, 3, 1, April 1994, pp. 18–46.

Sandholtz, Wayne, 'Monetary Union: Tough Road Ahead, But No Road Behind', paper prepared for presentation at the Centre d'Etudes et de Recherches Internationales, Paris, 29–30 September 1994.

Santoro, Carlo M., *La politica estera di una media potenza* (Bologna: Il Mulino, 1991).

Schöllgen, Gregor, *Angst vor der Macht. Die Deutschen und ihre Außenpolitik* (Frankfurt/M.-Berlin: Ullstein, 1993).

Schwarz, Hans-Peter, *Die Zentralmacht Europas. Deutschlands Rückkehr auf die Weltbühne* (Berlin: Siedler, 1994).

Smyser, W.R., *The Economy of United Germany. Colossus at the Crossroads* (New York: St Martin's Press, 1992).

Thiel, Elke, 'Europäische Wirtschafts- und Währungsunion', *Aus Politik und Zeitgeschichte*, B 7–8/1992.

Vernet, Daniel, 'L'année des rois nus', *Le Monde*, 31 December 1991.

Wallace, Helen, 'Institutionalized Bilateralism and Multilateral Relations: Axis, Motor or Detonator?', in Robert Picht and Wolfgang Wessels (Eds), *Motor für Europa? Deutsch-französischer Bilateralismus und europäische Integration* (Bonn: Europa Union Verlag, 1990), pp. 145–157.

Wallace, William, 'Deutschlands zentrale Rolle: Ein Versuch, die europäische Frage neu zu definieren', *Integration* 13 (1990), pp. 13–20.

Weidenfeld, Werner, 'Zur Handlungsfähigkeit Westeuropas in der internationalen Politik', in Peter Haungs (Ed.), *Europäisierung Europas?* (Baden-Baden: Nomos, 1989), pp. 109–121.

Weidenfeld, Werner, 'Back on the European Agenda: Economic and Monetary Union', in Rolf H. Hasse, *The European Central Bank: Perspectives for a Further Development of the European Monetary System* (Gütersloh: Verlag Bertelsmann Stiftung, 1990).

6 German Foreign Policy and Domestic Politics

Roger Morgan

At first sight, issues of foreign and European policy arouse only minimal political controversy in Germany: German policy appears to reflect a national consensus whose outlines are well known, and there seems little reason to expect its course to change dramatically in response to pressures from the domestic political arena. Ever since the Social Democrats accepted the basic lines of Adenauer's Westpolitik at the end of the 1950s, and the Christian Democrats in turn accepted those of Brandt's Ostpolitik in the mid-1970s (in each case ending a period of acute party-political conflict), foreign policy has been marked by a high level of consensus between the various parties in successive Bonn governments. One reason for consensus and continuity is that the Free Democratic Party, by agreement with each of the two bigger parties in turn, has held the Foreign Ministry without interruption for over a quarter of a century, but there are other reasons too.

CONTINUITY AND CONSENSUS

The foreign policy announced by the 'new' Kohl government of November 1994 could certainly be described as representing both continuity with the past and a broad national consensus about how Germany's objectives in the outside world should be formulated. The basic goals of policy in the areas of 'European and foreign policy, security and defence', as agreed between the parties now holding office, are set out in section VIII of the Coalition Agreement signed in November 1994 (a month after their election victory) by Helmut Kohl for the CDU, Theo Waigel for the CSU and Klaus Kinkel for the FDP. (The order of their signatures is significant. In the recent election, while Kohl's CDU had suffered only small losses, and Waigel's CSU had chalked up a slight increase, Kinkel's FDP had seen its support drop from 11 per cent to under 7 per cent of the vote, and its status in the new coalition was correspondingly and demonstratively reduced: instead of holding, as previously, five cabinet posts to the CDU's ten and the CSU's four, the FDP now only had three.)

The Coalition Agreement[1] promises a European policy devoted to further integration (described as essential for Europe's economic competitiveness, environmental protection, technological renewal, immigration control and success in the fight against organized crime), with particular emphasis on stabilizing 'the reform states of Central and Eastern Europe', and bringing them into membership of the EU 'as soon as the preconditions for this are present'. Further stated goals include 'partnership' with the ex-USSR and the stabilization of the Mediterranean region. The active external and internal development of the EU, including Franco–German cooperation as a 'core element', is to cover the establishment of Economic and Monetary Union 'in accordance with the Treaty, i.e. with the strict observance of the convergence criteria laid down in the Treaty and adherence to the time-table'.

In developing the Common Foreign and Security Policy of the EU, the governing coalition promises to work for greater use of majority voting in this area; for active policies of stabilization towards the EU's eastern and southern neighbours, and a 'development' of its relations with North America; for a strengthening of the operational capacity of the Western European Union; and for 'an independent European security and defence identity through the comprehensive building up of the WEU as the European pillar of the Atlantic Alliance and as the defence component of the EU'.

Further goals for the EU's development include intensified cooperation in police and judicial affairs (the implementation of the Schengen Agreement and common policies on asylum and refugee questions) and institutional reform (to be sought at the 1996 Inter-Governmental Conference) to strengthen the democratic legitimacy and political effectiveness of 'ongoing European integration'.

Specific pledges which reflect Germany's domestic political situation include a commitment to involve the Land governments in the preparation of Germany's position at the Inter-Governmental Conference, and an interesting (and detailed) promise to limit the growth in the EU's competences, and even to consider returning some powers to national governments, in the name of 'subsidiarity'. Financially, Germany's position in terms of payments and receipts in the EU budget is to be improved, EU subsidies which harm competition are to be drastically reduced, and in world trade the EU must be employed as an instrument to achieve an 'open, multilaterally organized system'.

On security issues, the coalition promises to work for the strengthening and (gradual) enlargement of NATO, and for a parallel strengthening of the CSCE (now OSCE) and 'intensive partnership with Russia', 'so that no new lines of division emerge in Europe'. Germany's armed forces must be adequate to contribute both to defence and to 'international crisis management' (i.e. UN peacekeeping actions and the like), subject in each case to the constitutionally required approval of the Bundestag. Finally, Germany's contributions to global economic development programmes (directed to 'the attack on poverty, humanitarian aid against need and catastrophe, the blocking of streams of refugees, limitation of population growth', etc.) are to be 'linked with the shaping of the EU's development policy'.

The goals of European, foreign, and security policy set out in these formal paragraphs serve as guidelines for German officials in the conduct of day-to-day affairs. Strictly, of course, they are only binding for the parties of the present coalition (CDU, CSU and FDP), but the main opposition party, the SPD, would have little or no objection to most of them. This is particularly true as far as European policy is concerned: how could it be otherwise, when the presidency of the European Parliament has passed from a German Christian Democrat (Egon Klepsch) to a German Social Democrat (Klaus Hänsch) as the latest decision of a permanent Grand Coalition in which their two (European-level) parties have dominated the Parliament for decades?

But even on the more controversial subjects like German participation in UN peacekeeping, it is unlikely that the text of the Coalition Agreement would have been substantially different if it had enshrined a revival of the Social–Liberal coalition of 1969–82, or of the Grand Coalition of the three years which preceded it. Only if the 1994 Bundestag election, against expectations, had brought Rudolf Scharping into office at the head of a 'red–green' coalition between his SPD and the Greens/Alliance 90, would the passages about military alliances and military preparedness perhaps have been weaker, and those about environmental and development issues stronger.

However, the fact is that the German voters fairly decisively rejected this kind of government: even though the Greens/Alliance 90 won slightly more votes than the FDP (7.3 per cent to 6.9 per cent), their 49 parliamentary seats, together with the 252 of the SPD, fell well short of the 337 needed for a majority, which Kohl's existing coalition narrowly achieved.[2]

The 'Bottom-up' Preferences

In fact the election of October 1994 showed that the near-unanimity on foreign policy achieved by the main parties (the 'top-down' consensus set out in the Coalition Agreement and tacitly supported by the SPD) corresponded very closely to the 'bottom-up' preferences of the German voters. The parties backing the consensus achieved together 84.9 per cent of the votes cast, while the two 'dissident' parties represented in the Bundestag – the Greens/Alliance 90 and the Party of Democratic Socialism or PDS (directly descended from the former SED) – scored 11.7 per cent between them, and the only other significant force, the extreme right Republicans, with a mere 1.9 per cent, fell far short of the percentage needed for parliamentary representation.

The votes won by the different parties, of course, were based essentially on other considerations than those of foreign policy (which the polls showed to be the least important from the viewpoint of the voters), but they give a general indication of popular support for different foreign policy orientations. The 7.3 per cent of voters (throughout Germany) who supported the Greens/Alliance 90, or the 4.4

per cent (in and around East Berlin) who voted PDS, were on the whole sympathetic to a less military-orientated and 'capitalistic' external policy than the national consensus, whereas the 1.9 per cent (largely in Bavaria) who supported the Republicans tended to favour a more nationalist (strongly anti-European and often very anti-foreigner) viewpoint. Their existence certainly influenced the positions of other parties to a small extent: left-wingers in the SPD who wished to see a Red–Green coalition expressed support for the views of the Greens/Alliance 90, and Theo Waigel's CSU certainly benefited in Bavaria by echoing the anti-European diatribes of their Republican rivals. However, the overall significance of these fringe groups is marginal.

Foreign Policy

If the foreign policy line of the Coalition Agreement corresponds to a consensus among the political parties and has the consent of the vast majority of the voters, then we ought to expect the domestic 'input' into German foreign policy to be quite predictable. The main political forces will all agree in expecting the federal government to pursue the foreign policy mixture as before: pressure on Germany's EU partners for commitment to stronger European institutions and more active EU policies (including eastward enlargement) as the 1996 Inter-Governmental Conference approaches, comes and goes; a commitment to maintain NATO as the main security instrument, at the same time as building up WEU and OSCE (in partnership respectively with France and Russia); and a very gradual upgrading of Germany's military involvement in selected UN or NATO peacekeeping missions.[3] But if this is the case, how can there ever be any surprises or changes of direction in Germany's foreign and European policies? How can Germany's foreign partners ever fail to find her totally 'berechenbar' ('predictable' or 'calculable'), the way the Federal Republic has always devoutly aspired to be?

There are several answers to this. One is that Germany's actual implementation of the general principles of the Coalition Agreement, in the real world of international politics, is bound to be subject to the conflicting pressures of various powerful forces. For instance, when or if the time comes for the later stages of Europe's projected Economic and Monetary Union to be implemented, both the Bundestag and the Bundesbank will have the right to judge whether Germany's European partners meet the necessary criteria: the Bundestag may find it hard to reach agreement on this point, and any agreement reached even there is likely to be based on a less restrictive interpretation of the rules than that of the Bundesbank. And we have only to ask how the Bundestag might approach a decision on the sending of German military personnel on a UN mission to Algeria, say, or to Macedonia, to realize that the outcome would be unlikely to be simple or certain. There is also the important fact, indicated very clearly in the Coalition Agreement, that the federal states or Länder of the Federal Republic, already vociferous when European integration touches the policy areas within their responsibility (and most of them also now ruled by parties opposed to the Kohl government), will insist on a large say in German policy towards the EU's future development. In some cases this may not be unwelcome to Bonn – the argument that certain possible EU policy deals would not be 'sellable' to the Länder might even be useful – but in other cases it seems likely to produce conflict.

Perhaps the domestic sources of the possible cross-pressures on German foreign policy – the sources from which internal politics might impinge on the consensual pursuit of the general objectives proclaimed in the Coalition Agreement – can be divided into four categories. Conflicts and surprises might result from:

1. the temporary 'capture' of German policy by a determined interest group;
2. the exigencies of coalition politics, in which one minister or another takes action designed to enhance his 'profile' against political rivals;
3. influence exercised on the Federal Government by other powers in the German institutional system, in particular the federal Länder;
4. a possible increase (even though temporary) in the influence of one or another of the 'extreme' political forces dismissively mentioned above.

1. 'CAPTURE' OF POLICY BY AN INTEREST GROUP

The phenomenon of the temporary but effective seizure of control of foreign policy by a group with a special interest is one to which the German foreign policy 'machine' may be especially prone, because of the relative lack of experience of most foreign policy questions among Germany's political and admi1nistrative élites. During the 40-year history of the Federal Republic before unification, every aspect of its foreign relations was linked more or less directly to the great national objective of overcoming or ending Germany's division: Europapolitik, alliance or Bündnispolitik, Westpolitik, Ostpolitik, and development aid or Entwicklungspolitik, were all conceived and executed in relation to Deutschlandpolitik. It is not surprising that among German experts, as Ludger Kühnhardt puts it, 'there were always more *Deutschland-Politiker* than *Aussenpolitiker* – in both German states'.[4]

The German party system, and the penumbra of policy think-tanks and informed journalism accompanying the foreign policy process, were almost always capable of a serious and comprehensive debate on any issue linked in any way with Deutschlandpolitik: on Berlin questions, on relations with the DDR, or on the complex links between West European integration or NATO weapons-deployment and national unity. This understandable concentration on 'the German problem', however, left Germany short of people – whether politicians, academic experts or media commentators – capable of submitting the new problems of the post-unification era to the same kind of treatment.

It was against this background, in 1991, that a small group in Germany succeeded in rapidly mobilizing support for the diplomatic recognition of Slovenia and Croatia, and was able to make this an objective of Bonn's policy, carried out amidst considerable international controversy in the winter of 1991/92.

When Slovenia and Croatia declared their independence from the Yugoslav Federation in June 1991, the position of the German government and of all the main parties was the same as that of the EC's other member states: the unity of Yugoslavia should be maintained on the basis of recognition of democracy and human rights, particularly those of minorities. Already, however, strong pressure within Germany for the recognition of the seceding republics was building up. Kohl's foreign affairs adviser Horst Teltschik received a secret visit from a Croat emissary, and the Republic of Croatia established a 'foreign office' in Stuttgart to mobilize public support; in May a demonstration of several thousands of Croatians (closely linked to the CSU) took place in Munich; and a relentless campaign for recognition was waged by the influential *Frankfurter Allgemeine Zeitung*.[5]

Germany's political parties were quick in demanding a change in Bonn's position. The general secretary of Kohl's own CDU, Volker Rühe, argued early in July 1991 that Germany could not refuse the yardstick of self-determination to the Yugoslav Republics 'when we achieved the unity and freedom of our own country through the right of self-determination'.[6] In Foreign Minister Genscher's party, strong doubts about maintaining Yugoslavia's unity were expressed in June by Martin Bangemann, vice-president of the EC Commission,[7] and in early July the party adopted a policy of recognizing the new republics.[8] Representatives of the SPD, the main opposition party, including its foreign policy spokesman Norbert Gansel, had also by now begun to demand a change of line. In early July the state government of Hessen (ruled by an SPD–Green coalition) offered material help to Slovenia and Croatia, arguing that 'the FRG could no longer hide behind the EC, whose indifference could well be explained by the constraints felt by members with minority problems of their own'. In a further demonstration of the wish of Germany's federal states to make their mark on policy – an issue with more general significance – representatives of all 16 states in the Bundesrat (thus including representatives of all Germany's mainstream political parties) voted for recognition of Slovenia and Croatia if the Yugoslav military attack continued.[9]

By mid-July, when Genscher had been subjected to intense pressure by all parties in the Bundestag's foreign affairs committee, a change in Bonn's policy seemed inevitable: by the end of the month, Germany was taking a position opposed to that of most of its EC partners.

The 'Ethnic Lobby'

The ensuing controversies, and the further strains which arose from Germany's unilateral recognition of the two new republics in December 1991, have been fully analysed and documented.[10] The aspect of the episode which is of interest here is that Germany's political parties, finding themselves confronted by an unexpected challenge in the field of foreign policy, reacted, with little hesitation or reflection, by adopting the view of an unrepresentative minority inside their country, which they thus allowed to 'capture' German policy for a brief but decisive period.

Their motives were no doubt varied. For a tiny minority on the right, atavistic memories of Germany's war-time alliance with Croatia or of Slovenia's Habsburg past may conceivably have played a role, but a far more important legacy of the past was the perception of Milosevic's Serbia as a new Hitlerian Germany whose aggression ought to be resisted. For the CSU, links with Bavaria's large immigrant Croat community (including religious affinities) were important, while the CDU could hardly reject the popular agreement (constantly drummed out by the *Frankfurter Allgemeine Zeitung*) that Germany had no right to refuse self-determination to the two republics only a few months after achieving its own unity in the name of this very principle. The FDP was moved by a mixture of principle (recognition of the republics became the policy of the Liberal International) and the practical fear of being out of tune with Germany's changing public opinion. As for the SPD, it was clearly stung into action partly by the realization that its serious underestimate of Germany's desire for quick unification the previous year had contributed to its electoral defeat in December 1990. In its compensatory eagerness to tell the German people what they seemed to want to hear, and to score party points against Kohl, the SPD went very far: when the party's parliamentary leader, Ulrich Klose, told Kohl, in the name of self-determination, that the German government had the choice as to whether Europe's future would be dominated by 'alliance thinking' or 'the idea of freedom', there was at least a faint echo of his predecessor Kurt Schumacher's denunciation of Konrad Adenauer 40 years earlier as 'the Federal Chancellor of the Allies'.[11]

When Kohl, addressing the CDU's first all-German party conference in Dresden in mid-December, proclaimed the EC's reluctantly granted agreement to recognize Slovenia and Croatia as a resounding success for German foreign policy, he was right at least in the sense that the Bonn government had pressed its EC allies to agree to what the majority of the German people now clearly wanted.[12] On the other hand his foreign minister, Genscher, was also right when he indicated that German policy had shifted at least partly in response to the 'ethnic lobby' of some half a million Croats, and to the political support they had mobilized in Germany.[13]

The tensions between Germany and her Allies, provoked by differences in policy in the episode just sketched, have no parallel in the five-year experience of German foreign policy since unification. (As another example of a difficult moment, due in some participants' view to the line taken by powerful forces inside Germany, some observers would cite the European currency drama of September 1992 and the role of the Bundesbank therein; but the origins and nature of this crisis were in fact very different.) Perhaps the fact that the Slovenia–Croatia episode has remained unique is due to a firm decision by the makers of German foreign policy not to let this kind of 'capture' of policy by a special interest, however worthy, occur again. If so they have been successful – so far.

2. THE STRESSES OF COALITION POLITICS

As a result of Germany's electoral system and the behaviour of its voters, virtually every government since the beginning of the Federal Republic has been a coalition between two or more parties. The only exception is the one-party administration which Adenauer was able to form after his electoral triumph of 1957 – though even then his party, 'the Union', contained the special element of the Bavarian CSU, led by the redoubtable and independent-minded Franz Josef Strauss.[14] Furthermore, the coalition arrangements have, at least since 1966, invariably resulted in the chancellor and foreign minister (the latter usually also vice-chancellor) belonging to different parties. As head of government the chancellor, of course, has a leading role in foreign policy, and can often exclude the foreign minister from important negotiations and decisions altogether, though the foreign minister, with the resources of a large ministry at his disposal, can usually find ways of retaliating. As the parties they lead are in constant competition with each other (as well as with the opposition) for the support of the public, there is a built-in tendency for each party leader/minister to seek ways of enhancing his public 'profile' at the expense of his rivals/colleagues.

The effects of this have included some striking changes of roles and emphasis, and occasionally some public differences of opinion between the two leading representatives of German foreign policy. Usually their common interest in remaining in office, on the basis of their 'Coalition Agreement', and in promoting German interests effectively, have led to a harmonious though changing division of labour. Timothy Garton Ash, analysing the differences in Foreign Minister Genscher's role in different coalitions before and after 1982, writes that while Schmidt had taken the leading part in attempting to develop Germany's relations with the East and above all Moscow, Genscher had, partly for substantive, partly for party-political reasons, established himself as the high priest and guardian of Germany's relations with the West, and above all with Washington. When Kohl set out to re-emphasize West Germany's vital relationship with the West, Genscher presented himself as the high priest and guardian of Germany's relations with the East.[15]

Kohl and Kinkel

In the years before unification the interaction between two powerful politicians, each with an entrenched position in relation to foreign policy and each with legitimate political ambitions for his own party, sometimes led to different points being emphasized, or different 'contributions' being offered, in the discussion of such issues as arms control or East–West relations in general. Since 1992, when Klaus Kinkel replaced Genscher as the FDP's party leader and as foreign minister of a Germany now unified, this situation has shown some elements of continuity and some of change. The main continuity perhaps lies in the fact of inter-party rivalry. Its terms, however, have changed. The FDP, having been drastically reduced in its parliamentary strength in October 1994 (and in fact removed altogether from the European Parliament and from three state parliaments elected on the same day as the Bundestag), now seems to stand on the brink of total ruin. After the further disastrous blows to the FDP's position in the Landtag elections in 1995 (most critically in North Rhine–Westphalia on 15 May), their position as extremely junior partners in Kohl's coalition has become highly precarious. If the FDP were to sink in national opinion polls towards the point of potential disappearance from the Bundestag at the next election in 1998, thus removing any prospect of the present coalition continuing, Kohl and his colleagues would appear to be only prudent in exploring, even before 1998, the possibilities of an alternative 'Grand Coalition' with the SPD, which would thrust the FDP into opposition even if it won representation in the Bundestag. If such a 'Grand Coalition' (perhaps led by Schäuble or Rühe after a resignation by Kohl in 1997, with Lafontaine as vice-chancellor and foreign minister) were to take office a year before the 1998 Bundestag election, and then to continue after an election victory (now perhaps with Lafontaine as Chancellor), the FDP would face a period of opposition, or worse, of a much more protracted and acute kind than it endured when it was last removed from national office in 1966. All this is speculation; but the fact is that Kinkel's FDP is now fighting for its life, and this only heightens the need for the foreign minister (even though he resigned as party chairman after the elecoral débâcle in May 1995) to enhance his party's 'profile' whenever the occasion arises.

From the CDU's point of view, perhaps paradoxically, there is an interest in letting this happen: Kohl's chances of keeping the present coalition alive depend on keeping the FDP alive too, and, as the last election showed, this now requires a considerable degree of support from the CDU. Kohl himself thus appears to be willing to allow Kinkel a considerable degree of freedom to be seen to be making German

foreign policy – not, however, including the vital sector of
Europapolitik, on which the chancellor wants to make his
own high-level mark as the EU's Inter-Governmental Conference approaches. On the other hand, a new dimension
in the inter-ministerial politics of foreign policy is now apparent: tension not so much between the Foreign Ministry
and the Chancellor's Office as between the Foreign Ministry and the Defence Ministry. During the cold war years,
the respective roles of these two departments were fairly
distinct: while the Auswärtiges Amt ran foreign policy (essentially political, partly economic), the Defence Ministry
was occupied with defence planning, with 'security policy'
in a largely military sense, and with Bonn's role in the US-
led NATO. In the very different world of the 1990s, while
some of the classic NATO-related tasks still remain, the substance of Germany's 'security policy' is at the same time
broader and vaguer: its concerns range from possible German participation in military operations 'out of area' to the
implications of possible German membership of the UN
Security Council, and from participation in international
humanitarian aid missions to defining the precise content
of the 'Common Foreign and Security Policy' prescribed by
the Maastricht Treaty, and its complex links with the WEU
as well as NATO.

This agenda obviously brings the civilian officials and
military planners of the Defence Ministry much more actively into issues hitherto handled largely by the Foreign
Ministry's diplomats. The potential for conflict thus increases,
and this effect is augmented by the fact that the Defence
Ministry's political head, Volker Rühe, as a leading contender
for the succession to Chancellor Kohl, has good reasons for
trying to enhance his own public 'profile'.

Kinkel and Rühe

This conjuncture helps to explain why the three years since
Kinkel and Rühe assumed their present ministerial posts have
been marked by a series of often conflicting messages to
the outside world. Observers in Bonn, by the spring of 1995,
were noting that the foreign minister, faced with acute pressure by the desperate position of his party, was tending to

become inconsistent and sweeping in his statements about German foreign policy: after stressing the need to work seriously on North–South relations and human rights, he would abruptly switch his rhetorical priorities to Germany's future role in UN peacekeeping and its claim to a seat in the Security Council. Again, declaring grandly that the now unified Germany must 'come down from the spectators' stand' of world politics, he gave the impression that he, not Defence Minister Rühe, was the man responsible for finding new tasks for the Bundeswehr in the post-cold war world. At this point, it was said, Rühe was forced to put on the brakes: he had to point out that there were limits to Germany's military role and that no-one should think of 'sticking little flags all over the world map' to mark spots where German soldiers were keeping guard for the UN, or imposing peace by force of arms.[16]

It became clear that Kinkel's Foreign Ministry, in pursuing the minister's aim of a German seat in the Security Council, was stressing the desirability of a greater international role for the German armed forces: Bundeswehr units, it appeared, might be sent to Nagorny-Karabach, or para-medical staff to Kuwait, as well as the existing German units engaged in specific roles in Bosnia (in NATO's AWACS aircraft) or in Somalia.

In contrast to suggestions of this kind, as minister actually in charge of the armed forces, Rühe was observed to be preaching great caution and great concern to keep German soldiers out of politically delicate or militarily dangerous situations abroad. While it was true that in the background Germany's political and constitutional processes were working towards the conclusion reached in the summer of 1994, that the Bundeswehr might indeed be committed to specific UN and other collective actions abroad (if the Bundestag gave its specific approval each time), differences of emphasis in the statements of the two ministers persisted. One observer summarized Kinkel's and Rühe's contrasting statements on Somalia, on NATO enlargement, on relations with Russia and on Germany's role in UN peacekeeping missions, as signifying 'their conflicting claims to leadership in foreign and security policy'. Indeed, if the foreign minister can be said to be guilty of trespassing on to the territory of the defence minister, the latter in turn has been accused of touring the world like a foreign minister, making foreign policy speeches on his travels to America and elsewhere.[17]

Because of the inextricable interconnections between 'foreign' and 'security' policies, and the political interests of the FDP and CDU as represented by Kinkel and Rühe, ambiguities of the kind described will continue to be a phenomenon that Germany's partners will have to live with. Other examples of the same kind of thing may well arise, for instance in the preparation and carrying through of the EU's Inter-Governmental Conference due in 1996. Even though there is likely to be a clear understanding (as in 1990–91) that the Foreign Ministry is the 'lead department' for political affairs and that Theo Waigel's Finance Ministry has the same role for economic and monetary ones (both coordinated by the Chancellor's Office), the fact that the three politicians involved belong respectively to the FDP, the CSU and the CDU cannot remain without influence.

In sum, any area of German foreign or security policy which involves the overlapping responsibilities of any of the ministries of foreign affairs, defence, finance and perhaps agriculture, as well as the pervasive overall responsibility of the Chancellor's Office, may at times be characterized by less than total coherence and by mild to serious discord. This is one of the prices to be paid for a democratic system designed, in effect, to make coalition government the norm.

3.   THE IMPACT OF THE FEDERAL LÄNDER

The foregoing discussion has considered the influence on foreign policy of various internal forces, including special interests, and of party politics as conducted inside coalition governments. Most of the forces so far discussed are without a significant territorial basis (or if they are territorial, like the CSU and the PDS, this is not relevant to the argument). We now turn to consider the foreign policy influence of the territorial units of the Federal Republic themselves, the governments of the Länder.

Thanks to the power of these governments in Germany's federal system, there has been a tendency since the earliest years of the republic for their representatives to influence the foreign policy positions of their respective parties, or of the federal government, or both. Examples of this include the way in which the SPD came to adopt a 'European' position by about 1960, partly because the SPD heads of government in Berlin, Hamburg, Lower Saxony and elsewhere assessed the value of 'Brussels' more positively than did the party's national leadership in Bonn; or the additional impetus to Franco-German *rapprochement* given by the south-western states of Baden-Württemberg and Rheinland-Pfalz; or the CSU's role in defending the interests of Bavarian agriculture both in Bonn and in Brussels.

These historical examples, however, could be said to have a relatively low profile: the 1990s have seen the growth of a more assertive 'foreign policy' role for the Länder. This more active role (exemplified by the July 1991 appeal of all 16 Land governments for the recognition of Slovenia and Croatia, mentioned above) appears to have been stimulated by two main factors: on the one hand the development of European integration into policy areas which the Land governments regard as their responsibility, and on the other hand the reorganization and reassessment of the German federal system stimulated by reunification.

New EC/EU Role of the Länder

The European dimension of the enhanced role of the Länder – documented in the Coalition Agreement's pledge that they will be given due influence on matters concerning them in the forthcoming Inter-Governmental Conference – has been developing on a broad front for some time. In May 1988, during the interval between the Single European Act and German unification, the Commission's president, Jacques Delors, addressing a conference of German Land prime ministers in Bonn, gave a list of policy areas in which, as he said,

> the federal Länder, together with the Community, can actively support a process of European integration: culture, education and training, radio, television, agricultural policy, health policy, environmental protection, foodstuffs law, transport policy, an active policy in support of small and medium enterprises, an active policy for research.[18]

This catalogue of Land-related issues, coming from the side of the Commission, reflected the long-standing interest of the Brussels institutions in developing relations with sub-national units of government, thus making the process of European integration more than one of quasi-diplomatic negotiations between the capitals of the member states. From the point of view of the German Länder, the opportunity for more active European links was more than welcome for two distinct reasons: firstly the Land governments could see the advantages of closer relations with 'Brussels', in terms of material resources and political influence; and secondly such relations, combined with a greater say in the shaping of 'European policy' in Bonn, would give them a defence against possible negative consequences of European integration in such fields as educational curricula or the content of television programmes. These at least were among the arguments used by representatives of the German Länder to win a greater share of influence on the relevant policy processes in Bonn (partly through an upgrading of the Bundesrat's involvement in EU affairs); a role in Germany's negotiating procedures in Brussels (through the direct participation of Länder representatives in the 1991 Inter-Governmental Conference and in the Council of Ministers and its subordinate committees); and now, as confirmed in the 1994 Coalition Agreement, the guarantee that such procedures will continue in the future.[19]

There is of course a strong party-political component in this assertion of the constitutional rights of the Länder in Europapolitik: all the Western federal Länder except Bavaria are now governed by coalitions in which the Christian Democrats are either absent or hold only a minority position (Bavaria itself is a special case), and even the CDU's prime ministers in the Eastern or 'new' Länder, particularly Kurt Biedenkopf in Saxony, are not automatically followers of the chancellor's line. As far as the issues of Europapolitik are concerned there is of course, as noted above, a broad consensus among the German parties, so there is no reason to expect dramatic conflicts between the positions of Bonn and the Länder in, say, the forthcoming Inter-Governmental Conference. As with the coexistence of different parties in the federal cabinet, however, the fact that Bonn and the Länder may be represented in Brussels by politicians with conflicting party interests must be identified as a possible source of occasional turbulence and discontinuity in the presentation of German interests abroad.

The New 'Länder'

As well as being stimulated by the course of European integration, the assertion of Länder interests in foreign relations has also received an impetus from the specifically German phenomenon of national unification. This expresses itself in several different ways. At the regional level, the 'new' Länder of Mecklenburg-Vorpommern, Brandenburg and Saxony are increasingly involved in trans-frontier cooperation with authorities in Poland (and also, in Saxony's case, in the Czech Republic) in the way that Germany's western and southern states have long been involved with their own foreign neighbours. There is also the general state of tension between the Eastern and Western parts of united Germany, which persists despite all the financial and other efforts being made to overcome it: it expresses itself in issues like the controversy over the transfer of the federal capital to Berlin, the sense of discrimination felt by many Easterners, and all the other frustrations which have brought such striking electoral success to the PDS. All these dimensions of the East–West divide in German politics are liable to have some effect on foreign policy. More specifically, and with more direct relevance to the question of the role of the Länder, we should note that the 'new' Länder of Eastern Germany have specific motives for seeking to develop active contacts of their own with the European Union.

In starting their existence with no national capital in Berlin to relate to, and with a sense of distance (in many senses) from Bonn, the 'new' Länder were also frustrated by the way in which the existing ones, on the eve of unification in 1990, hurriedly changed the voting rules of the Bundesrat: the purpose of this was to ensure that, while the newcomers could not muster a blocking minority even if they all voted together, the four biggest Western Länder had a built-in guarantee of being able to do so. Against this background, the 'new' Länder have an obvious incentive to seek the closest possible links with Brussels in their attempt to build up economic and social conditions in their part of Germany. They have found help in a variety of ways, including the support of experienced officials from West Germany and from Brussels, and the political ambitions of their leaders will certainly ensure that their special interests are taken into account in Germany's Europapolitik. The partners of the Federal Republic will find not only that Bonn's policies are strongly influenced by the general wish of the federal Länder to make their mark, but also that the Eastern Länder have a distinctive and significant role in this process.[20]

As mentioned above, the consequences of Germany's unification have included a reassessment and redefinition of the principles of the federal constitution. It is not possible to go into the details here, but one important effect of the constitutional revision is an enhancement of the rights of the Land governments *vis-à-vis* the federation, which will certainly – taken together with the party-political dimension which is inevitably present – have significant consequences for the conduct and perhaps the substance of German foreign policy.[21]

4. THE POSSIBLE INCREASE IN THE POWER OF THE 'EXTREMES'

The three previous sections, concerning the capture of foreign policy by eccentric groups and the effects of coalition politics and the federal system, were based largely on historical experience. A discussion of how German foreign policy might be affected by a growth in influence of one or more of the 'extreme' political parties must, in contrast, be essentially hypothetical: as we have seen, the German political system has so far excluded these 'extremes' from ministerial office, from any substantial influence on policy, and most of the time from parliamentary representation at any level. (The few exceptions to the last part of this statement include the presence of the extreme right National Democratic Party in some Landtage 25 years ago, and of six Republikaner in the European Parliament from 1989 to 1994, plus of course the success of the Greens – if indeed they are an 'extreme' party – since they entered the Bundestag in 1983.)

The putative influence of the anti-system or 'extreme' parties may be divided into two categories: first, the influence they may have had already in shifting the foreign policy positions of established parties, and second, the chances of their acquiring greater and more direct influence in the future.

Left Parties

As far as the influence of the 'extreme' parties on the positions of other parties is concerned, this amounts essentially to the possible effect of the Greens (and conceivably the PDS) on the left wing of the SPD, and that of the Republikaner on the right wing of the CDU/CSU. The SPD left, for a start, is vastly more susceptible to the ideas of the Greens than to those of the PDS: in fact, among many features which the PDS shares with the KPD (Communist Party of Germany) of the Weimar Republic, a generally bad relationship with the SPD features prominently. We thus have to consider mainly the influence on the SPD of the foreign policy ideas of the Green party: a stress on disarmament, Third World development and non-military approaches to European security. There is no doubt that there are overlaps and affinities between the Greens and the SPD: during the cold war period – and notably from 1982 to 1983, when the SPD split on the issue of tactical nuclear missiles and the party majority under Hans Jochen Vogel fought the 1983 election in opposition to the stationing of new missiles in Germany – many in the SPD have shown sympathy with the Greens' generally pacifist position. In the new situation of the 1990s, the issues have changed considerably, but not totally. Although the SPD's official view on defence policy (including possible 'out of area' operations) is now becoming ever closer to that of the governing coalition, there have been indications that the party might hesitate to maintain this position, especially in a crisis. In most parts of Germany the SPD is in competition with the Greens for the critical few per cent of voters which would allow it to overtake the CDU (the main exception to this is the area of the former GDR, where the SPD's main competitor is now the PDS): this inevitably means that the SPD is to some extent tempted to try to woo Green voters by adopting at least some 'atmospheric' components of the Green programme. As noted above, this has not affected the basic position of the SPD, but circumstances might occur in which it would. We shall return to this point.

When we turn to the other end of the political spectrum, and consider the ways in which the CDU/CSU's foreign policy may currently be influenced by the existence of forces further to the right, the evidence is at the same time very diverse and, on one point, quite precise. The first part of this statement refers to the way in which, ever since the Wende – the 'turning-point' symbolized by Kohl's appointment as chancellor in 1982 – the moderate right which he represents has often found it prudent to speak in patriotic and even near-nationalist tones in order to prevent support going to the true nationalists further to the right. All through the debates about Western defence in the early eighties, the significance of the 'historians' quarrel' about Hitler, the relations between the two Germanies while the wall still stood and the definition of German interests after reunification ('German interests' itself being a phrase much more frequently heard than before), the CDU/CSU and the press friendly to it, notably the *Frankfurter Allgemeine Zeitung*, have expressed positions clearly motivated in part by this consideration.

The Right Parties

The much more precise and concrete part of the story refers to the way in which Bavaria's CSU, faced with a challenge from the 'extreme' right Republicans (a party essentially based in Bavaria), deliberately set about defending itself by employing, among other means, a nationalistic rhetoric which at times even went beyond the terms associated with its first great leader, Franz Josef Strauss. After the shock of the European elections of 1989, when the Republicans won 14.6 per cent of the vote with a basically nationalist programme, the CSU leadership adopted a line of strident defence of German national interests against the unacceptable pretensions of Brussels: by 1993 the Bavarian party leader and minister President Eduard Stoiber was being compared, in his anti-European rhetoric, to Margaret Thatcher. His efforts appear to have contributed to the desired result: in the three critical elections in Bavaria in 1994, the Republican vote was reduced to 6.6 per cent in the European elections in June (not enough to win any seats when averaged out nationally), 3.9 per cent in the Landtag election in September, and 2.8 per cent in the Bundestag election in October. At the same time, the anti-EU tone and content of Bavaria's political discourse was certainly reflected in those passages of the Kohl–Waigel–Kinkel Coalition Agreement, quoted above, which pledged Bonn's new government to fight more strongly for Germany's financial interests in Brussels, to resist the transfer of new powers to the EU and to demand restoration of some already transferred. It is of course not clear how far this sort of argument, and related ones, will be taken in the future.

If we now turn to the other major question about the influence of the 'extreme' forces, that of their hypothetical say in German policy-making if they were ever to be appointed to ministerial office, this clearly must be answered in terms of a possible left-wing coalition, since a right-wing coalition including the Republicans seems unthinkable. As noted above, we are envisaging essentially the possible inclusion of the Greens in a coalition government with the SPD. Although it is true that the PDS is present as a substantial and apparently growing force in the Eastern part of Germany, its status as a direct heir of the discredited SED makes it untouchable as a coalition partner: the readiness of the SPD in Saxony-Anhalt merely to accept the parliamentary support of the PDS for a minority government, after a deadlocked Landtag election in June 1994, was deeply controversial, and is unlikely to form a precedent.

As for the Greens, there has been speculation ever since the late 1980s that they might one day enter a coalition government in Bonn, either in a bilateral partnership with the SPD (of the kind which governed Lower Saxony from 1990 to 1994 and is still currently in office in Hessen), or in the so-called 'traffic-light' combination including the FDP as well (thus green, red and yellow) which has been seen in Bremen and in Brandenburg. These experiences of governmental participation by the Greens at the Land level, however, tell us little about what their influence might be on the foreign policy of a federal government of which they might one day form part. As far as these things can be judged, it would appear virtually certain that the Greens, in the scenario we are considering, would be very much the junior partners in any conceivable coalition. Their presence in government would certainly imply a Coalition Agreement with a somewhat different wording from that of the 1994 version quoted above – whether or not the FDP was a party to it as well as the SPD – but the likely changes in the ensuing substance of German foreign policy might not be very perceptible. All that can be done at this stage is to register the possibility of this particular change as one that might introduce a new element into the politics of German foreign policy in the future.

CONCLUSION

This brief discussion has only been able to consider the impact of domestic politics on German foreign policy in a selective way. Among the many important themes which have been omitted, the international role of the German party-political foundations named after Adenauer, Ebert and Naumann, for instance, would deserve a chapter to itself.[22] However, the main sources of domestic political influences on foreign policy have been covered by our discussion of special political interests, of coalition politics, of the power of the Länder, and of the role of the extreme wings of the political spectrum.

Foreign policy itself is evolving in ways which make it likely that the involvement of domestic political forces will continue to grow. As well as the ever-growing interdependence resulting from the globalization of economic processes, there is a marked increase in transnational interactions in fields as diverse as migration, human rights, humanitarian actions, and policies relating to sport, language-teaching and the promotion of national cultures. All these areas, and many others, lend themselves to party political controversies, and the role of domestic politics in foreign relations – particularly in a period when political alignments and alliances in Germany are becoming less predictable – is likely to be much more significant than in the Federal Republic which the world has known hitherto.

NOTES

1. *Koalitionsabkommen für die 13. Legislaturperiode des Deutschen Bundestages,* Bonn, 11 November 1994.
2. The results of all the numerous German elections held in 1994 are conveniently presented in *Documents: Revue des Questions Allemandes* 5, 1994. All figures given here are from this source.
3. The main dimensions of German foreign policy are surveyed in the author's chapter 'Germany in the New Europe', in C. Crouch and D. Marquand (Eds), *Towards Greater Europe?* (Oxford, 1992).
4. Ludger Kühnhardt, 'Wertgrundlagen der deutschen Aussenpolitik', in Karl Kaiser and Hanns W. Maull (Eds), *Deutschlands Neue Aussenpolitik. Band 1: Grundlagen* (München, 1994), on p. 121.
5. Beverly Crawford, 'German Foreign Policy After the Cold War: The Decision to Recognise Croatia' (Working Paper of the Center for German and European Studies), University of California at Berkeley, August 1993, p. 15.
6. Ibid., p. 17.
7. Quoted in Mark Almond, *Europe's Backyard War: the War in the Balkans* (London, 1991), pp. 237–8.
8. Crawford, 'German Foreign Policy', p. 17.
9. Ibid.
10. As well as the study by Crawford, see Harald Müller, 'German Foreign Policy after Unification', in Paul Stares (Ed.), *The New Germany in the New Europe* (Washington, DC, 1991), esp. pp. 150–4, and Hans-Jürgen Axt, 'Hat Genscher Jugoslavien entzweit?: Mythen und Fakten zur Aussenpolitik des vereinten Deutschlands', *Europa-Archiv* 12, 1993, pp. 351–60.
11. Vogel's speech quoted in Crawford, 'German Foreign Policy' p. 17. On Schumacher's clash with Adenauer, see the latter's *Erinnerungen 1945–1953* (Frankfurt, 1967), p. 279.
12. Crawford, 'German Foreign Policy', p. 32 (Kohl's speech) and p. 26 (German opinion poll).
13. T. Garton Ash, *In Europe's Name* (London, 1993), p. 608.
14. See Strauss's *Die Erinnerungen* (Berlin, 1989), esp. pp. 297–334.
15. T. Garton Ash, *In Europe's Name,* p. 99.
16. See Werner A. Perger, 'Auf der Lauer', in *Die Zeit,* 3 March 1995.
17. Ibid.
18. Quoted in the author's chapter 'Political and institutional implications for the European Community', in W. Heisenberg (Ed.), *German Unification in European Perspective* (London, 1991), at pp. 97–8.
19. See R. Hrbek and S. Weyand, *Das Europa der Regionen* (München, 1994), esp. pp. 82–91.
20. See R. Morgan in W. Heisenberg, op. cit., pp. 99–104.
21. See R. Morgan and T. Christiansen, *Germany in the New Europe* (Oxford, forthcoming, 1997), chapter 2.
22. One of the few studies of this subject is M. Pinto-Duschinsky, 'Foreign political aid: the German political foundations and their US counterparts', *International Affairs,* Jan. 1991, pp. 33–63.

BIBLIOGRAPHY

Adenauer, *Erinnerungen 1945–1953* (Frankfurt: Fischer, 1967).

Almond, Mark, *Europe's Backyard War: the War in the Balkans* (London: Heinemann, 1991).

Ash, T. Garton, *In Europe's Name* (London: Cape, 1993).

Axt, Hans-Jürgen, 'Hat Genscher Jugoslavien entzweit?: Mythen und Fakten zur Aussenpolitik des vereinten Deutschlands', *Europa-Archiv* 12, 1993.

Crawford, Beverly, 'German Foreign Policy After the Cold War: The Decision to Recognise Croatia' (Working Paper of the Center for German and European Studies, University of California at Berkeley, August, 1993).

Documents: Revue des Questions Allemandes 5, 1994.

Hrbek, R. and S. Weyand, *Das Europa der Regionen* (München: Beck, 1994).

Koalitionsabkommen für die 13. Legislaturperiode des Deutschen Bundestages, Bonn, 11 November 1994.

Kühnhardt, Ludger, 'Wertgrundlagen der deutschen Aussenpolitik', in Karl Kaiser and Hanns W. Maull (Eds), *Deutschlands Neue Aussenpolitik. Band 1: Grundlagen* (München: Oldenbourg, 1994).

Morgan, Roger, 'Political and institutional implications for the European Community', in W. Heisenberg (Ed.), *German Unification in European Perspective* (London: Brassey's, 1991).

Morgan, Roger, 'Germany in the New Europe', in C. Crouch and D. Marquand (Eds), *Towards Greater Europe?* (Oxford, 1992).

Morgan, R. and T. Christiansen, *Germany's Role in the New Europe* (Oxford: OUP, forthcoming, 1997).

Müller, Harald, 'German Foreign Policy after Unification', in Paul Stares (Ed.), *The New Germany in the New Europe* (Washington, DC: Brookings, 1991).

Perger, Werner A., 'Auf der Lauer', *Die Zeit*, 3 March 1995.

Pinto-Duschinsky, M., 'Foreign political aid: the German political foundations and their US counterparts', *International Affairs*, Jan. 1991.

Strauss, *Die Erinnerungen* (Berlin: Siedler, 1989).

Part III: Policy Towards Germany

7 The Impact of German Unification on German–American Relations: Alliance, Estrangement or Partnership?

Lily Gardner Feldman

German–American relations since 1949 have displayed a remarkable, even astonishing continuity... US–German harmony was the result of, or at least coincided with, a world in port, not one at sea. Powerful anchors made sure that whatever the relative role or power of both countries, they could not drift apart... But the anchors, that were dug so firmly into the ocean bed, are dragging today. The flood is rising and the world is at sea. Can Germany and the United States, once stuck together, now float together?[1]

Christoph Bertram captures the central issues confronting analysts of the post-unification German–American dyad. Whether dealing explicitly with German–American relations or implicitly through extrapolating from German foreign policy in general, there have been three main American responses to the question of the relationship's seaworthiness.[2] They all share a recognition of the defining role the USA played in German unification,[3] but differ regarding five dimensions:

1. structural attributes (the degree of continuity and change; conceptions of German and American power; linkage between the bilateral relationship and the larger environment);
2. motivations (the relationship between domestic and international factors);
3. actors (governmental vs. non-governmental; homogeneous vs. heterogeneous);

4. content (functional areas of involvement; high vs. low politics; cooperation vs. competition);
5. trajectory of the relationship (optimism vs. pessimism).

This essay compares and contrasts the two more traditional conceptions of dyadic relations, alliance and estrangement, and then argues for a widening of the third lens through which German–American relations are viewed today: the partnership notion to which President Clinton alluded in his July 1994 characterization of the relationship as 'truly unique'.[4] Policy implications of the partnership approach are also drawn.

A THREATENED ALLIANCE

The first image is the traditional pragmatists' conception of German–American relations as an alliance. Not all the adherents to this view of German–American ties explicitly use the concept of 'alliance', but they all subscribe one way or another to the traditional definition offered by Holsti, Hopmann and Sullivan: 'a formal agreement between two or more nations to collaborate on national security issues'.[5] They exhibit different degrees of conviction, from mild to strong, but are joined in a realist perspective highlighting fundamental changes – in the international system, German and American power, and interests – that have attended German unification.

Change, Power and Interest

Stephen Szabo's analysis exemplifies a mild form of the alliance perspective. He proceeds from the assumption that 'there can be no doubt that the continuities of the cold war are gone and a fundamentally new German–American relationship will emerge after the transition period'.[6] The glue of the alliance, the external Soviet threat, has dissipated, and with it the 'strategic partnership' and 'security imperative' between Washington and Bonn, and Germany's dependence on the USA.

In this new setting, the projection of US power is

constrained by preoccupation with internal affairs and a con-
comitant effort to devolve power and responsibility 'to Germany as the leading power in Europe'.[7] Germany is
characterized as having the potential, but not yet the political will, to define and implement its national interests which
had largely been submerged before unification in the dominance of Moralpolitik over Realpolitik. The new Germany's
primary national interest is couched in classical realist terms:

> Germany has as its preeminent objective the need to avoid
> being forced back into a balance of power system as that
> which characterized Europe before both World Wars. Any
> revival of such a system would lead to counter alliances
> to German power and result in the encirclement of Ger-
> many and the revival of suspicion of German power and
> motives.[8]

Germany's commitment to European integration and the
Franco-German couple is essential for German security, and
'stabilization' to the East is not far behind. The need for
American power in Europe is seen in similar balance-of-power
terms. Germany's various interests are seen as more competing with one another than complementary.

The notion of Germany as a 'normal power' is central to
the alliance perspective. Even though Germany may still
exhibit some reluctance, it has begun the process of 'geopolitical normalization'. There is a prescriptive element also
to this school of thought, based on the assumption, using a
traditional military yardstick, that Germany did not pull its
full weight in the past, for example in the Gulf War: 'Part
of this normalization means that Germany must become a
responsible power which must help shape a structure for
peace and security and order in Europe, including the use
of force when necessary to maintain stability.'[9]

An unambiguous alliance perspective is offered by William
Odom, who describes the new environment for German–
American relations as a 'fundamental reordering of the
postwar system' that 'brings Washington back to the central
problems of this century: coping with rising German and
Japanese power, and checking Soviet ambitions'.[10] Defining
Germany's interests in traditional security terms, Odom posits
three options: 'going it alone, alliance with Russia, or alliance

with the United States'.[11] Never even entertaining a fourth, European option, he argues for the third course: a reformed NATO is the only conceivable choice for the USA and Germany. Yet, he is concerned about 'the unpredictable character of German nationalism'[12] which could lead Germany into 'going it alone'.

The sense of threat to the German–American relationship due to an excess of German power is what distinguishes Odom's traditional alliance perspective from Szabo's milder variant that sees the threat from an insufficient articulation of German power and leadership.

Actors, Motives and Activity

Both Szabo and Odom look to public opinion as bell-wethers for Germany's power proclivities, but find different realities and draw different conclusions. Consistent with traditional alliance thinking, Odom neglects completely other dimensions of the domestic environment that Szabo's analysis embraces. Nonetheless, while recognizing the reality of unification's economic demands and the vestiges of a pre-unification 'aversion to power politics', Szabo still views German domestic factors (and American) as a brake on German–American relations, not as a motor. He predicts a path of commercial rivalry in trade and monetary issues (without making the detailed connection between domestic need and international economic behaviour) rather than partnership.

These two realist variants are readily discernible in other analyses of German–American relations and one can also find analogues in assessments of German foreign policy and of Germany's role in Europe. Different analysts may choose to emphasize and elaborate particular concepts – 'normalization', 'geostrategy', 'Grand Strategy', 'national interest' – or particular challenges – Western Europe, Eastern Europe, Russia, Ukraine, denuclearization – but they share basic assumptions about unification representing a caesura in the German–American alliance, about the primacy of the NATO framework for German–US relations, about the growth in Germany's power potential, and a pessimistic outlook for the relationship if Germany declines, or seeks too vigorously, or is refused, realization of this potential for power, influence and responsibility.[13]

THE DANGER OF ESTRANGEMENT

This image predicts that the USA and Germany will grow apart, becoming either indifferent to one another or rivals. The burden of analysis in the second image of German–American relations rests on economic factors. While an assumption of Germany and/or the USA turning inward as a result of domestic economic challenges informed both the mild and strong alliance images, it was a secondary factor. Here economic conditions are the starting point for characterizations of the relationship.

Just as our first image was bifurcated by the perception of Germany as strong or weak, in this image of estrangement[14] there are milder and stronger variants distinguished by assessments of Germany's economic prowess. Whether Germany is inward-looking because of unification and increasingly indifferent to the USA on economic issues or outward-looking and asserting its power internationally as an economic rival to the USA, both variants entail a process of estrangement. And, as in the first image, there are analogues in analyses of German foreign policy in general and Germany's role in Europe, particularly in discussions of the concept of hegemony.[15]

The analyses of James Sperling and Robert Hormats illustrate the first, milder variant, while Jeffrey Garten and Richard Smyser represent the stronger form of economic image.

Continuity: The Primacy of Economics

While not denying at all the force of geopolitical change stressed by alliance advocates, in both branches of this school there emerges a greater sense of continuity for economic issues, with respect to their primacy internally for Germany and their perpetual potential as vexant or irritant in German–American relations. Sperling, for example, notes that the gargantuan burden of reconstructing Eastern Germany 'has produced a German foreign economic policy that has become *more* "national" in the calculation of interest; *more* brittle and inflexible in both content and execution'.[16] Both Sperling and Hormats couch their descriptions of the divergences between a weakened Germany and the USA (over exchange rates, interest rates, trade and general macro-economic policy) in terms of a ripening of tensions that pre-date unification. In detailing a 1991 episode of German intransigence in response to US pressure to lower interest rates, Hormats notes: 'This was but the latest example of a long-standing proclivity of the U.S. and Germany to hector one another on proper economic policy'.[17] Similarly, Garten was initially provoked before unification into his extended discussion of American, German and Japanese economic rivalry out of a sense among Americans 'that a crisis was brewing'.[18]

For all these analysts, the manifestation of German economic purposes divergent from those of the USA (or of other European countries) has clearly changed with unification, and, as Smyser suggests, their consequences are 'much more serious',[19] but the presence of national economic interests is hardly new.

Germany's Economic Power

In the view of Sperling and Hormats, the indelible consequence of unification for the transatlantic economy has been a weakened and less flexible Germany facing huge transfer payments to the East, large budget deficits and growing inflationary pressures. The USA faces its own economic challenges. Garten and Smyser concur with this assessment for the short term but, in comparing German and American power for the medium and long term, anticipate an ascendant Germany. Smyser points to an increase in 'German economic power and influence' and its impact on German–American relations:

> The most dangerous moment in any relationship is when a mutually-recognized and long-established balance of power between the partners shifts, especially if its shifts precipitately. Unification brought about such a shift in the German–American balance in the space of a year. Although Germany's weight in the relationship had been growing

for decades, neither the German nor the American government were prepared for the suddenness and the size of the shift. They have not yet adjusted to it.[20]

Garten is even more certain that 'there is no dispute about the growth of German power':

> [The] enormous expense of making unification work may well cause a pause in the nation's development as a major power, not only because of the preoccupation with domestic issues. But within several years, Germany is likely to emerge much stronger than it would otherwise have been – with a larger territory, a source of eager workers anxious to make up for lost time, and a new and spirited nationalism born of being a whole nation again.[21]

Actors, Activity and Outcomes

Alliance analysts set German–American relations in the larger context of NATO and transatlantic connections. In the estrangement image, the reference point is US–EU relations and the G7 framework. Garten and Smyser broaden the focus even further by embracing a global economic perspective, including the role of Japan. Their definition of internal actors is equally broad, sharing the Hormats and Sperling reference to the government and the Bundesbank, but also incorporating German firms' motives and behaviour. Garten includes various elements of German society, from educators to unions, in his development of an inextricable link between foreign and domestic policies.

Both sets of analysts describe tense economic relations between Germany and the USA. The milder form of German behaviour is relative indifference to the USA. Highlighting the self-absorption with domestic economic challenges, Sperling concludes that

> the external consequences of German domestic economic policy, ranging from the impact upon the level of interest rates to the level of economic activity in the rest of Europe and North America to exchange rate stability, appear to be at best of secondary interest to the Germans.[22]

Hormats offers an even more graphic formulation of indifference:

> In 1990 and 1991 relations between Germany and the U.S.
> were like those between two orchestras simultaneously play-
> ing different symphonies in the same concert hall, each
> so preoccupied with its own performance that it could
> scarcely make out, much less appreciate, the music of the
> other.[23]

The economic policy differences between Germany and the
USA adumbrated by Sperling and Hormats take on monu-
mental form in the analysis of Garten and Smyser, both of
whom posit markedly divergent economic philosophies and
practices that were kept in check during the cold war but
are now free to roam. Global competition, a concern with
competitiveness (that links internal economic and social
policies and potential to international position) and rivalry
are, then, the appropriate characteristics of the relationship.
The danger of separate futures is imminent for Smyser:

> The coordination of German–American economic policy,
> whether on trade or monetary issues, thus looms as a thorny
> and probably contentious question that will complicate
> relations continually and probably increasingly . . . Bonn,
> Frankfurt, and Washington need to find some kind of agree-
> ment, for in economic policy there can be no truly sepa-
> rate path. The temptation to find one may be great, but
> it does not truly exist.[24]

In Garten's thinking, separation already exists at one level,
as both the title and subtitle of his book, *A Cold Peace: America,
Japan, Germany, and the Struggle for Supremacy,* indicate. Rivalry, including 'for the allegiance of other nations in Latin
America, Eastern Europe, and Southeast Asia', is real but
not, however, absolute, in part because of the many other
non-economic aspects of relations and some modicum of
common economic interests:

> Tokyo and Berlin . . . are becoming neither pure partners
> nor pure rivals but a combination of both . . . We can no
> longer divide our world into good and evil. It's a crucial
> ambiguity we will have to learn to live with.[25]

As under-secretary of commerce for international trade in the Clinton administration, Garten muted the language of rivalry, but it is by no means absent:

> But perhaps worst of all is the conflict that can arise among competing industrial countries... It is easy to imagine the hard feelings that could emerge, for example between the United States and Germany in competing for major projects in China or Brazil. This rivalry of government inducements could undercut the cooperation we need in order to be able to continue to advance a common agenda of more open trade. It could easily strain foreign policy and security cooperation as well.[26]

Whether the process of estrangement is deemed incipient or entrenched, there is some hope for its derailment through a vigorous effort at transatlantic and global institution-building and enforcement, although the degree of optimism clearly differs between the milder and stronger branches of this approach, particularly on the question of leadership capacity.[27] The challenge all recognize in the German–American case of finding the appropriate balance between the reality of national economic diversity and the need for international agreement meshes well with the larger conceptual deliberations of scholars such as Miles Kahler who poses alternative political economy models for the post-cold war era,[28] of which German unification is obviously a vital part.

THE PROMISE OF PARTNERSHIP

The two images outlined above, alliance and estrangement, present different perspectives on the nature and robustness of German–American relations. Each of them usefully captures a slice of reality but, as partial foci, they inevitably ignore or downplay other dimensions of the relationship. The third image of partnership incorporates aspects of the other two images, but treads beyond a synthesis or reconciliation between contending views. It attempts a comprehensive, yet diverse, rendition of the relationship that gets to both the clarity and ambiguity of ties. The chief example of this approach appears in Daniel Hamilton's *Beyond Bonn:*

America and the Berlin Republic, a result of a Carnegie Endowment Study Group on Germany.[29]

A milder form of the partnership perspective characterizes Elizabeth Pond's analyses in which the degree of complexity and diversity in the relationship is less than in
Hamilton's treatment.[30] Analogues are present in re-exami-
nations of German foreign policy, particularly in discussions
of muted power, and a similar partnership framework has
also been employed to explain Germany's role in Europe.[31]

Continuity and Change in Purpose and Power

Whereas the alliance conception of German–American relations focuses on a sea change accompanying German unification, partnership – like the estrangement framework –
involves continuity and change in the wake of unification
as the 'nation that used to embody Europe's division finds
itself once more *das Land in der Mitte*':

> As the Berlin Republic's policy profile emerges, deep con-
> tinuities bind it to the highly successful structures of the
> Bonn republic . . . But to assume that the Berlin Republic
> will be the Bonn Republic writ large ignores the dynamic
> forces shaping a new democratic Germany. In fundamen-
> tal ways the Berlin Republic is similar to its predecessor.
> But it finds itself in a profoundly different situation.[32]

Identifying a clear growth in German power, the partnership school chooses to focus on greater symmetry with the
USA rather than the under-utilization of power (alliance)
or rivalry (estrangement). In Elizabeth Pond's words, the
old constraint of inequality has disappeared, but past patterns of behaviour remain:

> Rewriting the American–German and Euro-Atlantic secu-
> rity bargain in the post-wall era, then, should be the easi-
> est part of Europe's task in the 1990s. We have the habit
> of cooperation; we are enriched by it; and the United
> States will profit in this decade from having an equal ally,
> finally, in the new Europe.[33]

The larger reference point for those who emphasize German–American relations as an alliance was Europe, particularly

NATO. In the second image, the EU, the G7 and Japan constituted the larger framework. The partnership approach combines all of these elements and adds the OSCE as an important vehicle for German–US interaction, in part because of its very broad conception of security that combines traditional 'high politics' and newer 'low politics' definitions of security.

Unlike the first approach where there is some fear that US disengagement from Europe might be accompanied by greater involvement in Asia, and the second approach which envisions potential clashes between US–European and Japanese–US relations, partnership with Europe is not exclusive and the 'pivotal' bilateral partnership can 'act as a motor for multilateral purposes'.[34]

A new sense of ownership of power by a united Germany does not imply the sudden discovery of national interest as in the first image, nor does it concentrate today mainly on economic interests as in the second. Rather as a basis for partnership with the USA, it is a power that is both mindful of Germany's past and cognizant of the new demands of the future. Like the estrangement school, the partnership approach accepts that at times in the past Germany championed vigorously its interests, while at others it waffled assiduously. Germany has displayed, then, both in the past and since unification, a capacity for realism and responsibility.[35]

The Stimulus of Domestic Challenges

A similar sense of balance, which undoubtedly has to be recalibrated for a new era and a new context, is also to be found between the domestic and international environments. Instead of being a strait-jacket as in the first image (and part of the second), domestic challenges can act as a spur to the relationship through a process of mutual learning:

> Collaboration on domestic challenges provides the material for new coalitions. On a range of issues facing each country, such as health care reform, jobs, training workers, fighting drugs and organized crime, coping with immigration and dealing with the possibilities and problems of multicultural societies, there are opportunities to

compare different national experiences ... Strengthening
the German–American partnership begins at home ... domestic renewal is urgent and self-evident. It is an essential foundation for, not an alternative to, an active foreign
policy.[36]

Hamilton envisages new coalitions between Germany and
the USA in a broad range of areas.[37] In addition to traditional foreign policy actors at the national level (the first
image) and multiple contacts at the societal level (the second image), here priority is given to US states and German
Länder which have critical roles to play in the development
of economic ties between the two countries and in the resolution of a broader agenda of transnational issues from drugs
to the environment. There is also a need to give new impetus to the many institutionalized ties across societies, to
resupply the networks forming the undergrowth of the
relationship. For the new German–American societal coalitions particular emphasis is accorded the inclusion of Eastern
Germans who have only cameo roles in the first two images,
and then only in terms of their domestic economic plight.

Confrontation and Cooperation

Variegated actors mean multiple activity which appears in
this image as both confrontation and cooperation:

Recent bilateral tensions over the Gulf war, Bosnia, Iran,
interest rates and trade negotiations underscore the point.
Germany and the United States have different needs, obligations, and perspectives. There is potential for German–
American disagreement over China, the Middle East,
peacekeeping missions, monetary matters or investment
rules ... But the interests that coincide are weightier than
those that do not. The context for U.S. relations with Europe may have changed but bedrock American interests
in Europe endure.[38]

While recognizing the role of domestic and international
change in the five years since unification, Hamilton still finds
sufficient German–American societal, bureaucratic and policy
anchors to keep the relationship afloat. There is greater

optimism than in the other two images, especially if the two countries can strategically design the relationship's renewal (not starting over as in the alliance under threat, or an uphill battle as in the growing gulf between strangers). Germany and the USA can remain 'pivotal partners, both to each other and to the international order' if they refashion in strategic terms three key elements of the relationship: a new security bargain (bilaterally, institutionally and in the East); a new economic bargain (taking full cognizance of the EU's role); and a new environmental bargain (gripping by the horns old problems, openly anticipating new ones).

The prescription of continued partnership offers a broader conception of the relationship than the other two alternatives. It also conforms in many respects to the concept of the 'special relationship', including the 'foundations', 'operation' and 'endurance' aspects.[39] Contrary to popular belief, a 'special relationship' is not defined by harmony. It seeks cooperative and privileged relations over a broad panoply of policy ties (of which military security is but one), yet does not ignore conflict. Indeed, there are significant political and economic tensions between the USA and Germany – for example over barriers to US involvement in the electric power generation sector in Germany, and over Germany's intelligence and trade relations with Iran but they are balanced by cooperative relations.[40]

The hallmark of a special relationship is an ability to overcome crisis. This will depend upon the strength and resilience of institutional ties (both governmental and non-governmental), the shock absorbers that permit dialogue, resolution and anticipation of future problems. They may not be entirely visible in the German–American relationship now, but neither are they absent.[41] Rather, they have been obscured because of the tendency to zero in on the 'high politics' cooperative political and military aspects of the relationship or one element of 'low politics', namely conflict-laden trade dimensions. It is these other elements of the relationship, in policy and in society, that the Clinton administration is using as the raw material to renovate the German–American partnership and that Germans have long recognized as essential features of constructing regional and international cooperation.[42]

Public opinion in both countries is solidly supportive of German–American relations (75 per cent of Germans express pro-American sentiments; 66 per cent of Americans deem Germany a place of vital interest for the USA); while opinion in both countries attaches significant interest to domestic affairs, it can also be mobilized on international questions that have perceived domestic and local impact.[43]

THE PRACTICE OF PARTNERSHIP

The Bush administration had solicited Germany in spring 1989 to create with the USA 'partners in leadership'; earlier, during the Reagan administration, Ambassador Richard Burt had called for a 'mature partnership'. Only with unification has Germany become fully sovereign in the formal sense; only with unification can Germany be perceived and treated as an equal. It is the formalization of status that constitutes 'normalization' of Germany as an international power, the capacity to exercise self-determination. It is as much the fact that it chooses freely as what Germany actually does that will define normalcy and be the basis for genuine partnership with the USA.

The 1994 Bundesverfassungsgericht's decision on out-of-area military involvement completes the formal 'liberation' of Germany with regard to power. Germans and Americans both recognize the deeply internalized post-war value of restraint that will pose a psychological and practical brake on the unfettered use of miltary force, but this hardly precludes partnership. Indeed, Germany's June 1995 decision to alter precedent by using armed force outside the NATO area, in the form of air power (not ground forces) for the UN Rapid Reaction Force in Bosnia (as well as hospital personnel and logistical support), demonstrates its ability to combine voluntary action and historical constraint, while at the same time satisfying the USA. The indelible imprint of the Third Reich and the Holocaust are, of course, unique, yet, in its own way, the USA is also constrained militarily today by its past, that of the Vietnam War.

If one accepts that the old concept of sovereignty is no longer valid for any actor in the international system, having been 'perforated' innumerable times from every direction,[44] then one approaches an essential ingredient for German–US leadership in the post-cold war era: the fact that Germany and the USA are equally semi-sovereign, to use Pater Katzenstein's term.[45] The old concept of leadership, where problems, resources and choices were often clear and frequently implied American unilateralism, no longer obtains. Leadership now means the recognition of ambiguity and complexity, the honesty to transmit uncertain outcomes to publics before action, the recognition that burden-sharing rather than unilateralism is the only means. It requires a more realistic assessment of needs and resources such that countries like the USA and Germany do not succumb to the 'illusion of power' abroad (Senator Fulbright's term for the Vietnam era) or the ire of constituencies at home whose expectations have been raised far too high. Both National Security Adviser Anthony Lake and Foreign Minister Klaus Kinkel rhetorically, at least, seem to recognize the requirements.[46]

Neither the USA nor Germany has the capacity or the desire for singular leadership, whether regionally or internationally, but jointly, perhaps, there is some possibility of managing uncertainty, avoiding complete crisis or at least anticipating the consequences of failure. Each of those alternatives may render 'leadership' an unglamorous concept, but, as Jeffrey Garten has argued, it fits the messiness of the post-cold war era. Since 1993, and particularly since January 1994, both the USA and Germany have begun speaking and acting as revived partners. Until President Clinton's July 1994 trip to Bonn and Berlin, this was often done without fanfare but, as in other special relationships, what goes on in private defines the relationship as much as, if not more than, what proceeds under the public's glare. The content of that revival is important, but so are the consequences.

THE CONTENT AND CONSEQUENCES OF GERMAN–AMERICAN PARTNERSHIP

Content

For all the complaints about the absence of a policy focus in the external relations of Germany and the USA, or the fears that both are more interested in Asia, in fact a sense of purpose has been outlined on both sides of the Atlantic concerning German–American relations and, judging by trans-atlantic travel alone, the German–US relationship is a priority for both countries. Speeches by German and American leaders since 1993 share a number of features: identification of mutual needs, whether in the military (conventional and nuclear), economic (trade and investment) or trans-national (drugs, migration, environment) arenas; recognition of policy differences across the same areas (for example, Iran); reference to the common basis of federal systems; awareness of similar domestic challenges; celebration of the richness and depth of institutionalized societal ties.[47] In his call for a revival on the basis of 'commerce, culture, and commitment', then Ambassador Holbrooke summed up the challenges and the opportunities:

> [The] military component of the relationship no longer must cast so large a shadow over other dimensions of our partnership. The end of the Cold War liberated the German–American relationship from the need to focus narrowly on a common external threat. We are free to move beyond the armed truce of the Cold War to build a more durable peace in Europe ... We are free to press more vigorously for other common objectives: advancing prosperity and social justice at home, human rights, freedom, and market reforms abroad. Whereas the Cold War forced us to join forces to face a common external threat, the post-Cold War world offers us the opportunity to base our partnership less on external threats than on the common challenges facing our societies. Now that the time has come again to put the German–American partnership on a new footing, we can build on the habit of cooperation we developed during the Cold War without being limited by

it. We can and should devote attention to the security dimension without being consumed by it. And we can discover new affinities by rediscovering far older ones . . .[48]

In mutual learning both across the two societies and in areas of common foreign policy, rhetoric, plan and purpose are beginning to be matched by reality. The choices the two countries make at home will affect the form and quality of their bilateral relationship and the scope and purpose of their joint and international endeavours in the next decades. In addition to the growth in scholarly literature that draws comparison between the public policies of the two countries, policy debates in each country in key areas such as health care and industrial relations make reference to the other country. The US General Accounting Office, for example, has issued several reports on the German health care system and has examined the long-term care (Pflegeversicherung) debate in Germany.[49] The Commission on the Future of Worker–Management Relations, appointed by the White House and chaired by former Labor Secretary John Dunlop, drew on the German experience in highlighting the role of works councils.[50] The lessons are by no means one-way. German economics officials and industrial leaders point to the flexibility and innovativeness of the American labour market.[51]

Not all efforts to elicit understanding fare as well, as Germany witnessed in Washington with respect to the Berlin Document Center, the exhibition 'Against Hitler: German Resistance to National Socialism, 1933–45' and the restitution claim against Germany of the American citizen Hugo Princz.

The relationship has managed to overcome some key differences in the foreign policy realm. In the final analysis, Germany and the USA together provided leadership in the conclusion of the GATT Uruguay Round and the implementation of the Partnership for Peace. There has been coordination with respect to East-Central Europe and the former Soviet Union, combining strengths of resources and experience and jointly shouldering the risk of failure. On both Bosnia (the Bosnia–Hercegovina federation, the Contact Group, the arms embargo) and NATO enlargement,

Germany has been the lone EU country to appreciate consistently the American position and to offer active support wherever possible.[52]

Consequences

Even though Clinton used the term 'unique partnership' to avoid the exclusivity of the 'special relationship', there was still British concern about being isolated and passed over.[53] The danger that 'special relationships' or 'pivotal partnerships' are exclusive is real, as the German–American dyad amply demonstrated in June 1993 when the USA and Germany agreed (in the framework of the 1954 Friendship, Commerce, and Navigation Treaty) not to apply sanctions to one another in the US–EU dispute over government procurement of telecommunications equipment.[54]

The emphasis by both Kohl and Clinton on the need for European integration and their joint press conference with President Delors following the July 1994 US–EU summit in Berlin indicated a desire to be inclusive. The pace of US–EU institutionalization of ties since the beginning of the Clinton administration is another reflection of sensitivity to the appearance of choosing among Europeans; it also demonstrates a growing American acceptance of the EU as an international economic, political and security actor.[55] Already in 1992 and 1993, German political and business leaders conceived of the German–American relationship as a crucial circle to be embraced by a larger circle, the revitalized European–US relationship intimately connected to the larger international system. By the spring of 1995, this vision was repeated in greater detail by the German foreign minister and defence minister, and echoed by the American secretary of state and the American ambassador to Germany.[56] And Germany can still be singled out for special attention, as President Clinton emphasized during Chancellor Kohl's February 1995 visit: 'America has no better friend.'[57]

The linkage between the US–EU relationship and German–American ties, coupled with the priority in both fora and in Franco-German councils given to coordinated and joint action in Central and Eastern Europe, flies in the face of the prediction made by Timothy Garton Ash about the necessity of Germany to choose among its 'four options' for foreign policy priorities: deepening of the EC led by the Franco-German duo; widening the EU and NATO to embrace Eastern Europe; resuscitating the old Russo-German special relationship; and assuming the mantle of world power (in condominium with the USA).[58] While suggesting these are not 'absolute "either–or" choices', he does cast them as choices of priorities, for example, between 'the demands of [Germany's] special relationship with the United States and those of its special relationship with France'.[59] He argues that Germany cannot do all of these things, and certainly not at once. But his yardstick is the capacity of the individual nation-state, not the potential for burden-sharing offered by partnership and community.

Garton Ash's first option and the final one (at least its German–American partnership segment) have long been traditions for Germany: it is in both frameworks that Germany will be active with respect to the other two options, Central and Eastern Europe and Russia. Germany frequently made choices in the past, albeit not always with full transparence or dramatic flourish. It will continue to make choices now, as will the USA, not, hopefully, by muddling through, but by joining forces.

CONCLUSIONS: LAYERED PARTNERSHIP

In the past, and still today, Germany has been able to balance multiple identities and partnerships, even when its 'special relationships' – such as with France and Israel, or with France and the USA – were in conflict. It is now the USA that must elaborate more fully a 'layered partnership' with Germany and Europe that would include the following tiers:

1. Bilateral partnerships between the USA and individual countries, such as Germany, but also France, that must be complementary to the larger EU–US relationship in a fashion similar to the functioning of the Franco-German partnership in the context of the EU.
2. Societal partnerships that involve multiple actors in their own institutionalized arrangements, such as twinning

between cities and increasingly between regional units, as well as relations between non-governmental actors.

3. The internal partnership between the USA and the EU, involving mutual learning in areas of common concern, and mechanisms for heading off or resolving disputes.

4. External partnerships governing joint, parallel or separate US–European action in the international arena in both functional and geographic areas.

This may be a tall order for both Germany and the USA – both must work hard to prevent imbalance among the various parts, as well as bureacratic fragmentation – but it will be necessary if they are to be more than allies and want to avoid being strangers. Such a comprehensive concept of partnership is also essential if they want to pursue loftier goals than merely staying afloat. The intellectual and practical ingredients for a strengthened US–EU partnership, of which the German–American special relationship would remain a key part, have now been identified, as expressed in statements by Vice-President Leon Brittan and Secretary of State Warren Christopher in spring 1995.[60] Moving to the next stage, however, of choosing the right vehicle and implementing a new arrangement will have to await the 1996 presidential election in the USA and the Inter-Governmental Conference in the European Union. In the meantime, the German–American relationship will continue to demonstrate its capacity for change, consolidation and mutual learning, and thereby provide, in microcosmic form, a harbinger of the future US–EU relationship.[61]

NOTES

1. Christoph Bertram, 'US–German Relations in a World at Sea', *Daedalus* 121, Fall 1992, p. 119.

2. While the emphasis in this essay rests on American analysis, there is some secondary reference to German perspectives on German–American relations, on German foreign policy and on Germany's European policy.

3. This view is pervasive throughout the literature on German unifica-

tion, whether American or German, official or unofficial. Because it is undisputed and well-known, this essay does not consider the role the USA played in unification, but rather the implications unification casts on German–American relations. For comprehensive accounts of the process leading to unification, including the US role, see: Wolfgang Schäuble, *Der Vertrag. Wie ich über die deutsche Einheit verhandelte* (Stuttgart: Deutsche Verlags-Anstalt, 1991); Horst Teltschik, *329 Tage. Innenansichten der Einigung* (Berlin: Siedler, 1991); Manfred Görtemaker, *Unifying Germany, 1989–1990* (New York: St Martin's Press/Institute for EastWest Studies, 1994); Konrad H. Jarausch, *The Rush to German Unity* (New York: Oxford University Press, 1994); Elizabeth Pond, *Beyond the Wall. Germany's Road to Unification* (Washington, DC: Brookings Books, 1993); Stephen F. Szabo, *The Diplomacy of German Unification* (New York: St Martin's Press, 1992); M. Donald Hancock and Helga A. Welsh (Eds), *German Unification. Processes and Outcomes* (Boulder: Westview Press, 1994).

4. For President Clinton's remarks while in Bonn, see: *Financial Times*, 12 July 1994.

5. Ole R. Holsti, Terrence P. Hopmann and John D. Sullivan, *Unity and Disintegration in International Alliances: Comparative Studies* (New York: Wiley, 1973), p. 4.

6. See: Stephen F. Szabo, 'Unified Germany and the United States', paper presented to the SAIS/Ruhr Universität Bochum workshop, School of Advanced International Studies, The Johns Hopkins University, 7/8 July 1994, p. 1.

7. Ibid., p. 17.

8. Ibid., p. 25.

9. Ibid., pp. 23–24.

10. William E. Odom, 'The German Problem. Only Ties to America Provide the Answer', *Orbis*, Fall 1990, p. 486.

11. Ibid., p. 487.

12. Ibid., p. 489.

13. On German–US relations, see: Herman-Josef Rupieper, 'After the Cold War: The United States, Germany, and European Security', *Diplomatic History* 16, spring 1992; David S. Germroth and Rebecca J. Hudson, 'German–American Relations and the Post Cold War World', *Aussenpolitik* 43, 1, 1992.

For mild and strong realist perspectives on German foreign policy and on Germany's European policy, see: Hans-Peter Schwarz, 'Germany's National and European Interests. A Country with National Interests?', *Daedalus* 123, 2, spring 1994; Christian Hacke, 'Germany and the New Europe', in David P. Calleo and Philip H. Gordon (Eds), *From the Atlantic to the Urals. National Perspectives on the New Europe* (Arlington, VA: Seven Locks Press, 1992); Ronald D. Asmus, 'The Future of German Strategic Thinking', in Gary L. Geipel (Ed.), *Germany in a New Era* (Indianapolis: Hudson Institute, 1993); Ronald D. Asmus, 'Deutschland im Übergang. Nationales Selbstvertrauen und internationale Zurückhaltung', *Europa-Archiv* 47, Jahr 8, Folge, 25, April 1992; Wolfgang Krieger, 'Toward a Gaullist Germany? Some

Lessons from the Yugoslav Crisis', *World Policy Journal*, spring 1994; Thomas Kielinger, 'The Gulf War and the Consequences from a German Point of View', *Aussenpolitik* 42, 3, 1991; Philip H. Gordon, 'Berlin's Difficulties. The Normalization of German Foreign Policy', *Orbis*, spring 1994; Jacob Heilbrunn, 'Tomorrow's Germany', *The National Interest*, summer 1994.

The concept of 'normality' is not confined to the realist, foreign policy perspective. See, for example, an evaluation of Germany's internal character by Peter Pulzer in 'United Germany: A Normal State?', *German Politics* 3, 1, April 1994.

14. The term 'estrangement' is preferred to 'rift' because the latter implies a terminal condition whereas the former suggests a process.

15. Eckart Arnold, 'German Foreign Policy and Unification', *International Affairs* 67, 3, 1991. Michael Kreile, 'Übernimmt Deutschland eine Führungsrolle in der Europäischen Gemeinschaft?', in Werner Weidenfeld (Ed.), *Was ändert die Einheit?* (Gütersloh: Verlag Bertelsmann Stiftung, 1993). Andrei S. Markovits and Simon Reich, 'Deutschlands neues Gesicht: Über deutsche Hegemonie in Europa', *Leviathan* 1, 1992. Martin Walker, 'Overstretching Teutonia: Making the Best of the Fourth Reich', *World Policy Journal* XII, 1, spring 1995. Amity Schlaes, 'Germany's Chained Economy', *Foreign Policy*, September/October 1994. Norbert Walter, 'The Evolving German Economy: Unification, the Social Market Economy, European and Global Integration', paper presented in the series 'The New Germany in the New Europe', School of Advanced International Studies/The Johns Hopkins University, 18 April 1995.

16. James Sperling, 'German Foreign Policy after Unification: The End of Cheque Book Diplomacy?', *West European Politics* 17, 1, January 1994, p. 73, emphasis added. Compared to transatlantic relations, the degree of change seems to be far higher for Sperling in German positions regarding economic and monetary integration of the European Union where he sees a 'renationalised German economic policy' (p. 81) and 'Germany as Europe's dominant economy' (p. 73).

17. Robert D. Hormats, 'Patterns of Competition. United Germany and the United States: A New Partnership for the 1990s', in Steven Muller and Gebhard Schweigler (Eds), *From Occupation to Cooperation. The United States and Germany in a Changing World Order* (New York: W.W. Norton, 1992), p. 179.

18. Jeffrey E. Garten, *A Cold Peace. America, Japan, Germany, and the Struggle for Supremacy* (New York: Times Books/The Twentieth Century Fund, 1992), p. 5.

19. W.R. Smyser, *Germany and America. New Identities, Fateful Rift?* (Boulder: Westview Press, 1993), p. 77. See also his essay 'America and the New Germany', *German Issues*, 12 (Washington, DC: American Institute for Contemporary German Studies, 1993).

20. Smyser, op. cit., p. 124.

21. See Smyser, op. cit., p. 79; Garten, op. cit., p. 12.

22. Sperling, op. cit., p. 86.

23. Hormats, op. cit., p. 178.
24. See Smyser, op. cit., p. 84; and the section on 'Economic Philosophies and Macroeconomic Policies', pp. 74–79.
25. See Garten, op. cit., pp. 16, 19, and chapter IV, for a discussion of different economic histories.
26. Jeffrey E. Garten, 'The United States and Europe: Towards the 21st Century', remarks before the American Council on Germany, New York City, 9 March 1995 (Washington, DC: United States Department of Commerce, International Trade Administration, Office of Public Affairs), p. 21.
27. See: Sperling, op. cit., p. 93; Hormats, op. cit., p. 200; Smyser, op. cit., pp. 128–29; Garten, op. cit., chapter VII, 'The Leadership Vacuum'. As an administration official, Garten attempted to implement his ideas for European–American international economic leadership. See his 'The United States and Europe: New Opportunities, New Strategies', remarks before the European Union Committee of the US Chamber of Commerce Belgium, Brussels, 25 April 1995 (Washington, DC: Department of Commerce, International Trade Administration, Office of Public Affairs).
28. See Miles Kahler, 'Trade and Domestic Differences', in Suzanne Berger and Ronald Dore (Eds), *Convergence or Diversity? National Models of Production and Distribution in Global Economies* (Ithaca: Cornell University Press, 1995).
29. Daniel S. Hamilton, *Beyond Bonn: America and the Berlin Republic* (Washington, DC: Carnegie Endowment for International Peace, 1994).
30. See: Elizabeth Pond, *After the Wall. American Policy Toward Germany* (New York: Priority Press/The Twentieth Century Fund, 1990); Pond, *Beyond the Wall*, op. cit., chapter 17, 'Agenda for America'.
31. Karl Kaiser, 'Patterns of Partnership', in Muller and Schweigler, op. cit.. Gregor Schöllgen, 'Deutschlands neue Lage. Die USA, die Bundesrepublik Deutschland und die Zukunft des westlichen Bündnisses', *Europa-Archiv* 47, Jahr 5, Folge, 10, März 1992. Hanns W. Maull, 'Zivilmacht Bundesrepublik Deutschland. Vierzehn Thesen für eine neue deutsche Aussenpolitik', *Europa-Archiv* 47, Jahr 10, Folge 25 Mai 1992. Susanne Peters, 'Germany's Future Defense Policy: Opening Up the Option for German Power Politics', *German Politics and Society* 26, summer 1992. Clay Clemens, 'Opportunity or Obligation? Redefining Germany's Military Role Outside of NATO', *Armed Forces & Society* 19, 2, winter 1993. Wolfgang F. Schlör, 'German Security Policy', *Adelphi Paper* 277, June 1993. Jeffrey J. Anderson and John B. Goodman, 'Mars or Minerva? A United Germany in a Post-Cold War Europe', in Robert O. Keohane, Joseph S. Nye and Stanley Hoffmann (Eds), *After the Cold War. International Institutions and State Strategies in Europe, 1989–1991* (Cambridge, Mass.: Harvard University Press, 1993). Lily Gardner Feldman, 'Germany and the EC: Realism and Responsibility', in *The Annals of the American Academy of Political and Social Science* 531, January 1994. Gunther Hellmann, '"Einbindungspolitik". German Foreign Policy and the Art of Declaring "Total Peace"', paper presented at the XVIth World Congress

of the International Political Science Association, Berlin, August 1994.

32. Hamilton, op. cit., p. 13.

33. Pond, *Beyond the Wall*, op. cit., p. 268. See Kaiser, op. cit., pp. 148–149 on continuity and change.

34. Hamilton, op. cit., p. 9. For details of the scope of economic relations between the United States and Europe, see: Robin Gaster and Clyde V. Prestowitz, Jr., *Shrinking the Atlantic: Europe and the American Economy* (Washington, DC: North Atlantic Research/Economic Strategy Institute, July 1994).

35. See Hamilton, op. cit., p. 16.

36. Hamilton, op. cit., pp. 10, 23.

37. As special adviser to Ambassador Holbrooke in Bonn and subsequently as policy adviser to Assistant Secretary of State Holbrooke, Hamilton maintained the same emphasis on buttressing German and European–US ties through a variety of institutionalized societal relationships.

38. Hamilton, op. cit., p. 21.

39. On the development of the concept of the 'special relationship' and its explanatory power compared to other concepts such as alliance, interdependence, and integration, see: Lily Gardner Feldman, *The Special Relationship between West Germany and Israel* (London: Allen & Unwin, 1984).

40. Karen Donfried, 'German Foreign Policy and U.S. Interests', *CRS Report for Congress* 95–564 F, 3 May 1995 (Washington, DC: Congressional Research Service).

41. For indications, see: Ambassador Charles E. Redman, 'The United States and Germany: Sharing Values and Visions for the 21st Century', address to the Atlantik Brücke, Berlin, 14 February 1995.

42. Note, for example, that German scholars have been at the forefront of developing concepts that challenge traditional notions of international relations, whether transnationalism (Karl Kaiser), integration (Wolfgang Wessels), federalism and international relations (Franz Borkenhagen) or civilian power (Hanns Maull).

43. For German public opinion, see: Ronald D. Asmus, 'Germany's Geopolitical Maturation: Public Opinion and Security Policy in 1994', MR-608-FNF/OSD/A/AF (Santa Monica, CA: RAND, 1995). For American public opinion, see: John E. Reilly (Ed.), 'American Public Opinion and U.S. Foreign Policy 1995' (Chicago: Chicago Council on Foreign Relations, 1995).

44. The concept, by now deeply ensconced in the literature, belongs to Ivo Duchacek. See: 'Perforated Sovereignties: Towards a New Typology of Actors in International Relations', written before unification and the other seismic events of 1989, for Hans J. Michelman and Panayotis Soldatos (Eds), *Federalism and International Relations. The Role of Subunits* (Oxford: Oxford University Press, 1990).

45. Katzenstein's concept has been elaborated within the context of German domestic political arrangements. See: *Policy and Politics in West Germany: The Growth of a Semisovereign State* (Philadelphia: Temple University Press, 1987).

46. See Anthony Lake, 'From Containment to Enlargement', remarks to

the School of Advanced International Studies, The Johns Hopkins University, 21 September 1993; Klaus Kinkel, 'Verantwortung, Realismus, Zukunftssicherung. Deutsche Aussenpolitik in einer sich neu ordnenden Welt', *Frankfurter Allgemeine Zeitung*, 19 March 1993.

47. See, for example, Chancellor Kohl's speech to the National Governors Association, January 1994; the speeches by President Clinton and Chancellor Kohl in Bonn and Berlin, July 1994; the speeches by Clinton and Kohl in Washington, February 1995; the speeches by Ambassador Holbrooke in Potsdam (December 1993), Munich (March 1994), and Heidelberg (May 1994); the speech by Ambassador Redman in Berlin, February 1994.

48. Ambassador Richard Holbrooke, Heidelberg and Munich speeches, March 1994 and May 1994.

49. See, for example, United States General Accounting Office, 'German Health Reforms. Changes Result in Lower Costs', GAO/HEHS-95-27 (Washington, DC: General Accounting Office, Health, Education, and Human Services Division, 16 December 1994); 'Long-Term Care: Other Countries Tighten Budgets While Seeking Better Access', GAO/HEHS-94-154 (Washington, DC: General Accounting Office, Health, Education and Human Services Division, 30 August 1994); 'Long-Term Care. Current Issues and Future Directions', GAO/HEHS-95-109 (Washington, DC: General Accounting Office, Health, Education and Human Services Division, April 1995).

50. US Department of Labor and US Department of Commerce, Commission on the Future of Worker-Management Relations, May 1994, *Fact Finding Report* (Washington, DC: US Government Printing Office, 1994), 301-225-814/14422.

51. See, for example, 'Renewing the Social Contract: Management and Labor Relations in Germany's Changing Economy', *AICGS Seminar Paper*, no. 12, May 1995 (Washington, DC: American Institute for Contemporary German Studies/The Johns Hopkins University).

52. On Bosnia, see: Steven J. Woehrel and Julie Kim, 'Bosnia–Former Yugoslavia and U.S. Policy', *CRS Issue Brief*, 91089 (Washington, DC: Congressional Research Service, The Library of Congress, 4 April 1995); on NATO, see: Rick Atkinson and John Pomfret, 'East looks to NATO to Forge Links to West', *The Washington Post*, 6 July 1995.

53. For press reports of the Clinton visit and the issue of defining the relationship, see: *Financial Times*, 12, 13 July 1994; *Süddeutsche Zeitung*, 9, 11, 12, 13 July 1994; *Frankfurter Rundschau*, 9, 11, 12, 13 July 1994; *The Washington Post*, 15 July 1994.

54. See *The Wall Street Journal*, 14, 15 June 1993. *Financial Times*, 13, 14 June 1993.

55. For details of the institutionalization, see: Commission of the European Communities, Directorate General External Economic Relations, *E.C.–U.S. Relations: Progress Report*, no. 2, December 1993; European Commission, Directorate General Information, Communication, Culture, Audiovisual, *Progress Report on EU–US Relations*, no. 3, March 1994; European Commission, Directorate General External Economic Relations *Progress Report on EU–US Relations*, December 1994.

56. See, for example, Kinkel, 'Verantwortung', op. cit.; Helmut Kohl, 'Wir gewinnen mit Europa', speech to the Christian Democratic Union party convention, Düsseldorf, October 1992; Hans Peter Stihl, president of the German Conference of Chambers of Industry and Commerce, 'Ansprache anlässlich des Neujahrsempfangs der American Chamber of Commerce in Germany', Stuttgart, 27 January 1993; Edzard Reuter, 'Alle müssen an einem Strang ziehen', *Die Zeit*, 22 January 1993; Volker Rühe, 'America and Europe – Common Challenges and Common Answers', lecture given at Georgetown University, Washington, DC, 2 March 1995; Klaus Kinkel, 'German–American Friendship – the Transatlantic Agenda 2000', speech to the Chicago Council on Foreign Relations, 19 April 1995; Rudolf Scharping, 'The Atlantic Allies Have Responsibilities to Assume', *International Herald Tribune*, 14 March 1995; Secretary Christopher, 'Charting a Transatlantic Agenda for the 21st Century', address at Casa de America, Madrid, 2 June 1995; Redman, 'The United States and Germany', op. cit.

Calls for a new transatlantic partnership, including suggestions for a Transatlantic Free Trade Area and a US–EU Treaty, have also been made by German scholars. See, for example, Gunther Hellmann, 'EU and USA Need Broader Foundation: The Case for a Transatlantic Treaty', *Aussenpolitik*, 45, 3, 1994; Werner Weidenfeld, 'Jenseits des Selbstverständlichen: Europa und USA brauchen einen Neubeginn', *Europa-Archiv*, Folge 13–14, 1995; Reinhardt Rummel, 'Der Dialog zwischen der Europäischen Union und den Vereinigten Staaten. Erfahrungen mit der Transatlantischen Erklärung und Fragen ihrer Weiterentwicklung', Stiftung Wissenschaft und Politik, AP 2876, November 1994.

57. Office of the Press Secretary, The White House, 'Press Conference of the President and Chancellor Helmut Kohl', 9 February 1995, p. 1.

58. Timothy Garton Ash, 'Germany's Choice', *Foreign Affairs*, 73, 4, 1994.

59. Garton Ash, op. cit., p. 73.

60. Secretary Christopher, 'Charting a Transatlantic Agenda', op. cit.; Leon Brittan, 'The EU–US Relationship: Will It Last?', speech to the American Club of Brussels, 27 April 1995 (Washington, DC: European Union, Delegation of the European Commission).

61. For a review of transatlantic relations in 1994–95 and prognosis for the future, see: Lily Gardner Feldman, 'Transatlantic Relations', in *Jahrbuch der Europäischen Integration 1994/95* (München: Centrum für angewandte Politikforschung, 1995).

The concept of US–EU mutual learning through comparative public policy analysis is a major, innovative element in the European Commission's July 1995 report to the Council on 'Europe and the US: the Way Forward'.

BIBLIOGRAPHY

Anderson, Jeffrey J., and John B. Goodman, 'Mars or Minerva? A United Germany in a Post-Cold War Europe', in Robert O. Keohane, Joseph S. Nye and Stanley Hoffmann (Eds), *After the Cold War. International Institutions and State Strategies in Europe, 1989–1991* (Cambridge, Mass.: Harvard University Press, 1993).

Arnold, Eckart, 'German Foreign Policy and Unification', *International Affairs* 67, 3, 1991.

Asmus, Ronald D., 'Deutschland im Übergang. Nationales Selbstvertrauen und internationale Zurückhaltung', *Europa-Archiv* 47, Jahr 8, Folge 25, April 1992.

Asmus, Ronald D., 'The Future of German Strategic Thinking', in Gary L. Geipl (Ed.), *Germany in a New Era* (Indianapolis: Hudson Institute, 1993).

Asmus, Ronald D., 'Germany's Geo-political Maturation: Public Opinion and Security Policy in 1994', MR-608-FNF/OSD/A/AF (Santa Monica, CA: RAND, 1995).

Atkinson, Rick, and John Pomfret, 'East looks to NATO to Forge Links to West', *The Washington Post*, 6 July 1995.

Bertram, Christoph, 'US–German Relations in a World at Sea', *Daedalus* 121, fall 1992, p. 119.

Brittan, Leon, 'The EU–US Relationship: Will It Last?', speech to the American Club of Brussels, 27 April 1995 (Washington, DC: European Union, Delegation of the European Commission).

Christopher, Warren, 'Charting a Transatlantic Agenda for the 21st Century', address at Casa de America, Madrid, 2 June 1995.

Clemens, Clay, 'Opportunity or Obligation? Redefining Germany's Military Role Outside of NATO', *Armed Forces & Society* 19, 2, winter 1993.

Commission of the European Communities, Directorate General External Economic Relations, *E.C.–U.S. Relations: Progress Report*, no. 2, December 1993.

Donfried, Karen, 'German Foreign Policy and U.S. Interests', *CRS Report for Congress*, 95–564 F, 3 May 1995 (Washington, DC: Congressional Research Service).

Duchacek, Ivo, 'Perforated Sovereignties: Towards a New Typology of Actors in International Relations', in Hans J. Michelman and Panayotis Soldatos (Eds), *Federalism and International Relations. The Role of Subunits* (Oxford: Oxford University Press, 1990).

European Commission, Directorate General Information, Communication, Culture, Audiovisual, *Progress Report on EU–US Relations*, no. 3, March 1994.

European Commission, Directorate General External Economic Relations, *Progress Report on EU–US Relations*, December 1994.

European Commission, July 1995 report to the Council on 'Europe and the US: the Way Forward'.

Financial Times, 13, 14 June 1993; 12, 13 July 1994.

Frankfurter Rundschau, 9, 11, 12, 13 July 1994.

Gardner Feldman, Lily, *The Special Relationship between West Germany and Israel* (London: Allen & Unwin, 1984).

Gardner Feldman, Lily, 'Germany and the EC: Realism and Responsibility', in *The Annals of the American Academy of Political and Social Science*, vol. 531, January 1994.

Gardner Feldman, Lily, 'Transatlantic Relations', in *Jahrbuch der Europäischen Integration 1994/95* (München: Centrum für angewandte Politikforschung, 1995).

Garten, Jeffrey E., *A Cold Peace: America, Japan, Germany, and the Struggle for Supremacy* (New York: Times Books/The Twentieth Century Fund, 1992).

Garten, Jeffrey E., 'The United States and Europe: Towards the 21st Century', remarks before the American Council on Germany, New York City, 9 March 1995 (Washington, DC: United States Department of Commerce, International Trade Administration, Office of Public Affairs).

Garton Ash, Timothy, 'Germany's Choice', *Foreign Affairs* 73, 4, 1994.

Germroth, David S., and Rebecca J. Hudson, 'German–American Relations and the Post Cold War World', *Aussenpolitik* 43, 1, 1992.

Gordon, Philip H., 'Berlin's Difficulties. The Normalization of German Foreign Policy', *Orbis*, spring 1994.

Görtemaker, Manfred, *Unifying Germany, 1989–1990* (New York: St Martin's Press/Institute for EastWest Studies, 1994).

Hacke, Christian, 'Germany and the New Europe', in David P. Calleo and Philip H. Gordon (Eds), *From the Atlantic to the Urals. National Perspectives on the New Europe* (Arlington, VA: Seven Locks Press, 1992).

Hamilton, Daniel S., *Beyond Bonn: America and the Berlin Republic* (Washington, DC: Carnegie Endowment for International Peace, 1994).

Hancock, M. Donald, and Helga A. Welsh (Eds), *German Unification. Processes and Outcomes* (Boulder: Westview Press, 1994).

Heilbrunn, Jacob, 'Tomorrow's Germany', *The National Interest*, summer 1994.

Hellmann, Gunther, '"Einbindungspolitik". German Foreign Policy and the Art of Declaring "Total Peace"', paper presented at the XVIth World Congress of the International Political Science Association, Berlin, August 1994.

Hellmann, Gunther, 'EU and USA Need Broader Foundation: The Case for a Transatlantic Treaty', *Aussenpolitik* 45, 3, 1994.

Holsti, Ole R., Terrence P. Hopmann and John D. Sullivan, *Unity and Disintegration in International Alliances: Comparative Studies* (New York: Wiley, 1973).

Hormats, Robert D., 'Patterns of Competition. United Germany and the United States: A New Partnership for the 1990s', in Steven Muller and Gebhard Schweigler (Eds), *From Occupation to Cooperation. The United States and Germany in a Changing World Order* (New York: W.W. Norton, 1992).

Jarausch, Konrad H., *The Rush to German Unity* (New York: Oxford University Press, 1994).

Kahler, Miles, 'Trade and Domestic Differences', in Suzanne Berger and Ronald Dore (Eds), *Convergence or Diversity? National Models of Production and Distribution in Global Economies* (Ithaca: Cornell University Press, 1995).

Kaiser, Karl, 'Patterns of Partnership', in Steven Muller and Gebhard Schweigler (Eds), *From Ocupation to Cooperation. The United States and Germany in a Changing World Order* (New York: W.W. Norton, 1992).

Katzenstein, Pater, *Policy and Politics in West Germany: The Growth of a Semisovereign State* (Philadelphia: Temple University Press, 1987).

Kielinger, Thomas, 'The Gulf War and the Consequences from a German Point of View', *Aussenpolitik* 42, 3, 1991.

Kinkel, Klaus, 'Verantwortung, Realismus, Zukunftssicherung. Deutsche Aussenpolitik in einer sich neu ordnenden Welt', *Frankfurter Allgemeine Zeitung*, 19 March 1993.

Kinkel, Klaus, 'German–American Friendship – the Transatlantic Agenda 2000', speech to the Chicago Council on Foreign Relations, 19 April 1995.

Kohl, Helmut, 'Wir gewinnen mit Europa', speech to the Christian Democratic Union party convention, Düsseldorf, October 1992.

Kreile, Michael, 'Übernimmt Deutschland eine Führungsrolle in der Europäischen Gemeinschaft?', in Werner Weidenfeld (Ed.), *Was ändert die Einheit?* (Gutersloh: Verlag Bertelsmann Stiftung, 1993).

Krieger, Wolfgang, 'Toward a Gaullist Germany? Some Lessons from the Yugoslav Crisis', *World Policy Journal*, spring 1994.

Lake, Anthony, 'From Containment to Enlargement', remarks to the School of Advanced International Studies, The Johns Hopkins University, 21 September 1993.

Markovits, Andrei S., and Simon Reich, 'Deutschlands neues Gesicht: Über deutsche Hegemonie in Europa', *Leviathan* 1, 1992.

Maull, Hanns W., 'Zivilmacht Bundesrepublik Deutschland. Vierzehn Thesen für eine neue deutsche Aussenpolitik', *Europa-Archiv* 47, Jahr 10, Folge 25, Mai 1992.

Odom, William E., 'The German Problem. Only Ties to America Provide the Answer', *Orbis*, fall 1990.

Office of the Press Secretary, The White House, 'Press Conference of the President and Chancellor Helmut Kohl', 9 February 1995.

Peters, Susanne, 'Germany's Future Defense Policy: Opening Up the Option for German Power Politics', *German Politics and Society* 26, summer 1992.

Pond, Elizabeth, *After the Wall. American Policy Toward Germany* (New York: Priority Press/The Twentieth Century Fund, 1990).

Pond, Elizabeth, *Beyond the Wall. Germany's Road to Unification* (Washington, DC: Brookings Books, 1993).

Pulzer, Peter, 'United Germany: A Normal State?', *German Politics* 3, 1, April 1994.

Redman, Charles E., 'The United States and Germany: Sharing Values and Visions for the 21st Century', address to the Atlantik Brücke, Berlin, 14 February 1995.

Reilly, John E. (Ed.), 'American Public Opinion and U.S. Foreign Policy 1995' (Chicago: Chicago Council on Foreign Relations, 1995).

'Renewing the Social Contract: Management and Labor Relations in Germany's Changing Economy', *AICGS Seminar Paper*, no. 12, May 1995 (Washington, DC: American Institute for Contemporary German Studies/ The Johns Hopkins University).

Reuter, Edzard, 'Alle müssen an einem Strang ziehen', *Die Zeit*, 22 January 1993.

Rühe, Volker, 'America and Europe – Common Challenges and Common Answers', lecture given at Georgetown University, Washington, DC, 2 March 1995.

Rummel, Reinhardt, 'Der Dialog zwischen der Europäischen Union und den Vereinigten Staaten. Erfahrungen mit der Transatlantischen Erklärung und Fragen ihrer Weiterentwicklung', Stiftung Wissenschaft und Politik, AP 2876, November 1994.

Rupieper, Herman-Josef, 'After the Cold War: The United States, Germany, and European Security', *Diplomatic History* 16, spring 1992.

Scharping, Rudolph, 'The Atlantic Allies Have Responsibilities to Assume', *International Herald Tribune*, 14 March 1995.

Schäuble, Wolfgang, *Der Vertrag. Wie ich über die deutsche Einheit verhandelte* (Stuttgart: Deutsche Verlags-Anstalt, 1991).

Schlaes, Amity, 'Germany's Chained Economy', *Foreign Policy*, September/October 1994.

Schlör, Wolfgang F., 'German Security Policy', *Adelphi Paper* 277, June 1993.

Schöllgen, Gregor 'Deutschlands neue Lage. Die USA, die Bundesrepublik Deutschland und die Zukunft des westlichen Bündnisses', *Europa-Archiv* 47, Jahr 5, Folge 10, März 1992.

Schwarz, Hans-Peter, 'Germany's National and European Interests. A Country with National Interests?', *Daedalus* 123, 2, spring 1994.

Smyser, W.R., *Germany and America. New Identities, Fateful Rift?* (Boulder: Westview Press, 1993).

Smyser, W.R. 'America and the New Germany', *German Issues* 12 (Washington, DC: American Institute for Contemporary German Studies, 1993).

Sperling, James, 'German Foreign Policy after Unification: The End of Cheque Book Diplomacy?', *West European Politics* 17, 1, January 1994.

Stihl, Hans Peter, president of the German Conference of Chambers of Industry and Commerce, 'Ansprache anlässlich des Neujahrsempfangs der American Chamber of Commerce in Germany', Stuttgart, 27 January 1993.

Süddeutsche Zeitung, 9, 11, 12, 13 July 1994.

Szabo, Stephen F., *The Diplomacy of German Unification* (New York: St Martin's Press, 1992).

Szabo, Stephen F., 'Unified Germany and the United States', paper presented to the SAIS/Ruhr Universität Bochum workshop, School of Advanced International Studies, The Johns Hopkins University, 7/8 July 1994.

Teltschik, Horst, *329 Tage. Innenansichten der Einigung* (Berlin: Siedler, 1991).

United States General Accounting Office, 'Long-Term Care: Other Countries Tighten Budgets While Seeking Better Access', GAO/HEHS-94-154 (Washington, DC: General Accounting Office, Health, Education and Human Services Division, 30 August 1994).

United States General Accounting Office, 'German Health Reforms. Changes Result in Lower Costs', GAO/HEHS-95-27 (Washington, DC:

General Accounting Office, Health Education and Human Services Division, 16 December 1994.

United States General Accounting Office, 'Long-Term Care. Current Issues and Future Directions', GAO/HEHS-95-109 (Washington, DC: General Accounting Office, Health, Education and Human Services Division, April 1995).

US Department of Labor and US Department of Commerce, Commission on the Future of Worker-Management Relations, May 1994, *Fact Finding Report* (Washington, DC: US Government Printing Office, 1994), 301-225-814/14422.

Walker, Martin, 'Overstretching Teutonia: Making the Best of the Fourth Reich', *World Policy Journal* XII, 1, spring 1995.

The Wall Street Journal, 14, 15 June 1993.

Walter, Norbert, 'The Evolving German Economy: Unification, the Social Market Economy, European and Global Integration', paper presented in the series 'The New Germany in the New Europe', School of Advanced International Studies/The Johns Hopkins University, 18 April 1995.

The Washington Post, 15 July 1994.

Weidenfeld, Werner, 'Jenseits des Selbstverständlichen: Europa und USA brauchen einen Neubeginn', *Europa-Archiv*, Folge 13–14, 1995.

Woehrel, Steven J., and Julie Kim, 'Bosnia-Former Yugoslavia and U.S. Policy', *CRS Issue Brief*, 91089 (Washington, DC: Congressional Research Service, The Library of Congress, 4 April 1995).

8 Russia and Germany – from Enemy to Partner? A Contradictory Relationship

Vitaly Zhurkin

To understand the relationship between Germany and Russia, it must be understood that each power functions simultaneously at several levels (or incarnations) on the international scene. Germany is not only a mighty economic and political Western power but the strongest member of the EU and a formidable participant in the Atlantic community as well. Harmonization of these incarnations of modern Germany is not an easy task in itself. It takes a serious national effort to integrate the ambivalences of purely German national interests and Germany's European and Atlantic identities. Russia's role and fate is even more complicated and multifaceted. It is still a great power with particular interests and plays a rather ambivalent role in the CIS which is a weak and heterogeneous conglomeration. It tries to play a genuine role as one of the actors on the European scene. But above all, its actions and position are defined and formed by the acute economic and political crisis, uncertainties about Russia's future, domestic developments and events within the Russian federation.

Russia and Germany are obliged to deal with each other in this complex multidimensional set-up. It has become something of a conventional wisdom for analyses of contemporary German–Russian relations to start with the premise that we are dealing with the interaction of not only very old but also new states and societies. This premise is more accurate *vis-à-vis* the Russian federation but is also largely true as far as modern Germany is concerned. The re-unification of Germany – one of the greatest events in contemporary

European and world history – has and will have profound short- and long-term effects: this new state will, in the long run, increase the strategic power of Germany and will make it a more powerful and vigorous partner in Russian–German relations.

As for Russia, it really emerges as a new state in several senses. Firstly, Russia is a somewhat smaller actor on the international scene than the former superpower out of which it emerged (with about half of the population, two thirds of the economic potential and almost 70 per cent of the territory of the former Soviet Union). Secondly, Russia is a qualitatively new state which is trying, with varied results, to get rid of its totalitarian past and construct a market economy and a democratic society. Thirdly, Russia is still a considerable nuclear power (or nuclear superpower) and possesses many competitive resources: a vast land mass rich in natural resources (and not only energy); a skilled and educated labour force; a still strong scientific and research establishment; and a rich traditional culture.

In these new conditions, it is natural to appeal for the preservation of all that was positive in both former and contemporary German–Russian relations and to the enrichment of them whenever possible. In practice, relations between the two nations obviously cannot be a bed of roses, but, at a very general level, there seems to be a certain tendency for the positive elements in this relationship to outweigh the negative elements. Furthermore, the new framework of relations between the two states contains more constructive elements than before.

HISTORY

The historical background of the Russian–German relationship is extremely turbulent. In the last two-and-a-half centuries or so there have been many dramatic ups and downs. During the Seven Year War, Russian troops seized Berlin and, later, entered into alliance in the common struggle against Napoleon. There were decades of friendship and enmity in the 19th century and considerable dynastic ties between the imperial dynasties. The protracted battles of the First World War were yet another 'down' but peace brought the Rapallo Treaty between the two European post-war outcasts: a treaty which inaugurated considerable military and economic cooperation. The political confrontation of the 1930s led in turn to the Nazi–Soviet pact, one of the most repulsive treaties of 20th century history. The assault in June 1941 and the attempt of the German armies to conquer the Soviet Union developed into the fiercest fighting of the Second World War, and the defeat of the German armies spelled the end of Nazi Germany. In the post-war era of the cold war, Russian–West German relations continued to be full of contradictions: confrontation with the Berlin crisis of 1948 and the Wall in 1961, but at the same time the Moscow Treaty, normalization of relations and steady economic cooperation.

This history provides few lessons, with one major exception. Despite the accumulated history of conflict and grievances, Russian–German relations have, in general, steadily improved over the last three to four decades, to the extent that Soviet and Russian support (under Mikhail Gorbachev and later Boris Yeltsin) for German reunification was a dramatic historical volte-face, which did not occur in a vacuum. It is to the political framework of these relations that we will now turn.

POLITICAL FRAMEWORK

Contemporary political relations between Russia and Germany rest on quite a solid basis. By the beginning of the 1990s, the long-standing system of treaties and agreements which had developed over several decades culminated in the conclusion of the treaties on final settlement in relation to Germany, on good-neighbourliness, partnership and cooperation, and on development of large-scale cooperation in economic relations, industry, science and technology, *inter alia*. In sum, they constitute an extensive and deep legal foundation for the interrelationship in the last decade of the century. This is supplemented by a well-established practice of bilateral summits and other vital meetings whose results enrich the legal normative base of the German–Russian relationship and extend it into newer areas. For instance, the agreement on exchange of views and information on military and security problems is one of the most extensive ever signed with NATO members.[1] The level of mutual understanding is thus quite formidable.

Russia contributed crucially to this process, in particular by the position taken with respect to the reunification of Germany and by its approach during the process of the withdrawal of Russian troops from German soil. The strict adherence to the timetable and the cooperative approach to a myriad of large and small problems that the withdrawal brought about demonstrated the durability of this political will and the desire to sustain and extend the political framework.

The German government, on their part, were not passive at all in this and other areas of the relationship. German support for Russia in the G7, then EU and GATT in various ways cemented the elements of the special relationship which was developing. German–Russian cooperation in the CSCE helped to develop this organization in difficult times.

Naturally, it is still premature to speak of compatibility of socio-political systems. Modern Germany is a well-developed Western democratic state with a mature civil society. Russia for the time being has only just started constructing a democratic society. This is a period of trial and error. Russia has not yet decided what it is creating – Western-style democracy or something different; a kind of Eurasian society, a combination of democracy and some degree of authoritarianism or something else. It is, however, quite probable that the degree of compatibility between the two states will gradually grow. Traditional historic cultural ties between Germany and Russia will help a lot in this process.

This framework will not develop easily. Bilateral Russian–German political relations are not without problems, sometimes serious ones. There are difficult divergences of approach to issues of political and social institutions, democratic values, human rights. Considerable strata of German society reacted negatively to Russia's military action in Chechnya, losses of life and violations of human rights. Periodic conflicts emerge due to different attitudes to international developments (e.g. policy differences in relation to the Balkans).

But in spite of problems, differences and contradictions, Russian–German political relations represent, all in all, one of the most succesful examples of state cooperation. It was noted in Russia with satisfaction that not a single democratic party which entered the Bundestag after the general elections held in Germany in late 1993/4 questioned the foreign policy line of the German government in relation to Russia.[2] The elections proved that the framework and content of political relations is supported by an overwhelming majority of Germany's population. It is reciprocated by a similar attitude of a comparable majority of Russian citizens. The same could be said of support for economic cooperation between Russia and Germany.

ECONOMY

Both Germanies of the past as well as unified Germany have been formidable economic partners for the Soviet Union and now for Russia. Germany is the largest donor of financial and commercial assistance (and of humanitarian aid which has been particularly helpful in winter periods and has received a grateful response from Russian society).

But economic cooperation with the Soviet Union was not without drawbacks. A lot of financial aid disappeared in the 'black holes' of the Soviet economy, and the humanitarian aid partly vanished in the entrails of corruption. But this did not change the role of Germany as Russia's single most important economic partner.

Crisis and destabilization in Russia – which started before radical reforms but essentially accompanied them – coupled with the economic problems of German reunification created for the first time in many years a lull in Russian–German economic interaction in the early 1990s. In the period 1990–92 bilateral trade decreased by 50 per cent.[3] Further decline was essentially arrested in 1993 and Germany is still the biggest trade partner, accounting for one seventh of Russia's foreign trade. In 1994, total trade with Germany was roughly twice that of the second largest trade partner, the USA.[4] According to major international surveys, Germany provided about 60 per cent of external financial assistance to the CIS, mostly to Russia.[5] But aid has greatly decreased mostly due to Germany's own financial requirements after reunification. Investments practically stopped growing as well, though with about 8 billion DM, Germany accounts for 60 per cent of all foreign private investments.[6] Approximately half of Russia's foreign debt is owed to Germany.

A certain stability in economic relations since 1993 was the result of strenuous efforts on both sides. Germany prolonged repayment of Russian debts, signed new large contracts (in particular for Russian supplies of gas for 20 years) and increased technology transfer and consultative assistance. Russia is striving to put its economic house in order and improve conditions for foreign investors. Both work to expand and ensure export credits for German exports, though the situation continues to be tense: about half of Russian imports from Germany still have to be prepaid.[7] Yet there are reasons to believe that German–Russian economic relations will recover. One of the major reasons is a growing maturity in the new economic relations, a capability on both sides to pinpoint the most promising areas of mutually beneficial cooperation. A good example is a rather successful development of German technical-consultative assistance. After several not very fruitful attempts a system of priorities was drawn up. This includes help to small and medium-sized firms, structural reconstruction, agriculture, banking, infrastructure, privatization etc.

Another promising area is high technology. Both countries are engaged in practical cooperation in such fields as nuclear energy, space and the conversion of defence production. There are good prospects for cooperation involving European-wide infrastructure, in energy, transport and telecommunications.

A peculiar feature of Russian–German economic (and cultural) interaction is the comparatively well developed role of particular regional agreements. When the Russian federation was part of the Soviet Union it concluded partnership agreements with a number of states of the German Federal Republic: North-Rhine-Westphalia, Baden-Würtemberg, Lower Saxony. On the German side, this regional trend has been centralized. The Federal Republic of Germany has chosen several key regions with comparatively mature

economic and other infrastructure for more intense cooperation. First Vladimir and later Smolensk, Nizhniy Novgorod
and other provinces. Such regional diversification, which
Germany has cultivated more than any other Western partner, helps cement and deepen relations, assuring their
longevity.

THE EUROPEAN UNION

Russian–German economic relations are closely connected
with Germany's growing role in the European Union. An
intense debate has developed among Russian experts on how
the reunification of Germany will influence this role. Will
Germany distance itself from the EU and pursue a more
independent course or will it keep its renewed identity within
the EU? It seems that this dilemma is being quietly resolved.
Though the role of Germany in modern Europe has increased
substantially – and Germany has the economic power and
resources to move ahead alone – Germany is consistent in
its commitment to the EU and to developing within its framework. For Russia it will mean the necessity to take into consideration that economic (and probably not only economic)
relations with Germany will develop within the frameworks
and rules established in the European Union.

Naturally, the postures of both countries with regard to
the EU are radically different. Germany feels far more comfortable economically, politically and culturally within the
EU, and the quietly growing German role is conceded by
members as well as by non-members.

Russia's position is quite different. In 1994, Russia concluded an extensive and multifaceted treaty on partnership
and cooperation with the EU. The goal was clearly defined
but the ratification process will take between one-and-a-half
and two years. In order not to lose momentum, an interim
treaty was agreed on, consisting of provisions which do not
need ratification.

However, simultaneously a seemingly endless debate on
Russia's identity and role in the contemporary world is taking place, and there are voices raising exaggerated claims
as to Russian national interests, voices which have created

artificial hurdles to the framework of Russian–German relations. Politico-military actions such as the use of force in Chechnya received a highly critical response in the EU. Such actions can serve to destabilize Russia's role *vis-à-vis* Europe and even destroy the emerging partnership, though the EU continues to be committed to supporting democratic reforms in Russia. Thus there are voices and forces that could jeopardize the favourable relationship.

EUROPEAN SECURITY, O/CSCE, NATO

There are many similarities and common stakes in the approach of Russia and Germany to the problems of European security, a convergence with a considerable history. This has been manifest, in particular, in considerable mutual understanding and activities within the CSCE.

Germany, as some other Western powers, has eagerly supported Russia's attempt to arrest the proliferation of nuclear weapons on former Soviet territory.[8] Germany was an ardent supporter of the modernization of NATO which started with the London declaration of 1990 and continued at the Rome summit of 1992 with the creation of the NACC. Germany contributed to developing the idea of the Partnership for Peace in an attempt to reconcile Russia's objections against enlargement of NATO to the East, a process partly initiated by the drive of the central and East European states for membership of NATO.

Unfortunately, the attempt to build a permanent security arrangement around the Partnership for Peace was manipulated by NATO for its own purposes. Germany and the USA as well as other NATO Allies rather suddenly turned at the end of 1994 more resolutely towards the enlargement of the alliance to the East. Russia naturally reacted energetically and negatively. A serious knot of contradictions had emerged. The *bouleversement* as to the enlargement of NATO – though it will stretch over a number of years – poses a series of problems and threats for Russia. The most formidable of them is the threat of a new division of Europe, one which is harmful in itself and in which Russia will have to participate, however weakened and in crisis. The new

NATO turn towards enlargement was perceived in Russia as an anti-Russian action. And this perception can lead to the strengthening of nationalistic moods which will feed the forces of authoritarianism at home and assertiveness in foreign policy.

Around what is called in the West 'the new Russian assertiveness' in foreign and defence policies, another focus of contradictions is developing. When the first phase of the new Russia's foreign policy, oriented solely to the West, was completed, attempts to develop a more diversified approach to the outside world based on national interests were undertaken. The result was a growing concern abroad, including in Germany. Regrettably the new set of foreign policy contradictions is still unresolved and continues to darken the relations of Russia with Germany and other Western nations.

CIS

An important dimension of this controversy has developed around Russia's role and actions within the CIS. The processes involved in the Commonwealth of Independent States are multi-dimensional. They include economic, security, political and cultural dimensions. The most realistic of these dimensions is the sphere of economic cooperation. There is still no unanimity of opinion in Russia as to what is preferable – the promotion of economic integration with some or all CIS members or alternatively a policy solely devoted to the pursuit of national interests. This debate is far from over but, slowly and hesitantly, Russia is turning towards a policy of increasing integration. This process does not appear to create controversies with the West.

A quite different matter, however, is the field of conflicts, peacekeeping and the role of military forces. Russia complains of Western indifference towards the conflicts which are occurring in the post-Soviet geopolitical space and the West seems unable to participate in practical peacekeeping in these conflicts. Indeed Western opinion accuses Russians of unilateral action. The controversy unfortunately is growing, and mutual recriminations are increasing. It is still very difficult to foresee how these Russian–Western contradictions (described all too briefly here) will develop. It is even more difficult to calculate how they will influence German–Russian relations.

Still it might to be useful to examine the possibilities of working out a common or at least a compromise approach. A vital element of such an approach should be clear and unequivocal recognition by Russia of the sovereignty and independence of all other members of CIS, though one should recognize that Russia is increasingly doing this.

PROSPECTS

There exists a rather widespread model of prognosis related to Russian–German relations (and to a wider spectrum of international relations). This model usually includes three forecasted alternative scenarios: a pessimistic, an optimistic and a middle course which is usually an extrapolation of the present relationship. This middle course scenario is usually described as the most probable. However, in this case it would appear legitimate to dare to deviate from such an approach and to predict that the development of future German–Russian relations will lie between the middle course and the optimistic scenarios, for the following reasons:

1. (In spite of all the problems), the long historical development of the economic basis of the relationship, including the traditional compatibility of the German and Russian economies.
2. The moral–psychological *rapprochement* of the civil societies of both countries.
3. The multiplicity of common interests in Europe.
4. Areas of mutual approach to security problems.

In the history of Russian–German relations (as generally in international life) there were periods when the further development of the relationship depended more on Germany. There were times when it depended more on Russia. Evidently the progress of relations is a result of mutual bilateral efforts but some disparity often exists. At present the scope for optimism in the scenario mentioned above depends more on Russia for a number of reasons.

First, only political stabilization in Russia coupled with further democratization can ensure a reliable basis for the promotion of Russian–German partnership and cooperation. The tragic events in Chechnya are evidence of how this basis may be damaged (though fortunately not severed). But political catalysts of such or comparable types may eventually sever it.

Second, overcoming economic crisis in Russia together with the expansion of the reform process is the major condition for the expansion of trade and for industrial and scientific–technological cooperation. The prospects here are quite impressive. But they depend on Russia's ability to establish and expand the conditions for their realization. Third, a consistent and reasonable foreign policy course, one which inspires mutual understanding and partnership with other democratic nations, is also of great importance.

The above does not mean that Germany's role is passive. It is reasonable to expect that Germany should reciprocate in all these spheres. In some foreign policy disagreements, like the one involving NATO's enlargement, the German position from a Russian point of view was far from inoffensive. But the potential for cooperation exists in many areas and may grow. Germany can do a lot to develop it through bilateral actions and its own initiatives.

NOTES

1. *Rossiya i Sovremenniy Mir*, Moscow, N 2, 1994, p. 106.
2. *Diplomaticheskiy Vestnik*, Moscow, N 21–22, 1994, p. 65.
3. *Mezhdunarodnaya Zhizn*, Moscow, N 11, 1994, p. 102.
4. *Ekonomika i Zhizn*, Moscow, N 2, 1995, p. 19.
5. *Mirovaya Ekonomika i Mezhdunarodnie Otnosheniya*, Moscow, N 4, 1994, p. 104.
6. *Vneschnaya Torgovlya*, Moscow, N 4, 1994, p. 11.
7. Ibid., p. 10.
8. There was, however, an emotional explosion around nuclear plutonium materials which reached German soil from the East: though the origin of these materials is still controversial.

BIBLIOGRAPHY

Diplomaticheskiy Vestnik, Moscow, N 21–22 (1994).
Ekonomika i Zhizn, Moscow, N 2 (1995).
Mezhdunarodnaya Zhizn, Moscow, N 11 (1994).
Mirovaya Ekonomika i Mezhdunarodnie Otnosheniya, Moscow, N 4 (1994).
Rossiya i Sovremenniy Mir, Moscow, N 2 (1994).
Vneschnaya Torgovlya, Moscow, N 4 (1994).

9 The United Kingdom and Germany

Christopher Hill

> British relations with Germany since 1945 have been formed ... by an interaction between the traditional realism of Britain's political and professional diplomatic leadership and the emotional attitudes of hostility towards Germany of public opinion in Britain.[1]

INTRODUCTION: REALISM AND EMOTIONS

D. C. Watt's assessment of three decades ago might be thought to encapsulate the British attitudes to Germany which characterised the cold war era, but which became redundant almost from the moment of the first breach in the Berlin Wall on 9 November 1989: the double paradox of the contrast between insider sophistication, which was ultimately caught out by the pace of events in 1989–90, and popular xenophobia, which turned out to be less important than a sympathy for self-determination when German unification suddenly changed from taboo to reality. Indeed, it can be argued that Watt's analysis (no doubt accurate for its time) should now be inverted, with a range of political and official concerns about Germany's future now counterbalanced by a more relaxed attitude of the general public as the generations which fought two world wars move to the fringes of political life.

In this context, it is worth comparing two more recent remarks by key decision-makers of the 1980s – Lord Carrington and Margaret Thatcher. Carrington faced the question of European integration on defence:

> although there were ... political reasons ... which must inhibit the idea of a Europe primarily defended by a German Army and a British navy, we should, I thought

always be pressing further in that direction.[2]

Margaret Thatcher, by contrast, was less sanguine about the prospects for cooperation:

> Germany is . . . by its very nature a destabilizing rather than a stabilizing force in Europe. Only the military and political engagement of the United States in Europe and close relations between the other two strongest sovereign states in Europe – Britain and France – are sufficient to balance German power: and nothing of the sort would be possible within a European super-state.[3]

These contrasting views can be taken as harbingers of two competing views within the British political class on how relations with Germany should be handled in the uncertain decades after unification (for if anything is agreed within this class it would be that there are no new certainties to replace the old, and that the new Germany, through no fault of its own, represents a major challenge to all those involved in the diplomacy of European order). On the one hand there is the view, to be found in the more pro-EU quarters such as the Liberal Democrat and Labour Parties but more commonly than before also in the Foreign and Commonwealth Office and even the Ministry of Defence, that the European states should cooperate in taking ever more responsibility for their own defence and in working out some rational division of labour, even if it does not quite equate to Carrington's romantic land/sea dichotomy.

On the other hand is the view, expressed with characteristic bluntness by Baroness Thatcher,[4] that portrays the unified Germany as an embryonic leviathan, only temporarily inconvenienced by the costs of absorbing the new Länder and requiring a new round of balance-of-power politics so as to ensure that the European system falls into neither chaos nor hegemony – the twin dangers which British foreign policy has traditionally sought to avert. In such a round the European destiny of the United States would continue to be manifest and the other European 'great powers' would inevitably grow closer together.

National Interests Contra Supranationality

It should be noted that despite the obvious contrasts between these two differing views, they share an assumption about the continued separate existence of the member states of the European Union, and see no virtue in promoting integration as a way of transcending the problem of disproportionate national power – despite its logical attractions. The French (and indeed German) tendency to look for ways of locking Germany into identity-changing processes is not often echoed in Britain.[5] For the tying down of Gulliver would just as much bind his partners, and no British government, despite recent movement on the idea of European defence cooperation, could currently dare to suggest subordinating its own ultimate control of foreign and security policy to collective decision-making. Reinhardt Rummel has said that 'A German politician would never use the notion of "independence" in connection with the Federal Republic's foreign policy',[6] but the British equivalent has to pepper his (or her) speeches with the term.

To a degree this analysis bears out the proposition of Barbara Lippert et al. that German and British policy are essentially separated by a philosophical divide, between *integrationism* and *realism*, with Bonn still committed to a genuine union and to a common currency, and Britain always concerned to ring-fence 'national interests' from the encroachments of supranationality.[7] But the contrast is also a dangerous half-truth. For the whole British political spectrum now accepts membership of the EU as a central part of British domestic and foreign policy, *including* those derogations of sovereignty to which London has already signed up. 'National interests' have already been seriously redefined as a consequence of 33 years of first envisaging and then experiencing Community membership. The problem is with the future, that is with the possibility of continued dynamism and with the telos of a federal European state. For their part, of course, Germans do not subscribe to an uncomplicated version of the opposite position either, but that is not the concern of this particular paper.

The Approach

The approach taken here diverges from both the major positions outlined above. Little attempt is made to prescribe a policy for Britain in relation to Germany and therefore to the wider system in which Germany is embedded. Rather, the main objective of the paper is to relate the powerful historical experience of Britain and Germany to the apparent discontinuity represented by the end of the cold war and by German unification, and to ask whether Germany still represents, *in and of itself,* a major dilemma for governments in London – and whether it should do so. To this end a brief survey of the legacy of the past precedes an analysis of the impact of Germany's rebirth on British political society and on the perception of fundamental British foreign policy interests. This is done partly by looking at three particular issue areas: the internal functioning of the EU, the development of the CFSP and the problem of enlargement and a wider Europe. The broad conclusion arrived at concerns the enduring British failure to construct a special relationship with the Federal Republic, despite many particular achievements and points of convergence, and the likely impossibility of doing so. The future for Britain now resides less in the choice of preferred bilateral partners than in the working out of the best form of multilateralism in which to locate an Anglo-German relationship which has thankfully lost its historical drama.

HISTORICAL PROLOGUE

There is no point in pretending that for most of the 20th century Anglo-German relations have not been at least difficult and for long periods as disastrous as it is possible to get in the inter-state system. Great events do not have simple causes but certainly the rivalry and fear endemic in relations between London and Berlin played a major part in making two world wars possible. The inevitable scars of war continued to inhibit mutual relations after 1945, and it would have been a miracle had they not. On the British side the inhibition arose from a mixture of residual resentment at the suffering of war, and wariness of the emerging economic and diplomatic strength of the FRG; on the German side it was more a product of physical and political subordination, together with an eventual irritation at continuing British reminders of the past. But the genuine and phenomenal success of Franco-German *rapprochement*, with its many cultural manifestations, tends to blind us to the normally slower pace of healing between former antagonists. Recent events in the Balkans have made this point sharply. Looked at in this way, rather than in gloomy contrast to the Elysée Treaty, Britain and Germany have managed to reconstruct their relationship at almost all levels in an entirely satisfactory way, and for the most part conduct their official interaction through a civilized, if not intimate, discourse.

In any case, a longer perspective than that of 1904–45 will remind us of the fact that the British and the Germans have not been forever at each other's throats. The English monarchy has followed a German blood-line since 1714, while the Napoleonic wars and much of the century which followed saw Prussia and Britain on reasonable terms. The achievement of German unity through war in the 1860s did not cause major antagonisms at the time, and German culture and social development were widely admired in Britain a hundred years ago, as they are coming to be again now. Even the First World War did not wholly disturb the element of mutual respect that characterized this relationship between the two major states of protestant northern Europe, and Carsten has pointed out that the combination of Weimar democracy and guilt over Versailles led British diplomats to look fairly and favourably on their German counterparts in the 1920s[8] – perhaps, indeed, too much so, in terms of the slowness with which Hitler's revisionism was seen as a threat. It took the return of war to elevate the rabid anti-Germanism of a Robert Vansittart to the level of national policy, and even then British leaders took care to distinguish between Nazis and the German people – a theme that they were quickly to return to after the war and the tragic aberration of strategic bombing.[9]

ATTITUDINAL LAYERS

History affects the present, and present policy, at many different levels simultaneously, from relatively trivial squabbles over statues of old soldiers to the profound shaping of identity and institutions.[10] In this case we have to confront directly the question of whether the shattering experience of 1939–45 still hangs over British attitudes to Germany.

The answer is that it does, but to varying degrees and with varying consequences. As usual in policy analysis, it is important to distinguish between the major groups involved.[11] At the level of *the permanent bureaucracy*, those people who are engaged in a continual process of consultation and negotiation with the Federal Republic, 'history' is much more likely to mean the common experiences of the cold war and of Community membership than the Third Reich and all its associations. While officials are aware of the dangers of diplomatic freemasonry and of forgetting their own domestic constituencies, they are most unlikely to see the Federal Republic as a potential danger to European stability, even in its enlarged form. Indeed some of them even serve, on an exchange basis with their German counterparts, in German missions defending German interests, thus completing the circle which began in 1907 when Sir Eyre Crowe, despite his own German origins, wrote the famous Memorandum on 'the Present State of British Relations with France and Germany' which warned of an expansionist tendency in Berlin and moved London closer to Paris for what was to turn out to be the next half-century.[12] To some extent British and German officials have come, jointly if not exclusively, to conduct a form of foreign policy by committee in the post-war world, particularly since the arrival of the European Community's system of European Political Cooperation in 1970.

Political Parties

At the level of *political parties* the same will be true, but not so comprehensively. The years since 1980 have shown that holding office does not necessarily socialize even senior ministers, let alone their back-benchers, out of the nationalistic reflexes which were part of their political upbringing. Margaret Thatcher, Norman Tebbit and the late Nicholas Ridley were all too strong-minded to play the anti-German card simply to retain popularity with their little Englander supporters; they genuinely believed, if not always that Germany was a 'juggernaut' endangering the stability of Europe,[13] at least that Britain should not surrender its foreign policy leadership role to an inexperienced state whose image of a desirable European future – that of federalism – was rooted too much in its own unique experiences.

With the end of Thatcherism this attitude has been seriously weakened. The new generation of Conservative politicians are younger and are used to seeing Germany as an ordinary state. On the other hand the end of the cold war may have paradoxically created a new, if less virulent, strain of fear and competitiveness towards Germany, as the removal of four-power constraints and obvious potential for influence of a larger state combine to make Britain's position seem even weaker. Certainly the Federal Republic now looms as large in the political and psychological environments of British policy-makers as it has done for some time in those of the French. But this is also a sign of normality; power is always unevenly distributed, and as it becomes routinely accepted both that Germany in several respects enjoys significant advantages *and* that it does not exploit its power illegitimately, so British (or more correctly Conservative) politicians might be able to free themselves of their particular obsession with Germany. Douglas Hurd has already achieved this state of grace – he is reported to have lost his cool with Mrs Thatcher, for perhaps the only time, when she made some unguarded remarks about the Germans[14] – but this does not make him any the less tough a negotiator with Bonn (the similarity between 'Hurd' and 'Hürde', meaning 'hurdle', provided some amusement in Bonn during the early negotiations over unification).[15] Conversely a new and inexperienced Labour government under Tony Blair is more likely to err in relying too much on European solidarity than in beating the drum about Germany's historical mission.

For all political parties in Britain, generational change may be both weakening the old ties with Germany created by the experiences of war and post-war occupation, and reformulating them at a lower but more healthy level, obsession slowly being replaced by routine. The annual Königswinter conferences of the great and the good from both countries, together with the junior version set up to promote contacts among the successor generations, seem now an artificial device, rendered increasingly redundant by the range of contacts which British and German officials, academics, journalists and businesspeople enjoy by virtue of their daily business. Perhaps only the politicians still need the spur of a formal colloquium. On the other hand it must be admitted that British knowledge of German language and culture has declined steadily in most professions, unlike the reverse.

Popular Opinion

Finally there is the level of *popular opinion*, and its collective memories. As has been suggested above, there is some reason to believe that visceral anti-Germanism is much less prevalent than a regular reading of the *Sun* newspaper might suggest (a survey of British football supporters which showed that the team they most wished to see knocked out of the 1994 World Cup was Germany, may be balanced by the fact that all over north London youngsters were to be seen wearing Tottenham Hotspur shirts emblazoned with the name of the German captain, Jurgen Klinsmann, while other German players are now also taking advantage of the single market to play in Britain). A Mori poll of January 1990 showed that 45 per cent of British respondents already favoured German unification with 30 per cent opposed (admittedly in contrast to French and US figures of 61 per cent and 15/13 per cent).[16] Two months later, a clear majority of respondents thought that Nicholas Ridley should resign from the Cabinet after his description of the European Monetary System as 'a German racket designed to take over the whole of Europe', while 62 per cent (70 per cent in the 18–34 age-group) disagreed that a united Germany would 'pose a serious threat to peace in Europe in the future'.[17] A more recent (1994) survey on 'friendly feelings' has produced the finding that 69 per cent of respondents felt at least 'fairly friendly' towards the Germans, compared to 65 per cent towards the French.[18] It is true that Anglo-German school exchanges have foundered on British linguistic ineptitude and a paucity of available families to host German youngsters, but this indicates British reserve rather than hostility.[19] Certainly German university students are now flooding into parts of the British higher education system, for instance through the ERASMUS scheme, and they do not seem to meet with the resentment that many of their American equivalents have to suffer. Unfortunately this is once again one-way traffic; very few British students have the language and the ambition to study in Germany. Moreover, German universities are often forbidding places, even for young Germans.

It would be foolish to deny that despite this evidence British society still has the capacity to produce outbursts of vitriol against this or that example of supposed German arrogance, encouraged by a tabloid press which is the last bastion of Commonwealth, not to say old Dominion, influence in Britain. But just as outbreaks of racism do not wholly undo the less spectacular daily progress towards a multi-ethnic society, so the displays of xenophobia against Germany are decreasingly able to disturb a general appreciation of the possibilities for cooperation between the two countries. The continued cultural preoccupation with the last war, and with commemorative ceremonies, should not be taken as evidence of a persisting antagonism. Rather, it derives from feelings about the pity of war and of obligation towards those who died, after all, in a vital cause.

THE IMPACT OF GERMAN UNIFICATION ON BRITAIN

History, then, is being worked through in various ways and is not quite such a millstone around British policy as is often supposed. Nor has the shock of sudden German unity reawakened old paranoia. In the short term at least, and despite Mrs Thatcher's undoubted attempt to slow down the process in the first few months, Britain as a whole has seemed remarkably accepting about this major change in its immediate environment. Partly this was because there was almost nothing which even the iron lady could do to stop an accelerating popular movement, ably midwived by Helmut Kohl. Partly it was because it was associated with so many other dramatic and positive turns in international relations, not least the ending of 40 years of East–West tension.

None the less there have been significant consequences for Britain of the absorption of the GDR into the FRG, and some of these will only become apparent, in the nature of things, with the passage of time.

In practical terms, Britain suddenly faced a state with a population nearly 40 per cent bigger than itself, instead of 5 per cent as before. In land area Germany increased in size by 44 per cent, from a base of rough equality with Britain, and although in the short run its GNP increased by only 10 per cent it was already nearly half as big again as Britain's with a clear potential for further growth. Bonn tactfully soft-pedalled on the obvious implications for the balance of influence within EC institutions, but by 1994 its number of MEPs had risen to 98 out of 567, 11 more than Britain, with whom there was previously parity. This is all perfectly reasonable, and so will be the inevitable pressures for a greater say in council voting and in the Commission. They are a consequence of an increase in size which has put Germany clearly in a different league from its previous analogue countries, Britain, France and Italy. Whether the British have wholly woken up to the fact is to be doubted.

It is, indeed, at the level of perceptions, objectives and conceptions of self that the most important consequences of German unification for Britain will eventually be felt, and conversely where Germany will become aware of British reactions. It is possible, for example, as the extent of Germany's stronger position comes to dawn on opinion in London, that a sea-change could take place in attitudes towards European integration, along French lines. One foreign secretary once described continental aspirations to impose order on Europe as a system which 'aims at perfection, which we do not believe applicable to this century or to mankind . . . it is a vain hope, which England above all cannot pursue. All speculative policy is outside her power'.[20] This is the traditional aversion to both theoretical schemes and contiental entanglements – the two being inextricably entwined in British minds. But when interests are seen as sharply threatened, when existing policies are clearly no longer functional, then Britain is in fact perfectly capable of changing its view of a given enterprise from 'speculative' to 'realistic' or even 'inevitable'. This was the case both with the EEC and with decolonization, even if it is true that both changes were rationalized at the time as being wholly compatible with the continuation of British influence and independence in the world.[21]

If such a switch of basic position were to happen in relation to European integration, British governments would need to find a way of managing the same skilful tightrope walk conducted by the French between a traditional adhesion to the national state and a promotion of the European Union.[22] Changes in strategy may be made readily enough to accommodate new circumstances, but the underlying values and conceptions of interest which they serve will change far more slowly. The 'idea of Britain' which has proved so resistant to 'European' influences is no doubt an historical concoction, a myth like all other '*ethnies*' (or culturally homogeneous groups with family-like structures), but none the less persistent for that.[23] It is constantly changing, but at a pace too slow to be noticed by contemporary observers, like the erosion of mountain scenery. Moreover it is rather more likely to be transformed from within, through (say) the loss of Northern Ireland and/or Scotland, or the abolition of the monarchy (all now merely remote possibilities, instead of the unthinkable heresies they were in the 1950s), than through accommodation to changing external circumstances. As Germany has come together, so, conceivably, the United Kingdom could come apart.

There are, however, more concrete things to be said about British reactions to the new Germany in particular policy areas. These may be divided into three: intra-Union questions, CFSP questions and enlargement/pan-Europe questions.

In relation to the internal functioning of the Union, Britain has quickly felt the pressure of German financial difficulties as a result of unification. This has led indirectly to a certain questioning of the British budgetary rebates agreed at Fontainebleau in 1984. In the short and medium terms Germany will become less relaxed about its position as Community paymaster, and other net contributors will be the first to feel the pinch. *A fortiori* British requests for assistance on, for example, the Irish problem, will have to compete with German priorities in Eastern Europe (and will not be helped by Britain's various opt-outs). And Germany's resources naturally give it great influence over the smaller countries, as John Major found out when he had to climb down in March 1994 over the issue of the size of the blocking minority in council majority voting.

On some occasions London will be able to use Community mechanisms against Bonn, as in the first 'mad cow disease' affair, or that of M. Dehaene's candidature for the Commission presidency. On many others, however, the truth of the old maxim that free trade favours the strong (as it had Britain in the 19th century) will be brought home – as when Rover, the last British mass car producer, was taken over by BMW in 1994 and, more dramatically, when rises in German interest rates led directly to increased costs for British mortgage-holders. The most important single dispute in recent years between the two countries, however, among the many relatively minor squabbles, was that over the events which led to 'black Wednesday' in September 1992, and the enforced withdrawal of the pound from the exchange rate mechanism (ERM) of the EMS. The British government made no secret of the fact that the Bundesbank had been guilty at least of insufficient support of the pound, and at most of undermining its position by leaking the view that DM 2.95 was too high a rate for sterling to be able to maintain in the ERM. The loss of face for the Major government involved in this policy volte-face was high, and to some extent the Bundesbank was made a scapegoat. As it happens, the decoupling from the ERM has given the British economy a certain temporary leeway, as devaluations tend to do, and the experience will probably make future British chancellors take serious pause before once again making a formal linkage with the Deutschmark core of European monetary integration.

CFSP, WEU and Enlargement

In the area of foreign and security policy cooperation the differences between German and British preoccupations are evident, but this has not prevented the two countries from settling down into an effective working relationship which goes beyond the diplomatic service exchanges mentioned earlier, into matters of substance. To be sure there were some nervous flare-ups soon after unification, largely over Yugoslavia. There is no doubt that London was irritated and concerned over an apparent German desire to force the pace of European involvement in the Balkans (as over the recognition of Croatia and Slovenia in December 1991) without taking commensurate responsibilities. But the FCO grip over policy meant that there was little of the forceful language against a putative new sphere of German influence that came out of Paris at this time. Since the surmounting of that crisis, both sides have regained a sense of proportion and begun to work out a rough division of labour, whereby Britain still takes the lead where military action is required and Germany is more active diplomatically and economically, especially in the area of the old Warsaw Pact and USSR. The two states are even partners in the new 'contact group' on the Balkans, from which Italy is excluded.

Nor do alarm-bells ring so loudly in London over the Eurocorps or German enthusiasm for building on the WEU. The British government has partly come round to seeing some virtues in European defence cooperation and partly understands more fully the continuing lack of desire inside Germany for a military role in the world. For the foreseeable future it still seems more likely that Britain will be encouraging Germany to participate more in international peacekeeping activities than seeking to deter it from unilateral assertiveness.

In the last policy area under consideration, that of enlargement and the question of the wider Europe beyond the EU, there are still by the nature of things many loose ends in the policies of both London and Bonn. The two policies have converged in the 1990s from different starting-points, it being well known that the one favours a simultaneous widening and deepening and the other widening as a preventive measure against deepening. It is also probably the case that Britain has become committed to the ratcheting upwards of expectations on enlargement partly because it would prefer to see German influence over MittelEuropa exerted inside the EU than more freely outside it, in which case the centre of gravity of Germany's own interests would almost certainly also move eastwards, re-creating the divide in the continent that has just been overcome, albeit along a different fault-line.

The principal open question that remains, of course, in relation to Eastern Europe and to enlargement, and one that is no less important for Germany than for an anxious Britain watching on the sidelines, is the extent that 'Europe' can and should be redefined to include not only the former client states of the USSR, but also large parts of Russia and the old CIS. The dynamics of German trade, aid and investment, together with culture and language, are already forcing the priorities of the EU to swing more in an easterly direction, and even a Scandinavian enlargement, together with a semi-enlargement towards the Visegrad states, would reinforce this move dramatically at the expense of the geopolitically peripheral states like Britain. From this perspective Germany and Britain must in the end have different views on foreign policy priorities, despite their current agreement on enlargement, by virtue of their geographical positions. Britain does not wish to, and cannot in fact, become seriously involved in the international politics of central Europe, as it could not even in the days of greater British power during the 1930s. It might thus be forced towards the outer rings of the concentric circles in an enlarged EU tilted more towards the East. The agony of indecision over integration or sovereignty would then at last be over, solved by its sheer irrelevance in the face of events on the ground.

CONCLUSION

Britain has failed to prise open the Franco-German coupling, and it has even failed to establish a solid, predictable relationship with the Federal Republic. Anglo-German relations have too often been interrupted by misunderstandings which are rooted in very different outlooks and historical experiences. On the positive side of the balance sheet, these difficulties are no longer caused by the shadow of the Second World War, newspaper headlines notwithstanding. Nor has the revolution which created a new, united Germany yet produced serious problems between what are, after all, effective working partners in a number of established multi-lateral contexts.

From the British viewpoint what is needed is the ability to go beyond the old, essentially balance-of-power-based approach to diplomacy (even with allies), which has recently produced a revival of Anglo-Italian initiatives to match those of Bonn and Paris, and which delighted in Berlusconi's appointment of the Brugiste Antonio Martino to the Farnesina. Britain is no longer a 'great power' and it no longer needs a high-profile specifically German policy (although this is not to say that bilateral relations will not continue to be an important part of the complex web which is modern international politics). If Britain continues to emphasize special partnerships, in its personifying way, it will continue to be disappointed, as such a policy hands too much leverage to the love-object, especially when the relationship is asymmetrical. The USA, for instance, has increasingly focused on Germany (or Japan) as its preferred 'partner in leadership'.[24] If, conversely, Britain focuses on special fears and antagonisms, it will be conjuring up unnecessary difficulties by applying the thought processes of deterrence to relationships that, at least within the EU, are far too complex to be reduced to them. The cross-cutting cleavages of institutional complexity do not lend themselves to the pursuit of classical realist strategies. Furthermore, in historical and psychological terms Britain needs to stop defining itself in terms of Germany, whether seen as dangerous rival or economic panacea. When the British do so, they fall into the very '*Angst*' and 'inferiority complex' that Mrs Thatcher's famous Chequers seminar is supposed to have seen in the Germans.[25] Fortunately, and despite the opportunity for regression represented by the shock of German unification, there are signs that Britain is at last beginning to get Germany into perspective.[26]

NOTES

1. D.C. Watt, *Britain Looks to Germany: British Opinion and Policy towards Germany since 1945* (London: Oswald Wolff, 1965), p. 13.
2. Lord Carrington, *Reflect on Things Past: the Memoirs of Lord Carrington* (London: Collins, 1988), p. 229.
3. Margaret Thatcher, *The Downing Street Years* (London: HarperCollins, 1993), p. 791.
4. An honest Chancellor Kohl is said to have preferred to the more feline support of other Allies, not least because it made his own pronouncements seem so reasonable by comparison. See David Marsh, *Germany and Europe: the Crisis of Unity* (London: Heinemann, 1994), p. 44.
5. Throughout this paper 'Britain' will be used interchangeably with 'the United Kingdom' in the interests of readability.
6. In Reinhardt Rummel, 'Germany's Role: "Normalität" or "Sonderweg"?', in Christopher Hill (Ed.), *The Actors in Europe's Foreign Policy* (London: Routledge, 1996).
7. See Barbara Lippert, Rosalind Stevens-Strohmann, Dirk Gunther, Grit Viertel and Stephen Woolcock, *German Unification and EC Integration: German and British Perspectives* (London: RIIA/Pinter 1993), pp. 5–7, and Ch. 11.
8. 'In general, the British diplomats, officials and officers concerned with Germany during this period showed understanding and knowledge; they cannot be accused of anti-German bias or of insular arrogance': F.L. Carsten, *Britain and the Weimar Republic: the British Documents* (London: Batsford, 1984), p. 296.
9. On Vansittart and the way in which he soon discovered a new enemy after the war in Soviet communism, see David Wedgwood Benn, 'Germany: Britain and the Enemy Image', *The World Today* 46, 10 (October 1990).
10. A problem analysed more fully in Christopher Hill, 'The Historical Background: Past and Present in British Foreign Policy', in Michael Smith, Steve Smith and Brian White (Eds), *British Foreign Policy: Tradition, Change and Transformation* (London: Unwin Hyman, 1988). See also, among the burgeoning literature on 'the lessons of the past', Yaacov Y.I. Vertzberger, 'Decision-makers as Practical–Intuitive Historians: the Use and Abuse of History', in the same author's *The World in their Minds: Information Processing, Cognition and Perception in Foreign Policy Decision-making* (Stanford: Stanford University Press, 1990).
11. Ralf Dahrendorf has also emphasized the 'many layers' in 'the complicated relationship between Britons and Germans'. See his *On Britain* (London: BBC, 1982), pp. 141–144.
12. On current cooperation between the two diplomatic services, see 'Diplomatische Zusammenarbeit', *Frankfurter Allgemeine Zeitung*, 13 November 1992, and Steve Crawshaw, 'True Brits work for the other side', *The Independent*, 15 July 1994. On Sir Eyre Crowe see Zara Steiner, *The Foreign Office and Foreign Policy, 1898–1914* (Cambridge University Press, 1969), pp. 108–118. In a nice twist, Brian Crowe, a descendant

of Sir Eyre, is now head of the CFSP machinery in the Council of Ministers' Secretariat in Brussels.

13. The phrase is Margaret Thatcher's, in relation to a meeting with President Mitterand in December 1989: 'It seemed to me that although we had not discovered the means, at least we both had the will to check the German juggernaut', *The Downing Street Years*, pp. 796–797.

14. 'The Good, the Great and the Ugly: No. 62, Douglas Hurd', *The Independent Magazine*, 28 May 1994. The source was apparently Charles Powell.

15. An endnote I owe to Fred Halliday; see his 'Lying Abroad' (a review of Kissinger's *Diplomacy*), *London Review of Books*, 21 July 1994.

16. 'Two Views on Germany', *British Public Opinion*, February 1990.

17. *British Public Opinion*, August 1990. The poll was conducted on 13 July 1990. 48 per cent thought Ridley should resign, and 40 thought he should not. Mr Ridley left the government four days later. Interestingly, Baroness Thatcher barely mentions the affair in her memoirs.

18. *British Public Opinion*, September 1994. 17 per cent felt 'very friendly' and 52 per cent 'fairly friendly'.

19. John Ardagh, *Germany and the Germans* (Harmondsworth: Penguin, 1988), pp. 455–456.

20. Viscount Castlereagh on the Holy Alliance, 1820.

21. On the EEC see Christopher Lord, *British Entry to the European Community under the Heath Government of 1970–74* (Aldershot: Dartmouth, 1993), especially Ch. 2. On decolonization, see John Darwin, *Britain and Decolonisation: The Retreat from Empire in the Post-War World* (London: Macmillan, 1988).

22. Analysed by Henrik Larsen in terms of raising the national discourse to the European level. Henrik Larsen, *Discourse Analysis and Foreign Policy: the Impact of the Concepts of Europe, Nation/State, Security and the Nature of International Relations on French and British Policies towards Europe in the 1980s* (Ph.D. thesis, London School of Economics and Political Science, 1993). Britain can be seen, conversely, as having tried to drag down the European discourse to the national level.

23. For the mythology of nationhood in general, see Benedict Anderson, *Imagined Communities: Reflections on the Origins and Spread of Nationalism* (London: Verso, 1991) and for the 'invention of Britishness' see Linda Colley, *Britons: Forging the Nation 1707–1837* (New Haven: Yale University Press, 1992).

24. Christopher Coker, 'Britain and the New World Order: the Special Relationship in the 1990s', *International Affairs* 68, 3 (1992), p. 411.

25. The seminar, on 24 March 1990 and consisting of Mrs Thatcher, her advisers and various invited academic experts on Germany, was summarized in a memorandum written by the Prime Minister's foreign policy adviser, Charles Powell. This was subsequently leaked to *The Independent on Sunday* and reprinted in *Der Spiegel*. Other things the Germans were supposed to be prone to included aggressiveness, assertiveness, bullying, egotism and sentimentality. In some British readers this list rang bells closer to home. See Marsh, *Germany and Europe*, p. 45.

26. This view has been confirmed by recent events relating to the 50th anniversary of the end of the Second World War. The Duke of Kent's presence at the German commemoration of the bombing of Dresden, and the invitation to Germany to participate in VE Day activities in London designed to promote reconciliation, are hopeful signs.

BIBLIOGRAPHY

Anderson, B., *Imagined Communities: Reflections on the Origins and Spread of Nationalism* (London, Verso, 1991).

Ardagh, J., *Germany and the Germans* (Harmondsworth, Penguin, 1988).

Benn, D.W., 'Germany: Britain and the Enemy Image', *The World Today* 46, 10 (October 1990).

British Public Opinion, 'Two Views on Germany', February 1990.

British Public Opinion, August 1994.

Carrington, Lord, *Reflect on Things Past: the Memoirs of Lord Carrington* (London, Collins, 1988).

Carsten, F.L., *Britain and the Weimar Republic: the British Documents* (London, Batsford, 1984).

Christopher, Lord, *British Entry to the European Community under the Heath Government of 1970–74* (Aldershot, Darmouth, 1993).

Colley, L., *Britons: Forging the Nation 1707–1837* (Yale University Press, 1992).

Coker, C., 'Britain and the New World Order: the Special Relationship in the 1990s', *International Affairs* 68, 3 (1992).

Crawshaw, Steve, 'True Brits work for the other side', *The Independent*, 15 July 1994.

Dahrendorf, R., *On Britain* (London, BBC, 1982).

Darwin, J., *Britain and Decolonisation: the Retreat from Empire in the Post-War World* (London, Macmillan, 1988).

Frankfurter Allgemeine Zeitung, 13 November 1992.

Halliday, F., 'Lying Abroad', *London Review of Books*, 21 July 1994.

Larsen, H., *Discourse Analysis and Foreign Policy: the Impact of the Concepts of Europe. Nation-State, Security and the Nature of International Relations on French and British Policies towards Europe in the 1980s* (Ph.D. thesis, London School of Economics and Political Science, 1993).

Lippert, Barbara, Stevens-Strohmann, R., Gunther, D., Viertel, G., and Woolcock, S., *German Unification and EC Integration: German and British Perspectives* (London, RIIA/Pinter, 1993).

Marsh, David, *Germany and Europe: the Crisis of Unity* (London, Heinemann, 1994).

Powell, C., 'The Good, the Great and the Ugly: No. 62, Douglas Hurd', *The Independent Magazine*, 28 May 1994.

Rummel, Reinhardt, 'Germany's Role: "Normalität" or "Sonderweg"?', in Christopher Hill (Ed.), *The Actors in Europe's Foreign Policy* (London, Routledge, 1996).

Smith, M., Smith, S., and White, B. (Eds), *Brittish Foreign Policy: Tradition, Change and Transformation* (London, Unwin Hyman, 1988).

Steiner, Zara, *The Foreign Office and Foreign Policy, 1898–1914* (Cambridge University Press, 1969).

Thatcher, Margaret, *The Downing Street Years* (London, HarperCollins, 1993).

Watt, D.C., *Britain Looks to Germany: British Opinion and Policy towards Germany since 1945* (London, Oswald Wolff, 1965).

Vertzberger, Y.Y.I., 'Decision-makers as Practical–Intuitive Historians: the Use and Abuse of History', in Vertzberger, *The World on their Minds: Information Processing, Cognition and Perception in Foreign Policy Decision-making* (Stanford, Stanford University Press, 1990).

10 France and Germany
Yves Boyer

THE NEW PARAMETERS

Neither France nor Germany seem yet to have fully adjusted their external policy to the parameters prevailing on the world stage in the second half of the 1990s. This situation affects their bilateral relations and has consequences for the pace of the European integration process. On both sides of the Rhine, political leaders have had to redefine their countries' roles on the world stage and in European affairs. In this climate of transition, it seems as if Bonn and Paris feel uneasy with each other. This despite the fact that it is now three decades since the Elysée Treaty was signed[1] by Charles de Gaulle and Konrad Adenauer, and during these three decades both capitals have established a privileged entente which kept their relations at an unprecedented level of intimacy. Indeed, in the mid-1990s, one of the greatest challenges to the special relationship that continues to bind Paris to Bonn is to rediscover and reassert their reasons for giving such priority to this relationship and to adapt its parameters to a very different national, European and international situation. If, by misfortune, their *rapprochement* should lose its particular nature, the damage for Europe would be tremendous. Stability and prosperity in Europe continue to remain, by and large, a function of Franco-German entente and cooperation.

THE FRANCO-GERMAN LINKS

In this period of heavy weather what is the resilience of the link which continues to bond the two countries? Is the special relationship established between France and Germany doomed to lose its particularity? As pointed out by British observers, always prompt to anticipate a divorce between Bonn and Paris, 'it is too early to pronounce the Franco-German

241

relationship has so deepened it can survive unscathed any changes at the helm'.[2] In fact it seems that, for a variety of deep-rooted reasons, the marriage of interest between the two countries remains so solidly embedded that the current phase of turbulence will again lead the two countries to realize once and for all that neither Bonn nor Paris has any credible political alternative but to deepen their relationship.

Deriving from that basic assumption, it appears that the core of France's European policy is deliberately centred on the Franco-German axis.[3] This is a strategic choice made in the early sixties by General de Gaulle. His successors, from George Pompidou to Jacques Chirac, have constantly maintained this line with the necessary adjustments required by events. De Gaulle justified in very simple terms his policy of reconciliation with Germany:

> the two nations shall now cast out devils from the past; they shall acknowledge that they have to join for ever . . . the Germans have been really our enemies only since 1870. It is just three wars and three quarters of a century for the Germans and the Gauls who have elsewhere known so many wars in so many centuries . . . our greatest hereditary enemy has not been Germany, it has been England.[4]

STATE-TO-STATE RELATIONS

At the root of the spectacular Franco-German *rapprochement* lies an explicit political will of both countries to put an end to a disastrous relationship since German unity was accomplished by Bismarck. The prize is peace in Europe. The Elysée Treaty put an end to this troubled period. It opened the way to an intense cooperation between both governments and administrations as well as between ordinary citizens through various programmes aimed at promoting reconciliation between the two nations.

At the official level, the treaty set up enduring and in-depth mechanisms for cooperation. It created a strong political bond between Germany and France which is largely based on close and constant consultations. At the highest level, regular summits between the federal chancellor and the French president have been held twice a year since 1963. Thus, this cooperation entails a personal dimension. One of the very first measures a chancellor or a president takes once elected is to visit his French or German colleague. As an example, the day Chancellor Kohl was elected in 1982, he went to meet François Mitterrand. During the following ten years the two men met 115 times! When Jacques Chirac was elected in May 1995, the day after he was proclaimed president he went to Strasbourg to see Chancellor Kohl. At a meeting in Bonn in May 1996, the two leaders decided to meet informally every six weeks. French presidents and German chancellors have also made symbolic gestures to celebrate and illustrate the reconciliation between the two nations. Konrad Adenauer and Charles de Gaulle participated together in a mass in the cathedral of Reims, famous in French history, for it was here that the kings of France used to be crowned. In 1987, Helmut Kohl and François Mitterrand were hand in hand at in Verdun, commemorating the 70th anniversary of the bloodiest battle ever fought between the armies of France and Germany. In 1994, President Mitterrand decided to invite German miltary units from the Eurocorps to participate with their French counterparts in the traditional military parade on 14 July. It was the first time since 1945 that foreign troops had marched on the Champs Elysée.

At the ministerial level, informal consultations are organized which can take place almost immediately should an international problem or sudden issue arise. In 1982, it was decided to deepen coordination in the field of foreign affairs through regular meetings involving the foreign affairs and defence ministers of both countries. This close consultation process took on a new dimension when, in the late late 1980s, it was decided to establish a Franco-German defence council as well as a council for protecting the environment. A protocol to the Elysée Treaty was thus signed on 22 January 1988. At the same time a bilateral economic and financial council was set up between the two countries. Ministerial meetings every six months since 1963 have created strong links at all levels. In the field of defence, for example, the achievement is already impressive. The creation of Eurocorps, decided at a bilateral summit in La Rochelle, in May 1992, led to the development of an army corps with French and German units that were later joined by Belgian and Spanish units. The Eurocorps gives WEU real operational capabilities, based on impressive capacities. It possesses, for example, more heavy tanks than the whole British army. In the field of armament, cooperation remains intense and the creation in 1996 of a bilateral agency for armaments represents an important move towards standardization of military equipment for the Bundeswehr and the French armed forces. The development of standardized equipment and the deployment of the Eurocorps will certainly help to create a dynamic towards common military concepts and doctrines in the years ahead. This will represent a giant step towards an integrated European defence at a time when US military involvement in Europe will diminish significantly. The decision of 8 December 1995 made by Bonn to participate in the construction of the French Helios II spy satellite has been assessed as reinforcing Franco-German links at the strategic level. Despite very strong pressures from Washington to buy US-made satellites, Bonn opted for the European solution. Thus Paris and Bonn will possess, at the beginning of the next century, common means to evaluate crisis situations.

PARLIAMENTARIAN AND ADMINISTRATIVE LINKS

Parliaments have also been involved in this *rapprochement*. On important occasions, leaders of Germany and France have delivered speeches in the National Assembly or the Bundestag. During the Euromissile crisis, in January 1983, President Mitterrand made a decisive speech to the Bundestag in which he strongly advocated the deployment of Pershing II and land-based cruise missiles. During the Maastricht Treaty negotiations, Chancellor Helmut Kohl made a very convincing plea in favour of the treaty to the French National Assembly. And the prospect of monetary union helped to push the National Assembly and the Bundestag closer. It was also striking that, early in 1994, Jean-Claude Trichet, the governor of the newly independent Bank of France, presented his first public testimony to the Bundestag in Bonn a few days before he did so to the National Assembly.

Regular cooperation has also been established between French and German administrations. Organized by the French civil service's General Direction (Direction Générale de l'Administration et de la Fonction Publique) and its German counterpart through the Bundesakademie für Öffentliche Verwaltung, exchanges of personnel have taken place since the 1970s. Senior servants can, by an agreement of 1977, make short stays (between two and four weeks) in the other country's administration. At the Aix-la-Chapelle summit, in September 1978, longer stays – from six to twelve months – were also made possible. The Ecole Nationale d'Administration (ENA), which trains young French senior civil servants, receives German students each year: three were at ENA in 1994–95. Various ministries (finance, justice, interior, etc.) organize exchanges between French and German counterparts. In the field of internal security, before the Schengen agreement was signed, cooperation was institutionalized between German and French police forces and between intelligence services, particularly to coordinate the fight against terrorism. Police cooperation started in 1971 and was formalized by an inter-ministerial agreement of 8 April 1987.

PEOPLE-TO-PEOPLE

In addition to the *rapprochement* of various French and German administrations, close cooperation has also helped to create opportunities for a better understanding between ordinary people. Vigorous effort have been undertaken to promote exchanges between young people of each country through the Office Franco-Allemand pour la Jeunesse (OFAJ). Celebrating its 30th anniversary in 1993, the OFAJ declared that, since its creation, it has organized 160 000 meetings involving 4.8 million people. The success of OFAJ led Germany and Poland to establish a similar structure within the framework of the Polish–German treaty of 17 June 1991.

The reconciliation between French and German people also owes much to the twinning of cities. This phenomenon dates back to the early 1950s, before the Elysée Treaty was signed. It began with the twinning of Montbéliard, a French city in the Jura area, and Ludwigsburg on 31 May 1950.

Seven years later there were only seven twinnings between German and French towns. But this movement acclerated on the initiative of French mayors who belonged to the resistance during the Second World War and who decided to work for reconciliation between the two sides of the Rhine. For instance, a famous priest and hero of the resistance, Félix Kir, decided to twin his city, Dijon, with Mayence on 5 May 1958. The movement considerably helped to flesh out the implementation of the Elysée Treaty. Now 1400 twinnings link German and French cities which represent more than 80 million citizens.[5]

EUROPEAN INTERESTS

Once the wounds of the past had been largely forgotten and the rancours solemnly buried by Adenauer and de Gaulle, the Franco-German relationship acquired a new dimension. For the French this dimension consists of two closely inter-related ingredients.

Firstly, there is the basic assumption that the perpetuation of the Franco-German link remains in the deepest interest of the whole of Europe. The grim prospect of an EU unable to progress towards closer integration was outlined in the CDU–CSU paper of September 1994. This document warned of the danger of two blocs emerging in Europe: one centred on Germany, more favourable to free trade and open to the East of Europe, and another centred on France, more Colbertist and looking more towards the Mediterranean area. This scenario is a nightmare that both countries are keen to exorcize. The spectre of two Europes as outlined in the CDU–CSU paper found an echo in Paris when the minister for European affairs of the Balladur government, Alain Lamassoure, stated that if a fundamental and irreconcilable disagreement between Paris and Bonn were to occur, there would be two Europes.[6] In Paris and in Bonn it is still considered that the close alliance between the two capitals corresponds to an essential and vital need for reasons linked to history, geography and economy. The basis of this is a very simple reason that stems from a problem of historical dimensions: i.e. the role and the place of Germany in Europe.

As de Gaulle pointed out in 1965, 'the German problem is by exellence, the European problem ... the solution to such a huge problem could not be found otherwise than by Europe itself ... this is the foremost objective of French policy.'[7] German statements echoed this concern: 'the European Union is the only way which permits a reduction in German power. This is for Germany the only way to become normal.'[8]

The second ingredient of an enduring special relationship between Paris and Bonn is related to spheres of influence. Three factors are crucial here. One is the history of the expansionism of the former Soviet Union. A second is the permanent tendency of the United States, since the Second World War, to seek a benevolent domination of Western Europe. And, at the end of the 1990s, a third influence is the economic and trade rivalry between North America, Japan and Western Europe which, according to the French, should compel the Europeans to pool their resources in order to cope with hegemonic tendencies and trade competition.

There is, however, a strong belief in France that only the intimate alliance of France and Germany can provide the opportunity for Europe to deepen its unity and assert itself on the world stage. Unfortunately, most European countries are already either impotent, subdued by Washington, unable to resist its pressures or unwilling to assert European interests by diplomatic, economic or military means. Accordingly, deepening the Franco-German axis is the preferable, if not the only way, to escape impotence and exert influence on the European Union and its further developments as a kind of superpower. This widely spread French belief has been eloquently expressed by former President Giscard d'Estaing who wrote in 1991:

> experience revealed that all progress in the European construction started from joint Franco-German initiatives. If one day there were no longer these common efforts ... Europe will no longer progress ... when we will be 15 or 20, paralysis is almost certain. Europe then will need an engine, this engine is the Franco-German friendship. Our two countries want Europe to deepen. But not a single country is powerful enough to make Europe advance.[9]

DIVERGENCES

The relation between the two partners has, however, been an uneasy one. When ratifying the Elysée Treaty in May 1963, the Bundestag, in order to avoid displeasing Washington, added a preamble that immediately cooled Paris–Bonn relations. Later, when Ludwig Erhard succeeded Konrad Adenauer, the problem was exacerbated by the clear pro-American bias of Erhard. In January 1969, George Pompidou, who was elected head of state some months later, declared in Rome that France and Italy were closer to each other than to Germany whose industrial power posed problems.[10]

Other sources of friction between the two countries have appeared, particularly since the end of the cold war. Roland Dumas, former foreign minister under François Mitterrand, mentioned, for example, that during the German reunification process, differences arose between Bonn and Paris on the issue of the German–Polish border and later, at the beginning of the Yugoslavian crisis, on the Croatian question. Tensions reached a climax when, on these occasions, as recalled by Roland Dumas, both sides evinced a certain visceral agressiveness.[11] On EU enlargement and deepening, the agendas in each country were, at least initially, rather different, which provoked a degree of irritation. In the spring of 1994, for example, the German foreign ministry called in François Scheer, the French ambassador in Bonn, to complain about his comments to German journalists that Germany had taken a heavy-handed – and in Paris's view unhelpful – line in the negotiations to admit the Nordic countries and Austria to the EU.[12] After the visit of the German chancellor to Poland in July 1995, where Helmut Kohl declared that Poland will become part of the EU and NATO by the year 2000, suspicions about German aims were raised by French commentators. *Le Monde* published an editorial which stated that: 'if the ambitious goals defined by the Chancellor were to be delayed, the fault will be attributed to Germany's partners, in particular to France, portrayed in Bonn and in Warsaw as insensitive to the interests of Eastern Europe'.[13] On the German side, voices expressed concerns about the growing strain on the relationship between the two countries. In addition to political differences, there were problems in bilateral cooperation on industrial or defence projects. Bonn complained that in many cases there were imbalances between the two partners and advocated a strict equality. On this issue, there is certainly a greater effort needed by the French side to work with its German counterpart on the basis of strict parity. Greater German assertiveness in external affairs, however, led former Chancellor Helmut Schmidt to declare in 1994, 'since November 1989, cooperation between Bonn and Paris has been decreasing', adding that 'Germany shall become again a land of compromise'.[14]

THE STRATEGIC PACT

Despite divergences between the two countries, their political entente has proved, up to now, to be strong enough to overcome such bones of contention. What are the reasons for such a strategic pact?

There is obviously the feeling on both sides of the Rhine that European stability can no longer be guaranteed if basic agreement is not maintained between France and Germany. Without such agreement, Western Europe may return to a balance-of-power game, a game that can verge on latent civil war which, in the longer run, is synonymous with collective suicide. If France were to turn its back on the European construction, which horizon will Germany move towards? If Germany plays an independent role, will this re-create anti-German feelings in France that, undoubtedly, would inflict a deadly blow to the entente between the two countries?

There is indeed a very strange paradox in this relationship which is by no means a 'love affair' between the two sides of the Rhine. Both partners are tied by very strong common interests and the fear that, if old demons were again unleashed on the two sides of the Rhine, serious harm would be inflicted on each other and on Europe. This potential danger compels each partner always to seek compromise. There are many illustrations of this. For example, during the GATT negotiations in 1993, when France was isolated on the issue of agriculture, very few of its European partners supported it, so Germany instead played a very positive and constructive role. Another illustration occurred in June 1995, when President Jacques Chirac decided to resume nuclear tests before France would sign the Comprehensive Test Ban Treaty in 1996. Despite the very negative reactions of German public opinion, the German government understood immediately that this was a very sensitive issue for the French. Instead of adopting an unfriendly and irrational attitude, as was the case elsewhere in Europe, particularly in northern Europe, German political leaders took a low profile. Avoiding definitive reprobations and emotional declarations, they adopted a responsible attitude. The chairman of the CDU parliamentary group, Wolfgang Schäuble, outlined perfectly the official German position in declaring that:

> the announcement of a new campaign of nuclear tests complicates the debate on a common foreign and security policy in Europe . . . But, in order to make progress, we have to minimize problems between Paris and Bonn, whose respective positions on that topic are so different.[15]

Compromises are also effected by the French side. The most essential one is clearly in the monetary area. The French strongly believe that, in order to avoid jeopardizing the European monetary construction, they have no other credible choice than to follow the dominant monetary power in the EU, i.e. Germany. The debate on that issue is, however, very delicate in France where there is the feeling that Germany has transferred part of the unification costs on to its partners through a policy of high interest rates. Until now the partisans of the strong franc (*franc fort*) policy, which links the franc to the Deutschmark, have represented the dominant attitude which was followed by Mitterrand and Chirac. Both of them have, however, been under attack from within their respective camps where prominent leaders accused the *franc fort* policy, determined by German monetary policy defined by the Bundesbank, as largely responsible for the high unemployement rate in France. These leaders advocate a different policy which would put Germany and France on different courses in monetary affairs.

What appeared to be a risky gamble when de Gaulle and Adenauer set the rules of the game between the two countries, made of reciprocal compromises in order to reach common goals, proved to be possible. Undoubtedly this enduring and permanent process, based on consultations, brings benefits when it works, but were it to get seriously stuck, the prospects would be dire.

STABILITY

Together, Germany and France became co-managers of, and co-responsible for, the stability, unity and prosperity of the Western part of the European continent. This *mariage de raison* has created envy, if not suspicion and even anxiety, elsewhere in Europe, particularly in the United Kingdom. At the beginning of the Franco-German *rapprochement*, London did not believe it could work very long. When this diagnosis turned out be wrong, London has since tried either to insert a wedge between the two partners or to join them. Both strategies have failed. Obviously the Franco-German axis perturbs traditional British policy regarding the continent, as a former head of the Foreign Office states despairingly: 'I do not criticize the Franco-German partnership because for fifty years it has played an essential role in maintaining peace in Western Europe. But one cannot leave to those two States, as important they are, a monopoly as to ideas about Europe.'[16] In fact, in both countries, commitment to the Franco-German axis is felt to be greater than commitment to Europe. As has been reported by Jacques Attali, a former aide to President Mitterrand, Chancellor Kohl once said: 'for me, the Franco-German relationship is more important than Europe'.[17] Various French statements on the primacy of the Franco-German relationship, even on European construction, have echoed this sentiment.[18]

Now, in a very different international landscape from that which prevailed when the Franco-German entente was established, the *mariage de raison* has to be spelled out in a new covenant which will take into account the new situation in Europe and in the world after the end of the bloc system.[19] Accordingly, in preparing for the Inter-Governmental Conference (IGC) of 1996, the French appeared less worried about structures than about how to frame a new strategic agreement with Germany from which will derive mechanisms allowing the deepening and the enlargement of the European Union. With impressive unanimity, French political leaders – from the socialist party to the right-wing coalition backing President Jacques Chirac – are advocating a pragmatic approach to the future development of the European Union. They promote the idea of a European construction centred on three circles involving different perspectives and obligations, the inner circle of tightest solidarity and cooperation being built around France and Germany,[20] a view not so different from that which was emphasized in the CSU-CDU paper of September 1994. To put it more bluntly, today as yesterday, Franco-German entent remains the key dimension of the European construction. For Bonn and Paris nothing is more important than to preserve this entente. If Jacques Chirac and Helmut Kohl find a compromise on the reform of European institutions, the 1996 IGC will represent a real step forward. If not, the reforms will be merely cosmetic.

MUTUAL PERCEPTIONS

Does the fundamental importance of cooperation with Germany as it is perceived in Paris have the same resonance in Bonn? There has been abundant speculation that, after completing the costly reunification process, Germany may have a greater international margin of manoeuvre and may be tempted by hegemonic impulses *vis-à-vis* the European integration process.

There are as yet no signs emanating from Germany of such a shift. There are no indications that Germany is leaning towards self-assertiveness. Germany played a very minor role during the crisis in the Gulf in 1991–92. Even since, in July 1994, the constitutional court in Karlsruhe allowed German armed forces to be deployed outside Europe, there have been no signs that the German population favours such world activism. Furthermore, in terms of equipment, training and experience, German armed forces are far from ready to accept hastily a major role in out-of-area interventions.

The question of Germany's future is characterized not so much by an excess of strength as by Germany's reluctance to take its share in world affairs, an attitude that may directly or indirectly affect the European Union. Such issues arise because two trends are evident in Germany today. One is related to the very deep impact demography will have on Germany's future. The German population is indeed becoming rapidly older than that of any other European country, with the exception of Italy. The dependency ratio – i.e. the ratio of people over 65 to those in the 15–65 age group – rises from an average of 21 per cent in the EU in 1990 to 47 per cent in Germany against 39 per cent in France or in Britain.[21] It is estimated that in the year 2000, there will be 300 000 more deaths than births in Germany, and in 2030 this figure will rise to 600 000.[22] In these circumstances, Germany is in a very different situation from that at the beginning of this century when families of more than five people represented 44 per cent of all families against 5 per cent today. As a result, the country is likely to lose dynamism and will have to invest significant resources in health services for elderly people.

The second trend is related to the impact of the Second World War on new generations of German people. Apart from the idea of defending the homeland, the prospect of using force in international affairs evokes the darkest side of recent German history. Defence issues are seen by a significant part of the population at best as morally insane and at worst as unjustifiable. Such attitudes are illustrated by the very great number of young Germans who are conscientious objectors. Their number amounted to 131 000 in 1993, when the number of conscripts in the Bundeswehr at that time was 150 000.[23] There is clearly the fear in France that, instead of assertiveness, Germany leans towards a kind of neo-neutralism with the greatest reluctance to care about international problems beyond its East European *glacis*. According to former President François Mitterrand, in Germany, 'a lot of people want to go in that direction: leftist intellectuals are enthralled by neutralism, teachers are starting to talk this way'.[24]

If there is in Germany the dream of resembling a 'super Switzerland' there is, on the contrary, the dream in France of EU activism in world affairs, including security affairs. There is still a political consensus on the need for assertiveness in international affairs, even if this involves military forces. This cultural difference betwen the two countries may, in the future, come to pose the most serious obstacle on the road to further integration. Since the special relationship between the two countries is based on constant political consultations, adjustments and compromises, it will be essential to overcome these cultural differences.

THE FUTURE

In the future, the Franco-German entente may find new soil in which to grow, develop and deepen. The new international landscape of the late 1990s gives both countries a far greater margin of manoeuvre than during the cold wa when both saw their respective foreign and defence policies framed within narrow limits. The collapse of the bi-polar system opens new terrain in terms of common action. Since, in both countries, there is no serious credible and articulate alternative to the entente between the two sides of the Rhine, one can only echo what a long-time observer of the relations between the two countries declared quite convincingly: 'there is no future for France without Germany and vice versa'.[25]

NOTES

1. 22 January 1963.
2. David Buchan and Quentin Peel, 'Odd couple's testing tiffs', *The Financial Times*, 18 March 1994.
3. Alain Juppé, speech made at the Quai d'Orsay, 8 April 1993.
4. General de Gaulle quoted by Alain Peyrefitte, *C'était De Gaulle*, Ed. Fayard de Fallois (Paris, 1994), p. 599.
5. André Santini, 'Les jumelages franco-allemands', in: *Le couple franco-allemand en Europe*, Ed. Henri Ménudier (Université de la Sorbonne Nouvelle-Paris III, Ed. PIA, 1993).
6. Alain Lamassoure, interview, *Ouest France*, 2 February 1994.
7. General de Gaulle, press conference, 4 February 1965.
8. Karl Lamers, interview, *La Tribune Desfossés*, 7 February 1995.
9. Giscard d'Estaing interviewed in *Frankfurter Allgemeine Magazine*, 22 November 1991.

10. On the issue of permanent difficulties between Bonn and Paris, see: Jacques Morizet, 'Le traité de l'Elysée trente ans après', *Défense Nationale*, February 1994.
11. Roland Dumas, interview, *Le Figaro*, 3 September 1992.
12. 'Consensus de façade au sommet Franco-Allemand', *La Tribune Desfossés*, 1 June 1994.
13. 'L'Allemagne et la Pologne', *Le Monde*, 11 July 1995.
14. Helmut Schmidt, 'Quand l'Allemagne assassine l'Europe', *Globe Hebdo*, 11–17 August 1993. This text has also been published in *Die Zeit.*
15. Wolfgang Schäuble, *Le Monde*, 5 July 1995.
16. Douglas Hurd, speech at IFRI, Paris, 13 January 1995.
17. Jacques Attali, *Verbatim II*, quoted by Joseph Fitchett, 'Bonn–Paris Ties in Chirac Agenda', *International Herald Tribune*, 18 May 1995.
18. Alain Lamassoure said during a radio interview that 'we are not prepared to sacrifice the Franco-German entente to the process of European integration'. Radio Classique-Le Point, 31 May 1994.
19. 'France seeks to deepen ties with Germany', *Financial Times*, 20 February 1995.
20. See Alain Juppé, 'Quel horizon pour la politique étrangère de la France?', speech given for celebrating the 20th anniversary of the foreign ministry's policy planning staff, Paris, 30 January 1995.
21. Samuel Brittain, 'Defusing pension bomb', *Financial Times*, 16 March 1995.
22. Andrew Gowers, 'A story of births, deaths and marriages', *Financial Times*, 25 October 1993.
23. 'La Bundeswehr à court de munitions', *Libération*, 14 March 1994.
24. François Mitterrand quoted by Joseph Fitchett, op. cit.
25. Joseph Rovan, interview, *Le Figaro*, 17 May 1995.

BIBLIOGRAPHY

Brittain, S., 'Defusing pension bomb', *Financial Times*, 16 March 1995.
Buchan, D., and Quentin Peel, 'Odd couple's testing tiffs', *Financial Times*, 18 March 1994.
De Gaulle, General C., press conference, 4 February 1965.
d'Estaing, G., *Frankfurter Allgemeine Magazine*, 22 November 1991.
Dumas, R., *Le Figaro*, 3 September 1992.
Financial Times, 'France seeks to deepen ties with Germany', 20 February 1995.
Fitchett, J., 'Bonn–Paris Ties in Chirac Agenda', *International Herald Tribune*, 18 May 1995.
Gowers, A., 'A story of births, deaths and marriages', *Financial Times*, 25 October 1993.
Hurd, D., speech at IFRI, Paris, 13 January 1995.
Juppé, A., speech made at the Quai d'Orsay, 8 April 1993.
Juppé, A., 'Quel horizon pour la politique étrangère de la France?', speech, Paris, 30 January 1995.

Lamassoure, A., interview, *Ouest France*, 2 February 1994.

Lamassoure, A., radio interview, Radio Classique-Le Point, 31 May 1994.

Lamers, K., interview, *La Tribune Desfossés*, 7 February 1995.

La Tribune Desfossés, 'Consensus de façade au sommet Franco-Allemand', 1 June 1994.

Le Monde, 'L'Allemagne et la Pologne', 11 July 1995.

Libération, 'La Bundeswehr à court de munitions', 14 March 1994.

Morizet, J., 'Le traité de l'Elysée trente ans après', *Defense Nationale*, February 1994.

Peyrefitte, A., *C'était De Gaulle*, Ed. Fayard de Fallois (Paris, 1994).

Rovan, J., interview, *Le Figaro*, 17 May 1995.

Santini, A., 'Les jumelages franco-allemands', in: *Le couple franco-allemand en Europe*, Ed. Henri Ménudier (Université de la Sorbonne Nouvelle Paris III, PIA, 1993).

Schäuble, W., *Le Monde*, 5 July 1995.

Schmidt, H., 'Quand l'Allemagne assassine l'Europe', *Globe Hebdo*, 11–17 August 1993.

Part IV: Prospects

11 No Threats, No Temptations: German Grand Strategy After the Cold War

Josef Joffe

THE PAST AS PRELUDE

30 June 1995 was a watershed date in post-war German history. On that day, the Germans broke through the 40-year-old cocoon which had sheltered them so nicely against the pulls and pushes of world politics. By a comfortable margin, the Bundestag authorized the government to project force out of area – into the former Yugoslavia. Though the licence was not exactly a sweeping one,[1] it was revolutionary. For it empowered the government to send German troops into combat for the first time since the Second World War.

That was a drastic break with a jealously guarded tradition. Beyond national and alliance defence, so the cast-in-concrete consensus ran, German troops must never again be used abroad. This injunction had even acquired the weight of (alleged) constitutional taboo. Government after government, whether centre-left or centre-right, had reiterated that mantra until virtually everyone believed that the out-of-area ban was holy constitutional writ.

Actually, the Basic Law was more permissive than the purveyors of a strict prohibition claimed. Article 24, for instance, explicitly authorizes participation in systems of 'mutual collective security' and thus opened the way for (West) German membership in NATO and WEU. 'Collective security' is also at the heart of the UN Charter which enjoins member states to contribute military forces to the Security Council for peacekeeping and peace-enforcement (i.e. combat) purposes. When the Federal Republic acceded to the UN in

259

1973, it accepted all obligations under the charter – whence it follows that Bonn implicitly conceded its legal ability to honour these obligations.

Why then the stubborn insistence on stringent constitutional limits? The heart of the matter was never juridical but historical and political. Historically, it should not come as a surprise that a nation which twice in this century has failed so disastrously in war and thereafter succeeded so brilliantly in peace should remain so thoroughly chained to the habits of a 'civilian power'. But there was more than just the hold of memory.

First of all, this posture also proved to be immensely profitable. While the other Western powers squandered their blood and treasure on post-colonial or imperial ventures round the world, the West Germans were free to tend their own garden and to unleash an enduring 'economic miracle'. In the cold war era, Britain spent an average of 5 per cent of GNP on defence, the USA an average of 7 per cent. Yet the Federal Republic has never allocated more than 3 per cent. The societal gains of abstentionism were even more impressive. The Fourth Republic in France fell in the upheavals unleashed by the war in Algeria. A decade later, the Vietnam War similarly traumatized America. Compared to this kind of turmoil, the divisive debates in the Federal Republic (over rearmament in the 1950s and Euromissiles in the 1980s) look, in retrospect, like exercises in orderly democratic procedure.

Diplomatically, the politics of passivity turned a handsome profit, too. Whereas the United States, Britain and France took on a shifting array of enemies after 1945, the Federal Republic tried to offend none and to be friends with all – with Iraq and Iran, Israel and the Arabs, and – in the 1970s and 1980s – with the USA and the USSR. Conciliation rather than confrontation, and trade rather than war, was the credo of West German diplomacy – all the way to the Gulf War when Bonn reflexively tried to avoid an early commitment to the American coalition.

The constitutional limits on the use of force – or more precisely, the political interpretation of the Basic Law – must be seen in this context. It can be reduced to a simple moral: bitter were the fruits of war, sweet are those of peace. And the habits cemented by the profits of passivity die hard.

Yet after the great watershed of 1990/91 – marked by reunification, the collapse of bi-polarity and the demise of the Soviet Union – the constitutional court simply re-read the Basic Law and in the summer of 1994 decided according to the letter of the Basic Law. As a result of that verdict, the Federal Republic was suddenly free to do as it wished. It could engage in peacekeeping and peacemaking (i.e. forceful intervention), even in Gulf-type operations sanctioned by the UN. Yet it still took another year before the government actually decided to use its prerogative, as sanctioned by the constitutional court.[2] And it did so in a manner which highlighted continuity rather than rupture, a cautious rather than expansive view of Germany's role in the world. It acted because it had no other choice.

In the watershed summer of 1995, the issue was not really intervention out of area, but a far older claim on German policy: alliance loyalty. The decision was taken in the context of a probable withdrawal of Allied UN troops from the Bosnian theatre. Though the government had vowed that intervention in the Bosnian war was strictly *verboten*, it could not brush aside the claims of the alliance – a pillar in the overall structure of German foreign policy. No matter how strong the resistance to force projection, Bonn could not stand aside while French, Dutch or British forces were shot up during their retreat. Thus there was continuity in revolution: force projection in Bosnia as such, no; succour to Allied troops, yes.

The court's 1994 verdict had merely removed an artificial but very useful constraint. Along with the precedent of 1995, when parliament actually authorized (a very modest) force projection, that verdict makes for permissiveness, not for a programme.

And for a problem: What does a nation do with its liberated power in the post-bipolar age when the 40-year-old strategic threat has disappeared that previously posed all the major questions and delivered most of the major answers? In grand strategy, post-bipolarity is to affairs of state what post-modernity is to art, architecture and literature. In each realm the essential rule is 'no rule' – or: 'Anything goes.'

INTERNATIONAL STRUCTURE AND NATIONAL STRATEGY

Post-bipolarity is an age in which yesterday's demanding rules of state behaviour have evaporated along with the structure that gave rise to them. Bi-polarity was to strategy what the Bauhaus was to architecture: it imposed rules that were few in number, but unyielding in their implications.[3] The two key actors, the United States and the Soviet Union, and their allies were caught in a structural rivalry compounded by ideology that left no respite and no peripheries. And the essential rule could be summed up in one word: 'containment'.

The key structural features of the Forty Years War, also known as the cold war, were three:

1. Vast concentrations of ever-ready nuclear and conventional forces forever imposed a simple, but deadly rule on the antagonists: whoever shoots first shall die second. Hence war was out of the question, and so ultra-stability prevailed over deadly fear or murderous ambition. As a result, politics – and thus stability – became frozen wherever the balance of terror ruled. No matter how contested, borders remained cast in concrete; no matter how fiery, national ambitions remained in check.

2. Bi-polarity spelled control. Precisely because great power war implied mutual extinction, the United States and the USSR made sure 24 hours a day that unruly allies would not drag them into war. Even war between informal allies – above all, in the Middle East – was quickly squelched or contained by the superpower so that they would not be sucked into the quarrels of the small.

3. Bi-polarity made for stability within blocs and nations. Beholden to the security extended by patrons, clients took care not to affront their protectors. Running on a short leash of dependence, lesser allies accepted the discipline meted out by the strong. Amongst themselves, dependants remained on their best behaviour because of an overweening security threat from without. The rigorous integration of military forces repressed whatever temptations may have riled the soul. In the Soviet sphere, deviationism was swiftly suppressed by invasion. Even

internally, within states, discipline prevailed among unhappy nationalities, given the centralizing pressures exerted by the Cold War.

How did Germany fit into this structure? Bi-polarity was of
course anchored in the heart of Europe, where the global,
regional and intra-national balance came together at the
Elbe River. Here, the two superpowers, the two blocs and
the two Germanies were fused together in a triple-tiered
structure of ultra-stable confrontation. In Germany the United
States and the Soviet Union positioned the bulk of their
forward-stationed forces. Also between Rhine and Oder, the
two alliances deployed 1.3 million men plus thousands of
nuclear weapons. And the two Germanies with a total of
600 000 troops, countervailed each other in a peculiar kind
of stalemate that simultaneously harnessed and neutralized
German power.

During the cold war, Germany did not have to formulate
a grand strategy. Nor could it do so on its own. Grand strategy was virtually a given – imposed on the two half-coun-
tries by their position in the cold war system.

The German Democratic Republic had no choice whatso-
ever. As forward bastion of the Soviet Union, it was the strategic brace of the Muscovite empire in Europe. Possession
of the GDR allowed the USSR to encircle, contain and control its satellites. Given its enormous strategic value, the GDR's
freedom of choice was virtually nil, and thus East German
grand strategy was Soviet grand strategy writ small.

Though the Federal Republic boasted far greater sovereignty and autonomy, it, too, had to act on a stage – and
with a script – essentially provided by others. Bonn was not
free to choose its allies. The condition of rearmament and
rehabilitation was integration into the Western alliance. The
price was the *complete* subordination of its forces under Allied command and the dedication of its territory as a staging post for the West.

Script and stage, however, were gladly accepted by the
West Germans. Their security problem was a given, and its
name was the 'Soviet Union'. This problem had only one
solution for a country that shared a one-thousand mile border with the Warsaw Pact: 'deterrence'. Above all, West

Germany, lying across the invasion routes from the East, could not become the prime venue and victim of a Third World War.

Hence the primacy of deterrence. War must not be fought, but forestalled. And so the Federal Republic insisted on American nuclear weapons as well as on a massive Allied presence in a forward position on its soil. If the Soviets would have to attack the full panoply of NATO forces, if they would have to risk speedy escalation from the tactical to the strategic nuclear level, then they would value the *status quo* far more highly than expansion. The essence of German grand strategy during the cold war was to make the price forever dwarf the prize. And so West Germany became the most militarized space on earth, with about 800 000 Allied and German troops plus thousands of Allied nuclear weapons. To describe the strategic stage of the cold war in these terms is to dramatize the distance Germany and Europe have travelled since the summer of 1990 when Mikhail Gorbachev consented to the reunification of Germany within the West. In the autumn of 1994, the last of the Soviet troops, which once numbered 400 000, left the territory of Germany. Some Western troops will remain; the total for the Americans in all of Western Europe is to shrink to about 100 000, and most probably less – down from 330 000 at the height of the Cold War. The German army – 600 000 for the combined total of the FRG and the GDR – will come down to 325 000, more likely less. West German defence expenditures, once close to 3 per cent of GNP, are sliding toward 1.5 per cent for Germany as a whole.

These are the numbers, and they reflect a profound transformation of the stage on which future German grand strategy must operate. Today, Germany is encircled only by friends. Russian troops, once encamped in the heart of Germany, are stationed at a thousand-kilometre remove. Poland and the Czech Republic are no longer staging posts but buffers: indeed, these two countries as well as Hungary would join NATO today rather than tomorrow.

Never before in history has Germany, in whatever political guise, enjoyed such as a benign strategic setting. That is the key point of departure for all reasoning about Germany's future role. Nor does history offer much help. Take Bismarck, for instance, the greatest grand strategist of them all. He set out the essentials with dispatch and elegance. His enduring fear was France, bent upon *revanche* for the defeat in 1871. And his enduring *Angst* was the 'nightmare of coalitions', the all-European encirclement that almost ended the career of Frederick's Prussia. Hence, in the famous 'Kissinger Diktat', Bismarck formulated the following precept for the Second Reich: the basic purpose was to create a 'universal political situation in which all the powers except France need us and, by dint of their mutual relations, are kept as much as is possible from forming coalitions against us'.

The variations were many, but the purpose remained constant: guard against encircling coalitions and pursue Bismarck's goal with ever-mounting subtlety – some would say, with manipulation and deception – so that Germany's great rivals, above all its flanking powers France and Russia, should not join hands against the centre.

Today, however, the world is bi-polar no more, and multi-polar not yet. Neither straightforward containment, as dictated by bi-polarity, nor a Bismarckian policy of balance and manoeuvre, as prompted by the multi-polarity of the 19th century, can provide a *Leitmotiv* for grand strategy – whether for a world power like the United States or a regional power like Germany.

Today, there is no clear strategic solution because there is no clear strategic problem. Containment is obsolete because Russia, the white-blue-and-red successor of the Soviet Union, is not pressing on Germany and the West for the time being. And Bismarck's answer is not acute because Germany is surrounded not by enemies real and potential, but only by friends.

THE EUROPEAN STAGE IN AN AGE OF AMBIVALENCE

To get to grips with the issue, let us look at the contemporary stage – the European system. In some respects, the stage still looks like yesterday's. To begin with, the great Alliance of the cold war, NATO, is still in place. There is still an American SACEUR (the supreme NATO commander), an integrated force structure, a joint infrastructure, joint training and manoeuvres. There is also the West European Union, the purely European alliance that remained a paper compact during the cold war because it lacked the one element that allowed NATO to rule the roost: American membership. And there is still Russia. Unlike its predecessor, Russia lacks the distinction of 'first enemy'. But neither has Russia been promoted to the status of 'reliable friend'. The reasons are evident. Russia, though much diminished in comparison to the Soviet Union, is still too 'big' for Europe. It stretches across ten time zones, encompasses 150 million people, and harbours some 25 000 nuclear weapons.

Nor is Russia safely ensconced on the road to democracy, a system of governance which liberal thinking has traditionally endowed with pacific behaviour. Russia may best be described as 'Weimar Russia' as a country

- experimenting with democracy in the absence of a democratic past, let alone a civil society,
- trying out revolutionary economic reform in the midst of economic catastrophe,
- defeated in war (though only a 'cold' war), trying to find a place in the community of responsible great powers,
- without a clearly demarcated national space that is once more pushing Russia to restore its former empire by latent or open intervention in the southern 'near abroad'.

'Weimar' is an instructive analogy because, in 1918, Hitler was by no means pre-ordained. The First German Republic *could* have made it, if . . . One of the 'ifs' that did not materialize was an auspicious international setting. Instead of free trade, there was rampant protectionism. Instead of capital infusions, there was the steady drain of reparations. Instead of community with the victors, there was encirclement and discrimination.

The 'Weimar analogy' – meaning that the future can go either way – adds to the indeterminacy of German and Western grand strategy already described. It grows out of the ambivalence towards Russia. It is neither containment nor community – but a bit of both.

Containment runs the risk of a self-fulfilling prophecy: treat Russia as the main threat and it might turn into one. Community runs the risk of appeasement: allow Russia a freer hand, and that will favour neither the domestication of Russian power nor European stability. Too much community will encourage, and too much containment will frustrate Moscow, returning a resurgent Russia in either case to the anti-democratic, expansionist ways of yore.

An ambivalent threat like Russia does not for a concise grand strategy make. Is there a more definitive threat? Certainly Europe has not become more stable since the demise of the Soviet Union on Christmas Day 1991. War in Yugoslavia broke out in 1991. There has been latent war between Russia and Ukraine over the distribution of the property of the Soviet empire: nuclear weapons and the Crimea. There has been low-level war between factions, faiths and tribes on the southern edges of the former USSR. There has been real war in Chechnya where Russia brutally tried to reimpose imperial rule on a people claiming autonomy.

But these conflicts, as Europe has decided most clearly in the case of the former Yugoslavia, do not pose a security problem and thus do not make a case for action. Germany and Europe fear not military but socio-economic instability; they fear not foreign armies but foreign masses. Yet these are not matters of strategy proper, as tanks and planes are hardly capable of teaching market economics or turning back illegal immigrants.

What then *is* the nature of the stage on which German grand strategy must unfold? The best historical analogy is post-1815 Europe. In the aftermath of the Napoleonic Wars, the European system was distinguished by the following features:

- the defeat of France as prime hegemonic and ideological threat,
- the wary 're-socialization' of France into the community of the great powers,
- the residual fear of France's resurgence,
- the exhaustion of all the great powers, and hence the absence of a new dominant conflict,
- the fitful withdrawal of Britain, the great extra-European balancer and maritime power, from the continent,
- the emergence of nationalist and revolutionary challenges to the *status quo*, above all in Central and Eastern Europe.

Substituting 'Russia' for 'France', and the 'United States' for 'Britain', will yield a useful description of post-1990 Europe. The analogy can be pushed further. Post-1815 Europe tried to fashion an institutional framework for peace under the rubric of the 'Concert of Europe.' The 'Concert' was not so much an institution as it was an endless succession of conferences and committees that tried to adjust and adjudicate conflicts of interests.

In the absence of a new dominant threat, Europe functions similarly. There is a plethora of institutions: NATO, CSCE, WEU, the Visegrad States, the North Atlantic Cooperation Council (NACC), the 'Partnership for Peace', the European Union, the 'Eurocorps', German–American and German–Danish corps, a multinational Rapid Reaction Force under British command.

There is an endless ballet of meetings, summits and state visits. Documents are signed in plentiful profusion – such as the Charter of Europe, the Treaty on Conventional Forces in Europe or, most recently, the 'Partnership for Peace'. That none of these compacts and institutions really do or decide anything of import is not so much a matter of impotence as disinterest. Europe lacks that great, overriding security problem that used to galvanize attention, mobilize resources and focus national purposes.

Today, we live in the 'post-modern' age, where 'anything goes'. As in architecture and literature, old canons are discarded, and anybody can experiment with new combinations. If you don't like NATO, you can try out the 'Eurocorps'. If, on the other hand, you *do* like NATO as a tightly integrated organization, you don't enlarge it but offer various palliatives to would-be members – like NACC or the Partnership for Peace. If you like Russia, you offer a 'Strategic Partnership' to Moscow, as does the USA. If you don't like Russia, you press for the speedy admission of the East Europeans into NATO. Eclecticism rules everywhere.

FEW NECESSITIES, MANY OPTIONS

This holds true for the entire West, and it is doubly true for Germany. Germany, as explained earlier, did not have a national strategy during the cold war. That choice was not open to Bonn, but over time, dependence became a very comfortable habit. Now dependence has dwindled, safety has increased dramatically, and the freedom to act militarily without any restraint but a parliamentary one has been certified by the constitutional court.

But safety does not make for an easy grand strategy, nor for a clear purpose. This problem besets all great powers in the aftermath of the cold war. But as usual, Germany has to juggle more balls than most, and that task has made for a familiar response dating back to Frederick the Great's injunction to '*garder les mains libres*'. The contemporary version reads 'keep all options open', which breaks down into the following corollaries, but does not add up to a harmonious whole:

1. Maintain NATO and, above all, the US security tie as the ultimate insurance treaty against the resurgence of a Russian threat. As in the past, the Atlantic anchor and counterweight reassures not only Germany but also its neighbours by removing the sting of the country's power and centrality in the European balance.
2. At the same time, keep intact a continental option centred on the special relationship with France, as epitomized by the Franco-German corps. One part of this arrangement is fed by the sheer longevity of the relationship. The other part rests on hard-headed interest, with each of the two regarding (and manipulating) the other as an indispensable partner in the leadership of Europe. Yet this 'axis' contains numerous rivalries, and so there is ...
3. ... the countervailing imperative to limit dependence on France and take care not to alienate other European allies by preserving a subsidiary British tie. For some German interests – like free trade or the widening of the European Community – are better served by London than by Paris. So there are regular bilateral consultations and the air-mobile division (with Britain, Holland and Belgium) within NATO's Rapid Reaction Corps.
4. To complement this triple-tiered Western relationship, reunified Germany has not forsaken its Russian option, even though Moscow now has very little with which to

blackmail or to bribe Germany. In the past, West Germany's exposure to Soviet might and the Soviet veto over inter-German relations made for a good deal of propitiatory behaviour. But after the retraction of Soviet power, sped along by tens of billions in ransom money, the Moscow connection has dwindled into a latent option.

5. Hence the stabilization of Germany's immediate Central European hinterland is the more urgent task. Like Britain, Germany has been more eager than most to extend Western institutions eastward – at least to the Visegrad states. This strategy makes sense economically and geographically. Economically, these countries, above all the Czech Republic, are Germany's 'Mexico': next door, and with high productivity rates at a fraction of German wage levels. Their markets are ideally suited for penetration, but that requires political stability. Hence Germany is in the forefront of those who would attach the Central European quartet to the EU and to NATO while taking care not to do so too blatantly for fear of alienating Russia.

As should be self-evident, these five options do not add up to a coherent whole. The French connection does not harmonize with the Atlantic one, and the Central European option clashes with the Russian relationship as well as with the necessity of keeping the EU homogeneous for the purpose of 'deepening' and, more prosaically, of protecting the common agricultural policy against cheap competition. Other things remaining equal, German will thus pursue of strategy of diversification, balance and compensation, trying to give unto Peter without taking from Paul and to evade irrevocable commitment.

Above all, and in the absence of a resurgent strategic threat, united Germany will try to do what it knows best: to act as 'civilian power' and to eschew for as long as possible the ways of a traditional great power and hence the use of force. And why not? If a country is surrounded only by friends, it will seek to keep them. It will want to retain a paid-up insurance policy underwritten by the United States. It will try to protect its special relationship with France, even though barely contained tensions over free trade, the role of the United States, the evolution of the EU and, most generally, the end of dependence on France will make that marriage an ever more rocky one. Also, while stroking France, Bonn will not forsake Britain. Germany will seek to bring East-Central Europe into the EC and NATO orbit and, failing that, into its own. But it will pursue a 'Greater Central-European Co-Prosperity Sphere' with prudence, taking care not to alienate Russia or to stimulate Western suspicions.

For the time being, no hegemonial ambition or strategic conflict has emerged in Europe – though 'Weimar Russia', obeying Henry IV's deathbed advice to his son, may well try to 'busy giddy minds with foreign quarrels'. Russia remains the joker in the pack. But in benign contrast to 1919, the United States is determined to stay in Europe, and a main-stay of the old security order – NATO – is not cracking but merely shedding girth. The cold war has bequeathed an enor-mous tradition of cooperation to Western Europe, complete with a vast network of institutions and interdependencies which is being extended to the East. On this stage, German grand strategy will maximize options and minimize hard and fast commitments.

But when everything is tallied, one truth can hardly be gainsaid: autonomy is growing, and the old parameters *are* turning into variables because the bi-polar system that gave rise to them has disappeared. In such an indeterminate set-ting, no bet is a safe bet – save for one: that the past can no longer serve as prologue.

NOTES

1. The government was authorized to furnish logistical air support to UNPROFOR in Bosnia, to dispatch medics, and to provide NATO with reconnaissance aircraft over the former Yugoslavia and above all eight ECR *Tornados* to suppress Serbian surface-to-air missiles. For the details of the Government draft, see 'Der Bonner Regierungs-beschluss zur Untestüzung der Blauhelm-Soldaten in Bosnien', *Frank-furter Rundschau*, 27 June 1995, p. 5.
2. Even before the verdict of the Karlsruhe court, the government had begun to test the limits of a self-imposed policy of self-denial. It had dispatchted unarmed navy units into the Adriatic to help supervise the UN arms embargo against the former Yugoslavia. The German

air force flew in NATO AWACS planes that monitored Yugoslav airspace. (These two decisions actually led to the legal challenge before the constitutional court.) In the summer of 1993, a 1200-man Bundeswehr contingent under the UN flag was dispatched to Somalia, but that commitment was never tested under fire. And it was terminated, along with the American one, on 31 March 1994.

3. See the seminal article by Kenneth N. Waltz, 'The Stability of the Bipolar World', *Daedalus*, summer 1964.

BIBLIOGRAPHY

'Der Bonner Regierungsbeschluss zur Untestüzung der Blauhelm-Soldaten in Bosnien', *Frankfurter Rundschau*, 27 June 1995, p. 5.
Waltz, Kenneth N., 'The Stability of the Bipolar World', *Daedalus*, summer 1964.

Copenhagen Research Project on European Integration, CORE

CORE is an interdisciplinary research project on European integration. The project is directed towards a broad scope of topics including the political, legal, technological, economic and security dimensions of the European integration process. Researchers from various Danish research institutions participate in the project, mainly from the University of Copenhagen, the Technical University of Denmark, the Copenhagen Business School and the University of Roskilde. CORE was launched in 1992 and is receiving financial support from the Danish Social Research Council.

The steering committee of the project includes

- Associate Professor Morten Kelstrup, Institute of Political Science, University of Copenhagen, Chairman
- Research Director, Danish Institute of International Affairs, and Jean Monnet Professor Bertel Heurlin, Institute of Political Science, University of Copenhagen
- Professor Jan Kronlund, the Technical University of Denmark
- Professor, dr. jur Hjalte Rasmussen, Faculty of Law, University of Copenhagen
- Associate Professor Finn Østrup, Institute of Finance, the Copenhagen Business School

The project can be contacted at the following address:

CORE
c/o Institute of Political Science
Rosenborggade 15
1130 Copenhagen K
Denmark
Tel: +45 3532 3410
Fax: +45 3532 3399

CORE Publications

Books

Morten Kelstrup, ed., *European Integration and Denmark's Participation*, Copenhagen Political Studies Press, 1992.

Hjalte Rasmussen, *Towards a Normative Theory on Interpretation of Community Law*, Copenhagen Political Studies Press, 1993.

Gunnar Skogmar, *Nuclear Triangle: Relations Between the United States, Great Britain and France in the Atomic Energy Field 1939–1950*, Copenhagen Political Studies Press, 1993.

Teija Tiilikainen and Ib Damgaard Petersen, eds, *The Nordic Countries and the EC*, Copenhagen Political Studies Press, 1993.

Lykke Friis: *Den tyske magt. Tysklandsspørgsmålet fra Bismarck til Kohl*, Forlaget Politiske Studier, 1994.

Bertel Heurlin, ed., *Danmark og Den Europæiske Union*, Forlaget Politiske Studier, 1994.

Hjalte Rasmussen, *EU-ret og EU-institutioner i kontekst*, Karnovs Forlag, 1994.

Peter Nedergaard, *Organiseringen af Den Europæiske Union*, Munksgaard Forlag, 1994.

Hjalte Rasmussen, *EU-ret i kontekst*, GAD-jura, 1995 (2nd edition).

Birthe Hansen, *European Security 2000*, Forlaget Poltitiske Studier, 1995.

Bertel Heurlin, *Security Problems in Europe: 6 essays*, Forlaget Politiske Studier, 1995.

Working Papers

1/1994 Bertel Heurlin, *Post-Jugoslavien i et internationalt perspektiv – den internationale og den transnationale dimension.*

2/1994 Finn Østrup, *Economic effects of political instability.*

3/1994 Lisbeth Gundlund Jensen, *Den kommunale og regionale forvaltning i landene inden for EU.*

4/1994 Anne Knudsen, *Nations and Reason: a European Future.*

5/1994 Ulrik Jørgensen and Jan Kronlund, *Effekten af EU's Standardiseringsarbejde.*

6/1994 Allan Philip, Hjalte Rasmussen and Anders Torbøl, *Forholdet mellem Rom- og Maastricht-traktaterne og Edinburgh-konklusionerne: Den Danske Afgørelse.*

1/1995 Søren Riishøj, *Transition og transformation: Forandringerne i de central- og østeuropæiske lande efter 1989.*

2/1995 Lykke Friis, *Challenging a theoretical paradox: the lacuna of integration policy theory.*

3/1995 Morten Kelstrup, *Om det danske demokrati og den europæiske integration.*

4/1995 Peter Nedergaard, *Organisational Processes of the European Commission: Legitimacy and Efficiency.*

5/1995 Kirsten Thomsen, *Europæisk Integration: De regionale integrationsteoriers forklaringsstatus.*

6/1995 Finn Østrup, *Economic and Monetary Union.*

Index